the economics of black america

Edited by
HAROLD G. VATTER
Portland State University

THOMAS PALM
Portland State University

Under the General Editorship of
William J. Baumol, Princeton University

HARCOURT BRACE JOVANOVICH, INC.

HBJ New York/Chicago/San Francisco/Atlanta

ISBN: 0-15-518900-X

Library of Congress Catalog Card Number: 72-180997

Printed in the United States of America

preface

This work is designed primarily to meet the rapidly growing demand for a brief but comprehensive college-level survey of the socioeconomic problems black Americans face in their efforts to achieve full participation in a society dominated by whites. We judge that all departments of the social sciences, American studies programs, and other interdisciplinary courses will find the book appropriate for their purposes.

The book can be used as core material in a one-term course or it can be integrated into other courses as collateral material. It is not directed specifically to economics or sociology majors, although students in these fields and those in political science will find themselves most at home with the collection. While the level of the work is nontechnical, the material is challenging and conducive to active classroom discussions.

In designing a book for the social science college curriculum, we believe we have created something that will be of interest to every college student. This is no small part of our purpose since the subject matter should be of pressing concern to all Americans. The current slowdown in policy efforts is reason for alarm; millions of other people, both within and outside the United States, are almost as impatient for remedial action as black Americans are themselves. Our own sense of urgency in this matter, coupled with the conviction that people today are less informed about what might be done than they are about the facts of black status, account for our extensive study of policy alternatives in Part 2.

Much effort has been expended to produce an edited book that, we hope, closely resembles an original, cohesive manuscript. Although the selections vary greatly in length, all the selections should be viewed as passages in a text, passages that follow logically the thoughts that precede them and lead into succeeding passages. If we have accomplished our purpose, then no passage can be regarded as too brief, any more than a paragraph in an original statement can be regarded as too short. Some readers may feel that certain points have been inadequately developed. Applied to any book, such objections may be legitimate and suggest the need for further research on the part of the reader.

The book in substantial part is composed of the writings of blacks. We have been particularly careful to ensure that a wide spectrum of black thought is represented. However, in several instances we found it necessary to rely on white authors.

In devising the content and methodological position of the work, we profited immeasurably from the incisive comments of participants in the Curriculum Conference for Black Faculty Members in the Field of Economics held at Fisk University (April 17–20, 1969) and in the 1969 IBM-UNCF Summer Institute for Teachers of Economics held at the Atlanta University Center in Georgia. Our thanks for both opportunities go to the directors, Dr. Flournoy Coles at Fisk and James Hefner and Marcia Halvorsen at the Atlanta University Center. We are also indebted to the Portland State University students in Professor Palm's class on "The Economics of Race" (spring 1969) and to members of the Portland State Black Student Union for their influence.

We further wish to acknowledge substantive assistance from both the Economics Department and Social Science Division of Portland State University. Mrs. Bea Bowman, formerly of the department secretarial staff, and Mr. Thomas Gerity of the university library were especially helpful. Mr. Gerity devoted many hours of research time to locating and identifying bibliographic and specific sources and knows better than anyone else (except ourselves) the reams of material examined before sifting out the final product.

The work has also benefited from the observations of reviewers who, at various stages in the preparation of the book, offered valuable criticisms regarding selection, quality, comprehensiveness, and overall approach. These include Duran Bell, University of California, Irvine; Louis A. Ferman, Institute of Labor and Industrial Relations, University of Michigan; Daniel R. Fusfeld, University of Michigan; and Colin Wright, Northwestern University.

Harold G. Vatter

Thomas Palm

contents

Preface   iii

Contents   v

part 1
the status of black americans

1 Introduction   3

The differential status of black americans—Harold G. Vatter,   3

THE VICIOUS CIRCLE
Theory of the vicious circle—Gunnar Myrdal,   9

THE NEED FOR A SIMULTANEOUS, INTEGRATED ATTACK
A comprehensive approach—James Farmer,   13

2 Ideologies   14

INTRODUCTION—The Editors,   14
White racism—U.S. Commission on Civil Rights,   18

A SPECTRUM OF BLACK IDEOLOGIES
Militants and moderates—Kenneth B. Clark,   24
Excerpt from *The Autobiography of Malcolm X*—Malcolm X,   26
Integration now—Whitney M. Young, Jr.,   29

3 What Is Black Economics?   32

Is economics culture-bound?—Kenneth E. Boulding,   32
The limitations of standard theory—Thomas Palm,   35

4 Evolution of Black Poverty   43

INTRODUCTION—The Editors,   43

THE SLAVE HERITAGE
Discrimination, past and present—Alan Batchelder,   46
Back toward slavery—W. E. B. Du Bois,   51
The escape from the ghetto: immigrants and blacks—Kerner Report,   54

THE GHETTO

Formation of the black ghettos—Kerner Report, *58*   Central city—suburban fiscal disparities—Advisory Commission on Intergovernmental Relations, *64* The ghetto as an economic subsystem—Daniel R. Fusfeld, *68*

5 The Determinants of Income Differentials   71

INTRODUCTION—The Editors, *71*

Recent developments in income differentials—Manpower Report of the President, 1970, *75*   A century of personal wealth accumulation— Lee Soltow, *80*   Technological change and black employment— Dale L. Hiestand, *85*

UNEMPLOYMENT AND SUB-EMPLOYMENT

Critical significance of employment—Manpower Reports of the President, 1969 and 1970, *88*   Too few jobs in central cities—National Committee Against Discrimination in Housing, *91*   Too few jobs in rural slums— Rudolph A. White, *98*

PREPARATION FOR PRODUCTION INCOME

Determinants of productive intelligence—Alan Batchelder, *99* Results of segregated education—U.S. Commission on Civil Rights, *102* Black-white schooling and income differentials—U.S. Bureau of the Census, *105* Higher education for blacks—John Egerton, *106* Education and jobs—Mahlon T. Puryear, *109* Job attitudes—Mahlon T. Puryear, *113*

DISCRIMINATION IN RESOURCE MARKETS

The competitive market is color-blind—W. H. Hutt, *116* Inequality of opportunity in a competitive market—Alan Batchelder, *121* Management racial practices—Vernon M. Briggs, Jr., *122* Union racial practices—F. Ray Marshall, *131*

BLACK BUSINESS MOTIVATION

Limitations of the black businessman—Eugene P. Foley, *136*

MEASURING THE CAUSES AND EFFECTS OF DISCRIMINATION

Causes of variation in occupational achievement—U.S. Department of Health, Education, and Welfare, *139*   White gains and social costs from subordination of blacks—U.S. Commission on Civil Rights, *144*

6 The Black Consumer   149

INTRODUCTION—The Editors, *149*

The black consumer—Marcus Alexis, *151*   Patterns of black consumption— U.S. Department of Labor, *154*   Prices in black neighborhoods— Phyllis Groom, *166*   Race and housing values—George and Eunice Grier, *167* Inadequate consumption of health services—U.S. Department of Health, Education, and Welfare and U.S. Department of Labor, *170* Consumer Education—D. Parke Gibson, *174*

part 2
policy alternatives

Strategies to attack black poverty—Lester Thurow, *179*

7 The Choices Before Us   186
INTRODUCTION—The Editors, *186*
Recommendations to president nixon—Congressional Black Caucus, *187*
Strategy alternatives: a spectrum of policy opinions—Kenneth B. Clark, *197*
The vicious circle and poverty—Trienah Meyers, *199*
White racism—U.S. Commission on Civil Rights, *201*
REPARATIONS: PRO AND CON
For reparations—Whitney M. Young, Jr., *206*   Against reparations—
Kyle Haselden, *209*

8 Preparation for Production Income   211
INTRODUCTION—The Editors, *211*
Basic criteria for school desegregation—Neil V. Sullivan, *212*   Access to higher
education—Manpower Report of the President, 1970, *214*   Expanding
on-the-job training—William L. Henderson and Larry C. Ledebur, *216*
Education and jobs, or crime—Llad Phillips, Harold L. Votey, Jr., and
Darold Maxwell, *218*

9 Discrimination in Resource Markets   220
INTRODUCTION—The Editors, *220*
Employer job policies—U.S. Department of Labor, *221*
Bucking big labor in construction—a case study—Thomas J. Bray, *227*
Federal policy and job discrimination—Richard P. Nathan, *229*

10 Housing and jobs   233
INTRODUCTION—The Editors, *233*
The home and the factory—National Committee Against Discrimination in
Housing, *234*   Housing: private failures, public needs—
Chester Hartman, *238*

11 Prospects for Black Business   241
INTRODUCTION—The Editors, *241*
BLACK CAPITALISM: PRO AND CON
"To replace dependence with independence"—*Wall Street Journal*, *242*
"A dangerous, divisive delusion"—George Meany, *244*
A small business program for the ghetto—Eugene P. Foley, *245*
The black rural cooperative—Rural Advancement Fund, *248*

12 The Ghetto   252
INTRODUCTION—The Editors, *252*
Private enterprise in ghetto development—U.S. Council of Economic
Advisers, *253*   Corporate imperialism for the poor—Richard A. Cloward and
Frances F. Piven, *256*   Neighborhood power—Advisory Commission on
Intergovernmental Relations, *260*   "We don't all have to be in the ghetto just
to be brothers"—Clarence Funnyé, *261*

13 Income Maintenance   266
INTRODUCTION—The Editors, *266*
Cash grants for the poor—Sherwood O. Berg, *267*   Incentives and guaranteed
income—Michael J. Boskin, *270*   The nixon program and the rural poor—
Linda Hunt, Gary Hunt, and Nancy Scheper, *275*

14 Employment and the Price Level   281
INTRODUCTION—The Editors, *281*
A full employment policy is crucial—James Tobin, *282*   Employer of last
resort: a make-work technique—Thomas B. Curtis, *286*   Impact of inflation
on the poor—Robinson G. Hollister and John L. Palmer, *287*

Epilogue   291
A policy for the seventies—A. Philip Randolph, *291*

List of Authors   295

the status
of black
americans

1

introduction

the differential status
of black americans

HAROLD G. VATTER

Black Americans suffer poverty. They suffer it inordinately compared with the white population. Black Americans are deprived of quality education—more deprived than whites in the same income brackets. Blacks receive poorer housing and health services than whites do for the same dollar expenditures on housing, medical care, and hospitalization.[1] Life expectancy at birth for blacks remains notably shorter than that for whites. Even in the case of the black upper income group, there is a striking differentiation. In an early study of multiple earners, it was found that in almost 90 percent of upper-income nonwhite families it took two or more earners to attain that income, whereas among all upper income families multiple earners accounted for only about two-thirds of the total.[2]

Socially, black Americans are treated as an inferior race;

[1] On separate and unequal health consumption by blacks, see the *Report of the National Commission on Technology, Automation, and Economic Progress* (Washington: Government Printing Office, February 1964), pp. 111–35.

[2] Andrew F. Brimmer, "The Negro in the National Economy," in John P. Davis (ed.), *The American Negro Reference Book* (Englewood Cliffs, N.J.: Prentice-Hall, Inc., 1967), p. 266.

3

whites, even poor whites, are not. Thus blacks are not only a disadvantaged group in American society; they experience a *differential* disadvantage as well.

This differential exists in all significant economic and social matters in any comparison of all blacks with all whites. However, in a comparison of all blacks with the white poor, many economic differences are almost eliminated but the social differentials still persist. In a comparison of income and wealth criteria between the poorer blacks and a group of poor whites, many of the economic differences reappear and, of course, the social differences persist. Such comparisons can be made with respect to the status of black Americans, but in general the differential status concept that the editors employ in this book refers to all blacks and all whites. The chief reason for this emphasis is that we believe the ultimate goal of the contemporary American social consensus on the matter is to achieve a rough cross-sectional equality between the black and the white populations in all major socioeconomic respects.

We can consider the point made by Elizabeth Herzog, Myron Lefcowitz, and others that social scientists may have acquired ". . . the habit of attributing to ethnic background differences that may in fact derive chiefly from socioeconomic status."[3] Herzog cites Lefcowitz, for example, to the effect that when black and white children with similar family incomes are compared, "differences between them in educational achievement diminish."[4] But even she is prepared to go no farther than to argue that the differentials are reduced or perhaps "dwarfed" in the case of *poor* blacks and *poor* whites. Furthermore, the emphasis of this group of writers fails to appreciate, in our view, the full impact on the black individual of ghettoization, segregation, racism, and all their ramifications. Here are differences in kind. Only such failure can lead one to say "Slavery, *in fact,* can be viewed as— for some slaves and to some extent—an extreme version of poverty with a few repulsive additions."[5]

Black Americans have made material progress since slavery and reconstruction, but progress relative to *their* previous status and plane of living. All social groups will ordinarily share to

[3] Elizabeth Herzog, "Perspectives on Poverty 3," *Monthly Labor Review,* U.S. Department of Labor (February 1969), 47.

[4] *Ibid.,* 48.

[5] *Ibid.,* 48. (Our emphasis.)

introduction

some extent in the total growth of the economy. But in a society permeated by race discrimination and enjoying a high per capita income, the more pertinent comparison is between the advances made by all blacks and the advances made by all whites. Blacks will not tolerate and whites dare not permit the rate at which the proportion of black to white median incomes[6] closes to be so slow that approximate equality will take half a century to attain. Yet if the past performance (for example, from 1957 to 1967) is extrapolated, this is the estimate; the ratio has risen at a compound annual rate of one percent. The ratio of nonwhite to white life expectation at birth rose between 1920 and 1967 at an annual compound rate of only one-fourth of one percent. In the 1960's the movement of whites out of the below-poverty level was proportionately faster than the outward movement of blacks.[7] Indeed, between 1959 and 1968 in families headed by a female, there was a 16 percent decline in the number of poor persons among the whites, but a 24 percent *rise* among poor blacks![8] Clearly the "affluent society" contains a continuing status gap that suggests the abiding presence of forces hostile to the professed humanistic goals of Americans.

These hostile forces consist of contemporary white racism operating in the context of a differentially low black material status that has resulted from a long record of past discrimination. Together these forces tend to generate, if not counteracted from the outside, a *vicious circle* in which blacks come to market with poorer preparation than whites and that preparation is used as leverage by discriminating whites to reinforce the blacks' differential disadvantage. In vicious circle phenomena, as Gunnar Myrdal has declared, a change does not call forth countervailing changes but, instead, supporting changes which move the system in the same direction as the first change, but much farther. Because of such circular causation, a social process tends to become cumulative and often to gather speed at an accelerating rate.[9]

[6] A ratio that is notably lower in the South than it is in the North.
[7] U.S. Departments of Commerce and Labor, *The Social and Economic Status of Negroes in the United States,* 1969, BLS Report 375, Current Population Reports, Series P-23, No. 29, p. 22.
[8] Committee for Economic Development, *Improving the Public Welfare System* (Committee for Economic Development, 477 Madison Avenue, New York, N.Y. 10022, April 1970), p. 27.
[9] Gunnar Myrdal, *Rich Lands and Poor* (New York: Harper & Row, 1957), p. 13.

In other words, there is a systematic vicious circle of cumulative forces, both economic and *noneconomic,* that operates to sustain blacks in a uniquely disadvantaged condition of life. The economist's traditional presumptions are that factor owners are knowledgeable maximizers who will over time strive to raise their capacities to acquire income and wealth. However, this presumption is largely inappropriate for blacks because discriminatory phenomena in factor markets and product markets interact, *both* with each other *and* with discrimination in noneconomic institutions.

If not resisted by a multifaceted policy attack, the vicious circle could become a low-level disequilibrium trap imprisoning blacks in an ever-worsening spiral of poverty. Part 2 of this work is designed to present a spectrum of policy alternatives. But the vicious circle concept with respect to status is emphasized partly in order to assert that the policy attack, regardless of the alternatives selected, must move on all significant fronts in a simultaneous and integrated way. We are therefore embracing the "balanced-growth" approach to the task of black socioeconomic development.

The status of blacks has improved both absolutely and relatively, albeit at a snail's pace. Therefore we know that counteracting forces—not the least of which are the efforts of blacks themselves through ideological ferment and through migration and organization, for example[10]—have been at work to offset a purely downward cumulative movement. We are concerned here with the levels to which the countervailing influences upon the vicious circle have brought black Americans, together with the extent of the remaining gap between blacks and whites. It is presumed that it is the high purpose of the contemporary American social consensus to close this gap, although there apparently is much less of a consensus regarding the rate of that closure.

Part 1 of this book is devoted largely to the delineation and elaboration of the socioeconomic status of our 24,000,000 blacks and to the large gap separating them from the social norm. It

---

[10] From 1940 to 1954 the ratio of nonwhite to white family median income rose from .37 to .56. [See Tom Kahn, "The Economics of Inequality," excerpted in Louis A. Ferman, Joyce L. Kornbluh, and J. A. Miller (eds.), *Negroes and Jobs* (Ann Arbor: University of Michigan Press, 1968), p. 18.] This is an annual rate of increase of three percent. Its excess over the one percent from 1947 to 1967 probably reflects the higher migration rate in the earlier period, but other factors are no doubt also at work.

appears that there is a differential no matter which particular ordinary determinant of status is discounted or eliminated. And if, indeed, we hold constant *all* the customary determinants of differences in material status between social groups (*e.g.*, education, residence, family head), in the case of blacks vs. whites we find that there is still a "residual" difference in status (represented by income, for example). Although our measures of the pertinent determinants, such as the representation of education by years of schooling, may well be deficient and although there is certainly intercorrelation between determinants, such as income and area of residence, most students of the subject still agree that there is an important element of white racism, or "the propensity to discriminate" (past and present), in the observed status differences.

In the analysis of differential economic disadvantages of blacks, economists usually treat discrimination as a *residual* determinant. Of course, the residual notion always obscures interaction effects. For instance, in a recent discussion that attempts to segregate productivity differences from discrimination in employment with respect to black–white income differentials,[11] the writer acknowledges that "productivity factors may be the result of color discrimination in areas other than employment."[12] But the fact of current employment discrimination may well depress production performance. Furthermore, the "discrimination in areas other than employment" must include the accumulated effects of *past* disadvantages and discrimination as well as present discrimination. The matter is complicated even more by the apparent tendency for the intensity of discrimination to increase with the training of the individual black person. A black college graduate will earn less over his lifetime than a white high-school graduate.[13] With respect to social differentiation, discrimination is intuitively the *major* determinant, although again this is not easily disentangled from economic status.

The urban ghetto in both the North and the South has replaced the Southern agrarian environment as the chief single

[11] James Gwartney, "Discrimination and Income Differentials," *American Economic Review*, Vol. **LX**, No. 3 (June 1970), 396–408.

[12] *Ibid.*, 396.

[13] Dawn Wachtel, *The Negro and Discrimination in Employment* (**Ann** Arbor and Detroit: University of Michigan and Wayne State University, Institute of Labor and Industrial Relations, 1965), p. 1.

cultural vehicle for the perpetuation of the black differential disadvantage. This segregated subculture of poverty limits the scope of job opportunities by impeding mobility. The ghetto schools are materially-deprived institutions staffed by middle class personnel who are ill-equipped to transmit knowledge to and develop motivation in black children. Ghetto society has done little to relieve and may indeed have aggravated the endowment of family disorganization instituted by the slave system. The attendant insecurity is transmitted to children from generation to generation.

The ghetto is generally a place lacking many elements of cultural and educational inspiration. It is also strikingly devoid of accessible facilities for quality education, particularly higher education. In place of psychologically healthy recreational opportunities, ghetto recreational facilities place a high premium on immediate and transitory excitation. As Paul Ehrlich has pointed out, the congestion and lack of green space in the urban ghetto can have adverse effects upon mental health. The squalor of the ghetto environment tends to have a uniquely debilitating effect upon aspirations and undermines the black individual's confidence in himself.

The ghetto surrounds the black individual with similarly disadvantaged persons. This kind of homogeneity deprives the individual of role models that might be conducive to greater achievement. The ghetto is not, in McClelland's phrase, an "achieving society" (assuming it might, if given the choice, wish to be such). Enforced segregation in ghetto poverty and the associated white monopoly of privilege and affluence generate a hatred of higher material status rather than induce greater economic effort. These relationships are reinforced rather than mitigated by the combination of poor preparation for and employment discrimination in job markets that are located overwhelmingly outside the ghetto area.

The ghetto environment poorly prepares the individual for earning an income. Without the possession of tangible productive wealth and lacking much intangible wealth in the form of relevant training, the black worker is largely confined to (1) selling his labor services rather than his property services, (2) accepting low-paying jobs in the occupational hierarchy, and (3) suffering an inordinately high incidence of unemployment, underemployment, and casual work. These limitations would apply even in the absence of *current* discrimination in school placement offices, unions, employment agencies, business personnel departments, and the other institutions which make up our factor markets. Both past and current discrimination reinforce the inadequate preparation for productive employment that blacks carry with them to factor markets. This inadequate preparation is often used by whites to justify continued discrimination while, as mentioned before, the very awareness among blacks of employment discrimination may well lower their occupational horizons and preferences.[14]

When we turn to the consumer side of the private market, we again encounter constraints operating uniquely against equality of status for blacks: deprivation with respect to information about products, locational quasi-monopoly in the ghetto, price and quality discrimination by sellers, and inequality before the law. Thus differential consumer status reinforces differential producer status.

Here are the essential ingredients of the vicious circle. Hence this book is not, by and large, merely a study of poverty. It is more accurately a study of the American version of Apartheid.

[14] *Ibid.*, p. 3.

the
vicious
circle

theory of the vicious circle

GUNNAR MYRDAL

Throughout this inquiry, we shall assume a general interdependence between all the factors. . . . White prejudice and discrimination keep the Negro low in standards of living, health,

Abridged from pp. 75–78 in *An American Dilemma* by Gunnar Myrdal. Copyright © 1944, 1962, by Harper & Row, Publishers, Inc. By permission of the publishers.

[and] education. . . . This, in its turn, gives support to white prejudice. White prejudice and Negro standards thus mutually "cause" each other. If things remain about as they are and have been, this means that the two forces happen to balance each other. Such a static "accommodation" is, however, entirely accidental. If either of the factors changes, this will cause a change in the other factor, too, and start a process of interaction where the change in one factor will continuously be supported by the reaction of the other factor. The whole system will be moving in the direction of the primary change, but much further. This is what we mean by cumulative causation.

If, for example, we assume that for some reason white prejudice could be decreased and discrimination mitigated, this is likely to cause a rise in Negro standards, which may decrease white prejudice still a little more, which would again allow Negro standards to rise, and so on through mutual interaction. If, instead, discrimination should become intensified, we should see the vicious circle spiraling downward. The original change can as easily be a change of *Negro standards* upward or downward. The effects would, in a similar manner, run back and forth in the interlocking system of interdependent causation. In any case, the initial change would be supported by consecutive waves of back-effects from the reactions of the other factor.

The same principle holds true if we split one of our two variables into component factors. A rise in Negro employment, for instance, will raise family incomes, standards of nutrition, housing, and health, the possibilities of giving the Negro youth more education, and so forth, and all these effects of the initial change, will, in their turn, improve the Negroes' possibilities of getting employment and earning a living. The original push could have been on some other factor than employment, say, for example, an improvement of health or education facilities for Negroes. Through action and interaction the whole system of the Negro's "status" would have been set in motion in the direction indicated by the first push. Much the same thing holds true of the development of white prejudice. Even assuming no changes in Negro standards, white prejudice can change, for example, as a result of an increased general knowledge about biology, eradicating some of the false beliefs among whites concerning Negro racial inferiority. If this is accomplished, it will in some degree censor the hostile and derogatory valuations which fortify the false beliefs,

10   introduction

and education will then be able to fight racial beliefs with more success.

. . . Behind the barrier of common discrimination, there is unity and close interrelation between the Negro's political power; his civil rights; his employment opportunities; his standards of housing, nutrition and clothing; his health, manners, and law observance; his ideals and ideologies. The unity is largely the result of cumulative causation binding them all together in a system and tying them to white discrimination. . . .

Another corollary from our hypothesis is practical. In the field of Negro politics any push upward directed on any one of those factors—if our main hypothesis is correct—moves all other factors in the same direction and has, through them, a cumulative effect upon general Negro status. An upward trend of Negro status in general can be effected by any number of measures, rather independent of where the initial push is localized. By the process of cumulation it will be transferred through the whole system.

. . . it is likely that *a rational policy will never work by changing only one factor,* least of all if attempted suddenly and with great force. In most cases that would either throw the system entirely out of gear or else prove to be a wasteful expenditure of effort which could reach much further by being spread strategically over various factors in the system and over a period of time.

This—and the impracticability of getting political support for a great and sudden change of just one factor—is the rational refutation of so-called panaceas. . . . There still exists, however, another theoretical idea which is similar to the idea of panacea: the idea that there is *one* predominant factor, a "basic factor." Usually the so-called "economic factor" is assumed to be this basic factor. A vague conception of economic determinism has, in fact, come to color most of the modern writings on the . . . problem far outside the Marxist school. Such a view has unwarrantedly acquired the prestige of being a particularly "hard boiled" scientific approach.

As we look upon the problem of dynamic social causation, this approach is unrealistic and narrow. We do not, of course, deny that the conditions under which Negroes are allowed to earn a living are tremendously important for their welfare. But these conditions are closely interrelated to all other conditions of Negro life. When studying the variegated causes of discrimina-

theory of the vicious circle   11

tion in the labor market, it is, indeed, difficult to perceive what precisely is meant by "the economic factor." The Negro's legal and political status and all the causes behind this, considerations by whites of social prestige, and everything else . . . belong to the causation of discrimination in the labor market, in exactly the same way as the Negro's low economic status is influential in keeping down his health, his educational level, his political power, and his status in other respects. Neither from a theoretical point of view—in seeking to explain the Negro's caste status in American society—nor from a practical point of view—in attempting to assign the strategic points which can most effectively be attacked in order to raise his status—is there any reason, or, indeed, any possibility of singling out "the economic factor" as basic. In an interdependent system of dynamic causation there is no "primary cause" but everything is cause *to* everything else.

If this theoretical approach is bound to do away in the practical sphere with all panaceas, it is, on the other hand, equally bound to encourage the reformer. The principle of cumulation— in so far as it holds true—promises final effects of greater magnitude than the efforts and costs of the reforms themselves. The low status of the Negro is tremendously wasteful all around—the low educational standard causes low earnings and health deficiencies, for example. The cumulatively magnified effect of a push upward on any one of the relevant factors is, in one sense, a demonstration and a measure of the earlier existing waste. In the end, the cost of raising the status of the Negro may not involve any "real costs" at all for society, but instead may result in great "social gains" and actual savings for society. A movement downward will, for the same reason, increase "social waste" out of proportion to the original saving involved in the push downward of one factor or another.

These dynamic concepts of "social waste," "social gain," and "real costs" are mental tools originated in the practical man's workshop. To give them a clearer meaning—which implies expressing also the underlying social value premises—and to measure them in quantitative terms represents from a practical viewpoint a main task of social science.

the need for
a simultaneous,
integrated attack

a comprehensive approach

JAMES FARMER

. . . It is impossible to say that any one field of activity must be the focus of our major energies today because the problems which affect our children are so interrelated. The whole syndrome of problems affects them, and unless we work on all problems at the same time, the work we do on any one is bound to fail. Perhaps that is a cause of our past failures. We have been concentrating on a scale of priorities, saying that we will work on "A" first and when that is complete move to "B," not realizing fully enough that A and B are intertwined and while you are working on A, B is seeing to it that the work you do on A will be ineffective, and furthermore B is getting worse all the time. So we have to work at all the things—education, housing, jobs, welfare—all together.

From James Farmer, "The Plight of Negro Children in America Today," *Child Welfare*, Vol. XLVII, No. 9 (November 1968), 509. By permission of the publishers.

2 ideologies

Ideology refers to the ways people (individuals or groups) view their positions and roles in society, the ways they envision their relations with other individuals and in other social strata, and the ways they think society should be changed (if at all) in order to achieve their preferred social goals. In brief, ideology is one's perspective on the world. This chapter is placed early in the book because ideology influences both the treatment of blacks in society (Part 1) and the selection of policy options designed to deal with the problems of black status (Part 2). Indeed, ideologies provide an essential link between perceived status and what are thought to be the feasible and desirable policy choices. We therefore immediately proceed with a review of prevailing ideologies about the ways blacks and whites think they relate and should relate to each other.

There is lot less agreement about what to do than there is about the existing differential disadvantages of black people. Therefore, this chapter deals particularly with a number of ideological phenomena that carry substantial weight as hindrances or stimulants to effective policy.

White racism is discussed first in this chapter. Although recognition of its existence fails to pinpoint the specific policies required to attack the relevant problems, such rascism, as The National Advisory Commission on Civil Disorders declared, is essentially responsible for the subordinate status of black Americans and for "the explosive mixture which has been accumulating in our cities." When black people turn in anger against white

14

references to "the Negro problem" with the rejoinder that "there is no Negro problem; there is just a White problem," what they mean precisely is that white racism is the root of the matter.

Anthony Down's penetrating analysis which follows, like Howard Schuman's,[1] emphasizes *institutional subordination* as an even more virulent form of the racist disease than either overt, blatant chauvinism or unconscious racism ("that's real white of you, Bill"), and it is in this area that policy actions must be particularly concentrated. Nevertheless, Down's treatment suffers from some neglect of an important point stressed by Schuman—the widespread inclination of white Americans to assume comfortably that inequality can be overcome at any time by blacks if they simply exercise their "free will" to get ahead.[2] The remedy for this white article of faith will require great ingenuity and determination.

Because of the preeminent importance of deep-rooted white racism we will continue, in Part 2, Down's discussion on what white racism is with his unusually specific and lucid treatment of what white Americans can do to accelerate the demise of this social cancer. It is no accident that Bishop Stephen Spottswood, chairman of The National Association for the Advancement of Colored People, keynoted the association's 61st convention on June 30, 1970 by citing the "ominous" evidence of continuing racial division in the United States. Bishop Spottswood declared that "the White backlash on the one hand and the Black retreat on the other hand have combined to accentuate the racial polarity of which The Kerner Commission warned."

The general attitudes of blacks toward contemporary affairs in the United States and toward the white power structure in particular are also of great importance, especially for an appreciation of the pace and overall character of anticipated social change in the immediate future. Similarly, recent changes in white attitudes toward contact with blacks, the black protest movement, and the pace of interracial evolution are relevant to one's appraisal of what is desirable *and* feasible in the policy sphere during the coming critical period.

Black Americans are in overwhelming agreement on a number of basic matters respecting their status and their treatment by

[1] See Howard Schuman, "Sociological Racism," *Trans-Action, Social Science and Modern Society,* Vol. 7, No. 2 (December 1969), 44–48.
[2] *Ibid.,* 48.

the white majority. But they are in much less agreement on what steps to take to remedy their plight. This is to be expected; as sociologists know, almost every society, including black society, is parochial, and parochial societies generate ideological heterogeneity. The spectrum of black ideologies presented below expresses these conditions and, at the same time, is again focused upon the desired nature, direction, and pace of policy change. As historians aver, these desiderata are shaped by (1) the particular interpretation or image held by a given group regarding their conditions of existence, and (2) the group's implicit or explicit ultimate goals. How these two factors are interwoven and whether they are interwoven in a reasonably consistent way should concern the reader in the case of each group's particular approach. The reader will also observe that the socioideological groups frequently overlap.

A number of rather remarkable characteristics emerge from an observation of the ideological spectrum after a review of the source material. It seems clear that, in the long run, the great majority of black Americans favor integration (beyond desegregation[3] and certainly not the spurious "integration" of blacks emulating whites so bitterly scorned by Malcolm X).[4]

Despite the preference for integration, we found it extremely difficult to locate a current black statement in favor of "Integration Now."[5] Generally speaking, it is whites who project such a goal in the existing social context. The reasons are fairly obvious: the black movement for freedom and material equality today is possible only on the basis of a militant assertion of black unity and identity. This assertion appears again and again in the selections which follow, and has elsewhere been brilliantly defended by the black psychiatrist Franz Fanon. The assertion of a distinctive black identity is common to many ideologies and social movements among blacks. It is contained in the perspectives of

[3] The Survey Research Center reports that three-fourths of a sample group of blacks favored desegregation in 1968.

[4] In our judgment this also requires the demise of the ghetto. However, in the interests of objectivity, Part 2 will present some different viewpoints on ghetto policy.

[5] We did, however, in the statement by Whitney M. Young, Jr. which follows. The *Time* - Louis Harris poll in 1970 reported that 44 percent of all blacks respected Whitney Young, Executive Director of the National Urban League, "a great deal" and 24 percent "some, not a lot."

16   ideologies

both militants and moderates, separatists, black nationalists, Third World theorists, and Panthers. Even if this is a necessary aspect of the black struggle for a decent place in American society, and we do not question the proposition, it may nevertheless be true that separatism is a phase that eventually could turn into its Hegelian opposite and serve the purposes of racial integration. As Malcolm X puts it, "in the competitive American society, how can there ever be any white–black solidarity before there is first some black solidarity?"

Another remarkable characteristic of the ideological spectrum is that even given the hatred of white politics, white social practices, and the white power structure, the great majority of blacks accept the basic economic institutions of our "mixed" capitalistic order. A call for socialism, for example, is relatively rare, although possibly such sentiment exists without being widely articulated. The demand for local community political power is clearly envisioned as feasible within the framework of the existing economic order. Even the militant Black Panther program, which would certainly shift political power fundamentally toward the black community, contains in the economic sphere only the traditional liberal demands for decent food, clothing, housing, jobs, education, and the possession of property ("land").

A final notable characteristic of the ideological material which follows is its ambiguity in the treatment of power. Black power in some sense is certainly essential if black demands are to be met. But the hard fact is that, in the presence of even tacit white resistance and in the absence of broadscale active white support, blacks have little power. For a time, violence may achieve, probably has already achieved, some positive results. A large contingent of blacks, including a majority of the young, condone black violent protest. But it is not evident that civil unrest can yield lasting power for black Americans, and the majority of blacks abjure violence. Black power must rely heavily upon white guilt and black violence tends to destroy white guilt. On the other hand, black violence is basically a resistance phenomenon, not an initiated aggression, and is not likely to stop until whites first put a stop to violence in all its guises against blacks.

Clearly, given democratic institutions, power relations in the United States *can* shift in favor of black Americans only *if* there is some kind of alliance with the broad strata of white Americans. This seems to be both the dilemma contained in, and the solution to, the fundamental ambiguity of "Black Power." No one recognized this better than Malcolm X.

white racism

U.S. COMMISSION ON CIVIL RIGHTS

White racism exhibits itself in hundreds of ways in American society, and acts in hundreds of other ways that are not recognized by most citizens. Yet all of these can be usefully grouped into two basic categories: *overt racism,* and *indirect institutional subordination because of color.* (For convenience, the second category will be referred to as just *institutional subordination.*)

Overt racism is the use of color *per se* (or other visible characteristics related to color) as a subordinating factor. *Institutional subordination* is placing or keeping persons in a position or status of inferiority by means of attitudes, actions, or institutional structures which do not use color itself as the subordinating mechanism, but instead use other mechanisms indirectly related to color. . . .

Racism is one of those words that many people use, and feel strongly about, but cannot define very clearly. Those who suffer from racism usually interpret the word one way while others interpret it quite differently. This ambiguity is possible in part because the word refers to ideas that are very complicated and hard to pin down. Yet, before we can fully understand how racism works or how to combat its harmful effects we must first try to define it clearly even though such an attempt may be regarded as wrong by many.

Perhaps the best definition of *racism* is an operational one. This means that it must be based upon the way people actually behave, rather than upon logical consistency or purely scientific

From The U.S. Commission on Civil Rights, *Racism in America and How to Combat It,* Clearing House Publication, Urban Series No. 1 (Washington: Government Printing Office, January 1970), pp. 6–11 *passim.* The report was prepared by Dr. Anthony Downs.

ideologies

ideas. Therefore, racism may be viewed as *any attitude, action, or institutional structure which subordinates a person or group because of his or their color.* Even though "race" and "color" refer to two different kinds of human characteristics, in America it is the visibility of skin color—and of other physical traits associated with particular colors or groups—that marks individuals as "targets" for subordination by members of the white majority. This is true of Negroes, Puerto Ricans, Mexican Americans, Japanese Americans, Chinese Americans, and American Indians. Specifically, white racism subordinates members of all these other groups primarily because they are not white in color, even though some are technically considered to be members of the "white race" and even view themselves as "whites."

As a matter of further explanation, racism is not just a matter of attitudes: actions and institutional structures, especially, can also be forms of racism. An "institutional structure" is any well-established, habitual, or widely accepted pattern of action or organizational arrangement, whether formal or informal. For example, the residential segregation of almost all Negroes in large cities is an "institutional structure." So is the widely used practice of denying employment to applicants with any nontraffic police record because this tends to discriminate unfairly against residents of low-income areas where police normally arrest young men for minor incidents that are routinely overlooked in wealthy suburbs.

Just being aware of someone's color or race, or even taking it into account when making decisions or in other behavior, is not necessarily racist. Racism occurs only when these reactions involve some kind of subordination. Thus, pride in one's black heritage, or Irish ancestry, is not necessarily racist.

Racism can occur even if the people causing it have no intention of subordinating others because of color, or are totally unaware of doing so. Admittedly, this implication is sure to be extremely controversial. Most Americans believe racism is bad. But how can anyone be "guilty" of doing something bad when he does not realize he is doing it? Racism can be a matter of *result* rather than *intention* because many institutional structures in America that most whites do not recognize as subordinating others because of color actually injure minority group members far more than deliberate racism.

The separation of races is not racism unless it leads to or in-

white racism   19 volves subordination of one group by another (including subordination of whites by Negroes). Therefore, favoring the voluntary separation of races is not necessarily a form of racism. However, it would become racism if members of one group who wanted to cluster together tried to restrict the locational choices of members of some other group in order to achieve such clustering; for example, if whites tried to discourage Mexican Americans from moving into all-white neighborhoods or if a group of black students forced other black students to live in a specific dormitory. Furthermore, separation of groups is one of the oldest and most widespread devices for subordination in all societies. It is particularly effective in modern urbanized societies because it is extremely difficult, if not impossible, to provide different but truly equal opportunities and conditions for separated groups within an economically integrated society. . . .

For more than 300 years, overt racism was a central part of American life, particularly in the South. During these centuries, thousands of overtly racist laws, social institutions, behavior patterns, living conditions, distributions of political power, figures and forms of speech, cultural viewpoints and habits, and even thought patterns continually forced colored Americans[1] into positions of inferiority and subordination. It took the bloodiest of all American wars to abolish the most terrible form of legal subordination—slavery—just 100 years ago. . . .

In the past two decades, there has been important progress in striking down legal support for most of the forms of overt racism. The actual effects of many such forms of racism have been greatly reduced, too. Moreover, this type of conscious and deliberate subordination by color is now considered wrong by most Americans. As a result, many whites *believe* that overt racism—which is the only form they recognize—is disappearing from America.

Yet hundreds of forms of overt racism remain throughout most of the Nation. Examples are the deliberate exclusion of Negroes, Mexican Americans, and other colored persons from labor unions, law firms, school districts, all-white residential neighborhoods, college fraternities, and private social clubs.

[1] The terms colored and nonwhite in the remainder of this paper refer to Negroes, Puerto Ricans, Mexican Americans, Japanese Americans, Chinese Americans, and American Indians because this is how most whites really view and identify them.

. . . taken as a whole, Americans of color are still severely handicapped by the residual effects of past overt racism—plus the many forms of overt racism that still exist.

The deeply embedded effects of overt white racism will not instantly disappear if the white majority suddenly reduces or even eliminates the use of color as an explicit factor in making decisions or influencing its actions. Many whites now say: "All right, we recognize the injustice of overt racism. So we will stop using color as a factor in making decisions. Instead we will use other factors which are clearly and reasonably related to the activities and privileges concerned." Examples of these other factors used in making decisions are skill levels in relation to jobs, place of residence in relation to school attendance, ability to score well on entrance examinations in relation to higher education, self-confidence and leadership of whites in relation to job promotions, and savings plus present income in relation to buying homes.

Usually, the use of such factors is free from overt racism. Hence, it constitutes great progress in relation to most of American history. . . .

Nevertheless, even "merit employment" programs can conceal many forms of indirect institutional subordination by color. In fact, we can use the example of such programs to illustrate how present elimination of overtly racist action does *not* destroy or even significantly weaken the continuing racist effects of *past* overtly racist behavior. This can occur because many of those effects are embedded in institutional structures that no longer appear related to race or color.

Consider an employer who needs workers to fill certain jobs that demand advanced carpentry skills. Naturally, he requires that applicants have such skills in order to be hired. But what if the local carpenters' union excludes all Negroes and Mexican Americans as members? Then this very reasonable behavior of the employer has racist effects because of overt racism of another organization upon which he relies to carry out his own activities. Or what if unions accept minority group apprentices specially trained in local high schools, but the only high schools providing such training are in all-white neighborhoods, either too far from minority group neighborhoods for convenient attendance, or far enough to be placed in different school districts because all school district boundaries are based upon the "neighborhood proximity" principle? In this case, no decision-makers are using overtly racist principles. Yet the result clearly continues systematic subordination of minority groups by excluding them from important economic opportunities. Returning to the example, assume that the employer saves money by never advertising available job openings. Instead, he relies solely upon word-of-mouth communications from his present employees to their friends to find applicants—but all his present employees are white. This is an extremely widespread practice, since most workers find their jobs by hearing of openings from friends. Yet it has the effect of excluding nearly all minority group members from consideration for available jobs. Because of past overt racism, most whites have mainly white friends, particularly since they live in all-white neighborhoods.

Again, the employer is taking actions which are not overtly racist in either nature or intent—but which nevertheless have racist effects—that is, they subordinate people because of their color. In this case, these effects occur because the seemingly reasonable and "unbiased" behavior of the employer takes place in an institutional context that still contains profoundly racist elements remaining from three centuries of overt racism. . . .

This "invisibility" of institutional subordination is even more striking concerning those forms which result from *geographic exclusion* of minority group members from all-white areas, or *perceptual distortion* in the way people see reality. Overt racism —both past and present—is the main cause of the spatial separation of where most whites live from where most nonwhite minorities live. The major form of such racism is deliberate discouragement of Negro and other nonwhite families from buying or renting homes in all-white neighborhoods. Such discouragement is systematically practiced by white realtors, renting agents, landlords, and homeowners. This clearly racist behavior has become so well entrenched that many minority group members no longer even try to find homes in all-white areas because they fear they will "get the run-around" or receive hostile treatment from at least some neighbors. So the pattern of exclusion is continued—in spite of recent laws and court decisions to the contrary.

Yet dozens of other forms of institutional subordination are indirectly caused by the absence of nonwhites from white residential areas. For example, most new jobs are being created in suburban shopping centers, industrial parks, new office buildings, and schools or universities. But American suburban areas are overwhelmingly white in population (about 95 percent in 1966). So the suburban sources of new employment are usually far from where nonwhites live. . . . Even if they do get jobs in the suburbs, they have great difficulty in finding housing near their work. This difficulty does not result only from overt racism: it is also caused by zoning laws which deliberately discourage any housing serving relatively lower-income groups, or local actions which prevent use of Federal subsidies for such housing. Such laws are usually defended on grounds of "maintaining high community standards" of housing and open space, or protecting the existing residents from tax increases that would be caused by building more schools to serve new low-income residents.

All these conditions discourage minority group members from even trying to get suburban jobs. This perpetuates their exclusion from all-white suburban areas. Yet many of the best quality schools, housing developments, recreational facilities, and general residential environments are found in the suburbs. So most minority group members find themselves cut off not only from the fastest growing sources of new jobs, but also from many of the best amenities in American society. This is clearly racism or "institutional subordination."

. . . invisibility of institutional subordination occurs in part because minority group members themselves are "invisible" in the normal lives of most white Americans—especially white children. Most white children are brought up in neighborhoods where Negroes, Mexican Americans, and other nonwhite persons are totally absent, or constitute an extremely small minority— usually engaged in menial jobs. These children form an unconscious but deeply rooted mental image of "normal" society as consisting only of white people, and of all colored persons as "strange" and "different" from "normal people." This image is further reinforced by the world they see on television. . . .

. . . this perception of whites as the only "normal Americans" was further reinforced for more than 100 years by the elementary and other textbooks used in almost all American schools. The exclusion of minority group members from such texts is one more way in which millions of Americans were—and still are—made both "invisible" and "strange" in the minds of the white majority.

a spectrum of
black ideologies

militants and moderates

KENNETH B. CLARK

The basic structure, strength, and weaknesses of American society face increasing critical evaluation by a growing number of
young Negro intellectuals. Probably James Baldwin, novelist
and essayist, is the outstanding example of the most eloquent of
these younger Negro social critics. In a bitter exclamation of
futility and pessimism Baldwin quotes a prominent Negro, "I
am not at all sure that I *want* to be integrated into a burning
house." He quotes another as saying, "I might consider being
integrated into something else, an American society more real
and more honest—but *this?* No, thank you, man, who needs it?"

A further indication of the present mood of the younger Negro
intellectual is the fact that he is directing his critical barbs not
only at the inconsistencies and injustices inherent in American
racism but is becoming increasingly critical—or more overt in his
criticisms—of traditional Negro leaders and Negro organizations.
While there have always been criticisms of these individuals and
organizations from the more militant nationalistic groups of Negroes, it is significant in appraising the present mood of the
Negro, particularly in the North, to note the relatively new fact
that such criticisms, generally more reasoned and sober, are now
coming from younger Negro intellectuals. It is another index of
the complexity of the present level of strength and increasing
morale of the Negro that it is possible to view these criticisms as
evidence that the Negro in the North is now secure enough to
assume the difficult role of self-critic and to demand that the
Negro organizations become even more effective in obtaining
complete equality in the shortest possible time. . . .

As the lines of racial confrontation become more clearly

drawn, some of the basic dilemmas of the Negro people take the form of apparent ideological differences and conflicts. The most obvious of these differences is found in an analysis of the relationship between the tactics and philosophy of Martin Luther King, on the one hand, and the Black Muslim movement, on the other. These two approaches appear to be dramatically and diametrically opposed. Martin Luther King preaches a doctrine of "love for the oppressor" at the same time that he offers an effective social action technique of nonviolent, assertive demand for civil rights. The Black Muslims preach a doctrine of black supremacy, hatred of whites, and total separation of Negroes from whites, who are characterized as "blue-eyed devils," morally defective and therefore incapable of offering the Negro justice and equality. In spite of these apparent differences, it would be a mistake to ignore the similarities in these two movements: Each reflects the Negro's basic impatience; each accepts, as a fact, the assumption that if the Negro is to attain his rights, he must do so primarily, if not exclusively, through his own efforts; each is an assertive reaction against the dawdling, tortuously slow pace of desegregation by the majority of whites who seem to Negroes to desire racial peace at any price; and each is in its own way militant and uncompromising.

For purposes of analysis, however, the most significant similarity between these two movements is the fact that they represent a basic dilemma and ambivalence within the Negro people as a whole. The Black Muslims reflect the reality of hatred and resentment which Negroes understandably feel. The Muslims are honest and defiant in their extreme expression of this genuine and understandably human reaction to injustice. . . .

. . . Their philosophy and that of other black nationalist groups is rather simple and direct. It is a philosophy rooted in hatred and despair and reflecting the American racist simplifications of the importance of skin color. The dramatic twist which these groups give to American racism is that they preach the supremacy of blacks and the inherent degradation of whites. This reversal is dramatic, disturbing, and terrifying to whites and to some middle- and upper-class Negroes as well. . . .

Martin Luther King reflects another aspect of the general feelings of Negroes for whites. In preaching love he taps a part of the truth and, what is more, appears to have hit upon a highly effective strategy and weapon. In spite of pervasive problems of injustice, it is impossible for two peoples to have shared a common destiny for more than three hundred years without evolving bonds of identity and affection. The variations in skin color among American Negroes are all too striking and disturbing indications of the fact that the alleged hatred of the white man for the Negro was never complete and categorical. The Black Muslim's preachings of hatred of Negroes for whites, while a reflection of some aspect of the psychological reality, is also not complete. A major dilemma of the contemporary Negro, therefore, is to decide which aspect of his ambivalence should prevail; which is the more effective.

excerpt from
THE AUTOBIOGRAPHY OF MALCOLM X

The American black man should be focusing his every effort toward building his *own* businesses, and decent homes for himself. As other ethnic groups have done, let the black people, wherever possible, however possible, patronize their own kind, hire their own kind, and start in those ways to build up the black race's ability to do for itself. That's the only way the American black man is ever going to get respect. One thing the white man never can give the black man is self-respect! The black man never can become independent and recognized as a human being who is truly equal with other human beings until he has what they have, and until he is doing for himself what others are doing for themselves.

The black man in the ghettoes, for instance, has to start self-correcting his own material, moral, and spiritual defects and evils. The black man needs to start his own program to get rid of drunkenness, drug addiction, prostitution. The black man in America has to lift up his own sense of values.

Only a few thousands of Negroes, relatively a very·tiny num-

From Malcolm X with the assistance of Alex Haley, *The Autobiography of Malcolm X* (New York: Grove Press, Inc., 1966), pp. 275–378 *passim*. Reprinted by permission of Grove Press, Inc. Copyright © 1966 by Alex Haley and Malcolm X. Copyright © 1965 by Alex Haley and Betty Shabazz. (Also published in London by Hutchinson & Company Ltd.)

ideologies

ber, are taking any part in "integration." Here, again, it is those few bourgeois Negroes, rushing to throw away their little money in the white man's luxury hotels, his swanky nightclubs, and big, fine, exclusive restaurants. The white people patronizing those places can afford it. But these Negroes you see in those places can't afford it, certainly most of them can't. Why, what does some Negro one installment payment away from disaster look like somewhere downtown out to dine, grinning at some head-waiter who has more money than the Negro? . . .

The black man in North America was economically sick and that was evident in one simple fact: as a consumer, he got less than his share, and as a producer gave *least*. The black American today shows us the perfect parasite image—the black tick under the delusion that he is progressing because he rides on the udder of the fat, three-stomached cow that is white America. For instance, annually, the black man spends over $3 billion for automobiles, but America contains hardly any franchised black automobile dealers. For instance, forty per cent of the expensive imported Scotch whisky consumed in America goes down the throats of the status-sick black man; but the only black-owned distilleries are in bathtubs, or in the woods somewhere. Or for instance—a scandalous shame—in New York City, with over a million Negroes, there aren't twenty black-owned businesses employing over ten people. It's because black men don't own and control their own community's retail establishments that they can't stabilize their own community.

The black man in North America was sickest of all politically. He let the white man divide him into such foolishness as considering himself a black "Democrat," a black "Republican," a black "Conservative," or a black "Liberal" . . . when a ten-million black vote bloc could be the deciding balance of power in American politics, because the white man's vote is almost always evenly divided. The polls are one place where every black man could fight the black man's cause with dignity, and with the power and the tools that the white man understands, and respects, and fears, and cooperates with. . . .

Twenty-two million black men! They have given America four hundred years of toil; they have bled and died in every battle since the Revolution; they were in America before the Pilgrims, and long before the mass immigrations—and they are still today at the bottom of everything!

Why, twenty-two million black people should tomorrow give a dollar apiece to build a skyscraper lobby building in Washington, D.C. Every morning, every legislator should receive a communication about what the black man in America expects and wants and needs. The demanding voice of the black lobby should be in the ears of every legislator who votes on any issue.

The cornerstones of this country's operation are economic and political strength and power. The black man doesn't have the economic strength—and it will take time for him to build it. But right now the American black man has the political strength and power to change his destiny overnight.

. . . Why black Nationalism? Well, in the competitive American society, how can there ever be any white-black solidarity before there is first some black solidarity? . . . Even when I was a follower of Elijah Muhammad, I had been strongly aware of how the Black Nationalist political, economic and social philosophies had the ability to instill within black men the racial dignity, the incentive, and the confidence that the black race needs today to get up off its knees, and to get on its feet, and get rid of its scars, and to take a stand for itself. . . .

Every free moment I could find, I did a lot of talking to key people whom I knew around Harlem, and I made a lot of speeches, saying: "True Islam taught me that it takes *all* of the religious, political, economic, psychological, and racial ingredients, or characteristics, to make the Human Family and the Human Society complete.

"Since I learned the *truth* in Mecca, my dearest friends have come to include *all* kinds—some Christians, Jews, Buddhists, Hindus, agnostics, and even atheists! I have friends who are called capitalists, Socialists, and Communists! Some of my friends are moderates, conservatives, extremists—some are even Uncle Toms! My friends today are black, brown, red, yellow, and *white!*" . . .

I said that on the American racial level, we had to approach the black man's struggle against the white man's racism as a human problem, that we had to forget hypocritical politics and propaganda. I said that both races, as human beings, had the obligation, the responsibility of helping to correct America's human problem. The well-meaning white people, I said, had to combat, actively and directly, the racism in other white people. And the black people had to build within themselves much greater awareness that along with equal rights there had to be the bearing of equal responsibilities. . . .

I tell sincere white people, "Work in conjunction with us—each of us working among our own kind." Let sincere white individuals find all other white people they can who feel as they do— and let them form their own all-white groups, to work trying to convert other white people who are thinking and acting so racist. Let sincere whites go and teach nonviolence to white people! . . .

The goal has always been the same, with the approaches to it as different as mine and Dr. Martin Luther King's nonviolent marching, that dramatizes the brutality and the evil of the white man against defenseless blacks. And in the racial climate of this country today, it is anybody's guess which of the "extremes" in approach to the black man's problems might *personally* meet a fatal catastrophe first—"non-violent" Dr. King, or so-called "violent" me.

integration now

WHITNEY M. YOUNG, JR.

For both Negro and white citizens, democracy is a way of life, an ideal in which all share rewards as well as responsibilities. Indeed, without this concept, democracy has no meaning and certainly no permanence.

The sharing that I foresee is to be welcomed by whites as well as black Americans. There are people who seem to think that every advance the Negro makes is at the expense of whites, that the Negro only progresses as the white gives up his freedoms. My concept of integration is not one of either the white or the Negro giving up all that he is used to. After honest examination of the positive and negative elements in each of the two cultures, we will retain the best in each. Responsible white leadership and the mass media must, with honesty and sincerity, promote and teach the idea that integration is an opportunity for all Americans rather than an irritating and uncomfortable problem.

For the Negro, obviously it means a better opportunity for decent housing and education, jobs and living. But it is not a matter of Negroes giving up all that has been part of their community, their background and their culture and adopting all that is white. Out of the years of suffering and deprivation the Negro has developed certain qualities—humaneness, compassion, patience, and endurance—and certain values that should be useful to whites either as individuals or in organizations such as General Motors or the Bank of America.

It was these qualities of perseverance, patience, resilience, of ability to adjust and adapt that were the sustaining pillars of Negro life; they have made possible his survival in spite of everything. These qualities are important to this nation which finds itself in a situation of leadership that is severely challenged, one in which it must make compromises and must adapt. In the United Nations we are finding that in order to lead we must recognize the rights of others.

So, though there are many qualities stemming from segregation that the Negro wants to eliminate and should, the same is also true of white society. The white culture, as a result of a period of dominance and privilege, has developed certain unhealthy qualities—indifference to others, for one, and a tendency toward a sense of superiority and exclusiveness for another. . . .

Integration is an opportunity for white citizens to show to the whole world their maturity and their security. It is time for them consciously to proclaim the creative possibilities in that diversity from which they have unconsciously benefitted. People do not grow through similarity to one another. One grows from the stimulus of people who are different, people whose cultural backgrounds are heterogeneous. One contributes to the other. . . .

When you surround yourself with people who drive the same cars and have the same skin color and go to the same churches, clubs and parties and read the same books all you do is perpetuate a type of homogenized mediocrity. Probably no nation owes so much to diversity as does ours. We have benefited in myriad ways from the vast variety of contributions to our way of life by people of all manner of backgrounds. . . .

ideologies

. . . In the United States, with our mobility and our communications media, ours is a 24-hour-a-day, 365-days-a-year interchange with the rest of the world. And how much more we enjoy and absorb from life when we open our senses to the manifold varieties of "otherness" available to us. Men grow to the extent that they are the beneficiaries of diverse ideas, not through the process of having their ideas reflected and reinforced by people whose backgrounds and cultures are identical.

We are, through integration, seeking to help all our citizens realize their true, creative potentials and to move toward a new type of society that is not a replica of any past culture or any single group, but is a culture that has absorbed the best from each.

3 what is black economics?

is economics
culture-bound?

KENNETH E. BOULDING

. . . If the question, "Is economics culture-bound?" is to have any meaning, it must be interpreted to signify "Does the character of economists and the nature of their subculture affect the scope, the relevance, or the truth of the product in the shape of economics which they produce?" . . .

The subculture of economists, as it has existed now for nearly two hundred years, is very far from being a random sample of human populations or human cultures. It bears the genetic stamp of its British origin, of its eighteenth century birth date, of its connection with the larger scientific subculture and of its origins in what might be called the intellectual middle class. . . .

. . . within a developing society, like the United States, we do not really understand why some relatively poor segments of it, such as the blacks, on the whole are participating in the developmental process, though with about a thirty-year lag, while others, such as the Spanish-speaking Americans and Indians, hardly seem to be participating in the developmental

From Kenneth E. Boulding, excerpts from "Is Economics Culture-bound?" Paper presented at the American Economic Association annual meeting, New York, December 28, 1969. (mimeographed)

process at all. The problems here seem to be beyond the power of economic models to reach. . . .

One wonders whether culture-boundness may not have something to do with this relative failure. . . .

We cannot leave this subject without recognizing that economics has two cultures at least, although which is the most culture-bound is hard to say. Marxian economics and radical economics generally form a separate stream which has common origins with capitalist economics in the classical economists, but which has diverged very strikingly both from its source and from its "bourgeois" relation. Karl Marx, of course, came out of much the same social class and background as the classical economists. Like Ricardo, his father was a Christianized Jew and the Judeo-Christian influence is very striking in the whole Marxist system of thought.

The very existence of the Marxist split in economics, however, points up a still unresolved problem within the general body of the science, which arises perhaps because of the bias of classical and bourgeois economics toward individualism and towards the neglect of the economics of the group. . . .

. . . . Group decisions and community demands and supplies are somewhat alien to the traditional framework of economics. Hence, the problems which revolve around group life, community, group identity, public goods, the grants economy, identity and identification, benevolence, malevolence and so on have been neglected.

Part of the Marxist revolt indeed is a revolt against this individualistic bias. The Marxist solution, however, is quite inadequate. Class is a completely inadequate concept to bear the weight of the enormous complexity of group and integrative relationships. . . .

When we look at the economics of race, the individualistic bias of economic theory leads to an insensitivity to the problems of identity, especially group identity, which are so prominent now. We are going through an agonizing struggle to find the proper place of racial groups within the integrative structure. The liberal philosophy of integration owes a great deal to economics and the implicit assumption of economics that the individual is an individual no matter what his color, creed or national origin. This philosophy is now running into severe criticism because of its apparent denial of the reality of groups. We face a paradox here that, whereas the individual person is the only ultimate social reality, it is a reality which is sharply conditioned by the groups within which the person has grown up. The individual, furthermore, cannot even be an individual unless he has some sort of group identity. Just which group identities are the most fruitful, however, must remain an open question and we certainly cannot assume that a common skin color or a common anything automatically creates community and group identity.

Oddly enough, our statistical information system has a much stronger "racial" structure than does economic theory. In economic theory there is practically no recognition that race exists at all as a social phenomenon. In our statistics, however, especially in the census we categorize people by race quite without regard as to whether this is, in fact, the most significant and useful category.

. . . In different ways, neither economics nor statistics has recognized adequately that the problem of what groups are significant in society is both very important and not to be taken for granted and requires a great deal of research, most of which we have not done.

Whatever groups we decide are significant in society, it is clear that economists constitute one of them. There seems to be an inescapable dilemma here that intellectual products, like economics, are produced by intellectuals and intellectuals tend either to be middle class or to become so.

the limitations of
standard theory

THOMAS PALM

It is readily established, if not self-evident, that the socioeconomic status of Black Americans has not reached national living standards and that this racial differential is a social problem of potentially massive consequences.[1]

The very persistence of differential black poverty and subjugated social status over centuries argues that this is not a random event, that the result has been produced and maintained systematically. If the result is systematic, it should be possible to identify in general terms the mechanism by which it is engendered, i.e., it should be possible to develop a body of relevant theoretical propositions. It is not self-evident, however, what technique of study will lead to a clearest practical understanding of the origins and current nature of the problem and thereby contribute to a solution. Is there, or could there be, a "Black Economics" or a "Black Social Science" and, if so, what might be the scope and techniques of such a discipline? In particular, how well could economics function in such a role?

If the issues are conceived from the outset as primarily economic ones, they will tend to be examined with the established tools of orthodox economics—its definitions, standards of measurement, selected internal relationships, and "parameters." Although the procedures of modern economics on both the theoretical and applied levels have provided important insights into interracial relationships, there are three major limitations to the usefulness of established doctrines:

1. Since the usual generalizations about economic propositions are based on assumptions about human behavior and administrative arrangements typical of middle-class, white, western societies, the conclusions drawn may be irrelevant for groups with different ethnic-cultural backgrounds.

2. Since existing behavior patterns and social arrangements

[1] Part 1 of this book examines that differential. The reader should also consult John P. Davis (ed.), *The American Negro Reference Book* (Englewood Cliffs, New Jersey: Prentice-Hall, Inc., 1967) and Harry A. Ploski and Roscoe C. Brown, Jr. (eds.), *The Negro Almanac* (New York: Bellwether Publishing Company, Inc., 1967).

are the problem, a solution necessarily involves *changes* in them. But existing theory is built mostly on the assumption that patterns of interpersonal relationships and the social machinery are *given* (parameters). The distributions of income and resources among various groups within society, for example, have been taken as givens, instead of critical phenomena that require explanation and alteration.[1] In sum, while solution of the problem is necessarily largely dynamic, the bulk of existing theory is static, or at best comparative statics.

3. Since the issue of racism goes beyond the boundaries of the scientific method as conceived by the dominant positivistic school and into philosophical concern with aesthetics, semantics, and particularly ethics, the student of differential black status cannot limit his concerns to matters of logic and data. He cannot limit himself to positive science because judgments about the quality of life, the meaning of behavior, and moral worth influence the magnitude and relationships among the positive "scientific" variables.

Given these limitations, a knowledge of contemporary economic theory is nevertheless useful. On the microeconomic level, the assumptions that characterize "pure competition" lead logically to conclusions notably absent in the real world. By contrast, models of "imperfect competition" point directly to the consequences of the absence of knowledge, mobility, communication, and racial tolerance. In resource markets, concentration of economic power in the hands of a limited number of employers or employees indicates a restriction of employment opportunities, aggregate production, and, thereby, total real income. In product markets, similar concentrations of power lead predictably to a tendency to raise consumer prices through output reductions. Since these conclusions follow from the institutions assumed by the models, the policy implication is obvious: if the conclusions are realistic and intolerable, the causes must be altered.

The standard theory of exchange as developed, for example, by Gary Becker in his *The Economics of Discrimination*[2] leads

---

[2] Gary S. Becker, *The Economics of Discrimination* (Chicago: University of Chicago Press, 1957).

what is black economics?

to important (because they are useful) insights into the social nature and consequences of racism, even though the argument is based on static assumptions and on a model originally designed to examine international trade.

On the aggregative level, a policy conclusion such as that of James Tobin: ". . . the single most important step the nation could take to improve the economic position of the Negro is to operate the economy steadily at a low rate of unemployment"[3] is interesting precisely because, given developments in the theory of aggregative economic relationships, we now know that it is *possible* to manipulate overall levels of production and employment. Knowledge of causal mechanisms in the changing purchasing power of money is likewise of importance in the context of the already differentially low incomes of black Americans.

Applied fields such as industrial organization, labor economics, and public finance do identify conditions which make possible employer, employee, and governmental discrimination against (or in favor of) individuals or groups, thus identifying variables amenable to change. The preparation, recruitment, and commitment of a labor force and criteria for allocating nonlabor resources efficiently have long been studied in a nonracial context. The findings retain relevance in the current setting.

The discipline of economics can be applicable only to the degree that its major ideas (concepts), presumed relationships (assumptions), and forces treated as given (parameters) *are relevant*. How relevant are they?

Of these three components, economic concepts are the most generally cross-cultural. The basic problem of scarcity and the resultant necessity of choice are pervasive human concerns. Indeed the advantages of efficiency in the allocation of scarce resources are all the greater, the poorer the individual or group that must make the choices, since the consequences of a mistake are more grave. In a world of scarcity any decision to use resources to one end has as its real cost the foregone alternative.

The nature of the relationships among variables may, however, differ from group to group. The variables that are causally important may likewise vary. It is usually assumed that labor is responsive to wage differentials, that it tends to respond to opportunities for better earnings. However, data suggest that black

[3] See his article in the policy section (Part 2, Chapter 15).

workers are not as motivated, informed, and mobile as other workers. Whites need not fear racial hostility in responding to better wages or new job openings, whereas blacks have long encountered systematic rebuffs on such grounds. Systematic denial of educational opportunities, job information, and chances for promotion on the basis of merit likewise curtail response to apparent incentives. Such "noneconomic" barriers seriously qualify the assumption of labor mobility, and policy built on such an assumption will fall far short of the mark. Even when the black consumer knows that the quantity and quality per dollar is generally higher in suburban shopping centers than in ghetto stores, he again faces "noneconomic" barriers and he will not, because he cannot, respond in an *economically* rational way.

Since no human mind or computer can deal with all social variables simultaneously, at any one time it is necessary to consider only the relationships among some explicit variables and subsume the influence of other forces in the value of parameters. While the values assigned to such givens in the social scientist's models may be applicable in general, they may be seriously misleading when applied to subgroups within the society. When parameters do differ as a function of race, for example, the reasons for the difference need to be explored; they may well be primarily "noneconomic."

It is known that for the same income levels blacks tend to save *more* and to have *less* debt than whites. This implies that the vertical intercept or parameter of the black consumption function, as determined by *everything* that influences spending besides income, is the lower of the two. Besides contradicting the stereotype of the irresponsible black spendthrift, this differential parameter suggests the need to explore racial differences in the availability of credit and, indeed, the entire nature of the market for consumer goods.

The difference in the nature of the relationships of economic variables between the general society and black America can be traced in part to differential institutional requirements and opportunities. By "institution," we of course mean both the prevailing attitudes and beliefs held by members of a society and that society's administrative arrangements. Thus the economic ideas of production, consumption, and exchange have their existential counterparts in specific forms of industrial structure and market types. Institutions further include law, family, education,

what is black economics?

enforcement, and defense, as embodied in specific legislatures, homes, schools, police, and military establishments.

As Anthony Downs has written:

> For more than 300 years, overt racism was a central part of American life, particularly in the South. During these centuries, thousands of overtly racist laws, social institutions, behavior patterns, living conditions, distributions of political power, figures and forms of speech, cultural viewpoints and habits, and even thought patterns, continually forced colored Americans into positions of inferiority and subordination. It took the bloodiest of all American wars to abolish the most terrible form of legal subordination—slavery—just 100 years ago. . . .
> Yet hundreds of forms of overt racism remain throughout the Nation. Examples are the deliberate exclusion of Negroes . . . from labor unions, law firms, school districts, all-White residential neighborhoods, college fraternities, and private social clubs.[4]

Standard economic theory tells us that the receipt of income is largely governed by the productivity and quantity of resources that individuals can sell. But history and the other social sciences should make it clear that the access which black Americans have had to income-producing wealth, both as physical property and investment embodied in people, has been severely and intentionally curtailed by racism, as has the opportunity to sell such resources. The ability of money income, thus limited, to command goods and services has been cut further by restrictions placed on the black consumer as to what he may buy and from whom and where.

While the more offensive explicit restrictions directly based on race are being slowly stricken down, subtle, tacit institutional mechanisms, in many cases more powerful in their impact, remain. For example, the historical concentration of blacks into urban ghettos and rural slums today tends, in effect, to exclude them from the quality education available in suburban schools, from quality single-family housing units, and from the jobs generated on urban fringes by the industrial exodus from core cities. In many peoples' views it seems reasonable that young children attend neighborhood schools (lest they be bussed interminably),

[4] The U.S. Commission on Civil Rights, *Racism in America and How to Combat It.* Clearing House Publication, Urban Series No. 1 (Washington: Government Printing Office, January 1970), p. 7. The report was prepared by Anthony Downs.

that candidates for jobs present evidence of competence (lest, in a world of scarcity, they interfere with production), and that housing values be protected by zoning laws (lest savings be destroyed). It is quite possible to hold these and similar views without any racist intent, and most people perhaps do so. However, the effect of such views, given the denial of opportunity to attain an education, the denial of geographic mobility, and the resultant low incomes, may well be racist.

Therefore, the attempt to build a relevant "Black Social Science" is more likely to succeed if its generalizations are drawn from the study of actual institutions as they have evolved historically, rather than from the idealistic constructs of social philosophers. The reason for this assertion is that the *operational meaning* of social concepts is *what people do*. The student of differential black socioeconomic status is thus forced to go beyond the usual scope and methodology of economics—at least into sociology, psychology, history, and government—to recognize the causes of economic variables and to suggest policies to correct such variables.

Secondly, the management of social adjustment requires general theoretical propositions specifically designed to cope with change. The tools of contemporary economics were largely fashioned, however, for limited, static purposes. Their focus is nondevelopmental; their boundaries are constricted. Bauer and Yamey have stated the problem clearly:

> The analysis of the factors affecting the level, efficiency and growth of resources in an economy was outside the scope of the deliberations of economic theorists. The discussion was generally at a high level of abstraction, so much, indeed, that the principal, long-term determinants of income and wealth, such as the factors underlying the growth of capital, the size of population, the attitude towards work, saving and risk-bearing, the quality of entrepreneurship and the extent of markets, were considered as institutional forces or facts given, as data, to the economist. . . .
> . . . the problems of the growth and change of resources often raise issues which are of much greater practical significance than those of the allocation of given resources. . . . it has come to be realized that the high level of simplification adopted in economic theory in the decades before the recent war [World War II] abstracted from so many major factors that the variables retained for examination were not always or usually sufficiently important to help substantially

what is black economics?

with the fullest possible understanding and interpretation of phenomena, and particularly with the establishment of functional relationships. Though the analysis may have been logically correct and formally elegant, it dealt with too few of the influences affecting the situation, so that the results were of limited intellectual or practical interest. . . .[5]

So, for example, the static theory of comparative advantage logically argues that the existing distribution of scarce resources determines the pattern of specialization that is of greatest mutual advantage. Since black Americans own relatively little capital and therefore have a *relative* abundance of (largely) unskilled labor, they ought to specialize in selling that labor or in producing commodities which embody large amounts of such labor. The argument does not deal either with the questions of *why* blacks have such a shortage of capital or with what steps might be taken to increase that supply both in its physical sense and as human investment in productive skills, health, and mobility. Specialization on the basis of existing resource endowment is indeed an efficient *short-run* policy, but it ignores the point that the very intent of development is to change resource endowment in the direction of greater capital and managerial capacity.

That specialization on basis of current resource endowment may not only fail passively to prepare for the future, but can actively contribute to a deterioration of the unskilled worker's position, is cogently argued by Gunnar Myrdal.[6] Economic development for the individual can become self-sustaining only when critical minima in investment and social services are reached. Such resource owners have productivity, adaptability, and bargaining power on which to build. Unskilled workers do not.

The barriers facing the unskilled worker are multiplied by interlocked vicious circles. For example, low incomes make saving difficult; this in turn retards accumulation of wealth and human capital and tends to perpetuate low incomes. Such vicious circles, compounded by the deteriorating terms of trade unskilled workers face in an increasingly capital-intensive, technologically sophisticated economy, may well swamp the theoretically expected

[5] Peter T. Bauer and Basil S. Yamey, *The Economics of Under-Developed Countries* (Chicago: The University of Chicago Press, 1957), pp. 10–11 *passim.*

[6] See Gunnar Myrdal, *An International Economy* (New York: Harper & Row, 1956).

the limitations of standard theory   41

equilibrating processes of the "normally" functioning market economy. The results of market exchange under such conditions are likely to be counterproductive, particularly for the unskilled black worker who faces differential institutional burdens. To the degree that equilibrium analysis overlooks the importance of retrogressive, cumulative forces, its predictions cannot help but be fundamentally erroneous.

It can be said, then, that there *is* a "Black Economics" in the sense that what economists usually subsume in their "ceteris paribus," other-things-equal conditions become endogenous variables. These variables are drawn from phenomena usually "claimed" by other social disciplines. In this sense, then, "Black Economics" is "Black Social Science."

Finally, a discipline so conceived deserves a place in the sun only if it is created in the service of policy. The standard distinction between a scientific discipline and value judgments, however legitimate elsewhere, is spurious in this case. As the staff of *The Revue of Black Political Economy* put it in explaining their choice of title:

> We feel that, in America at least, for black people to effect any significant alteration in their economic position, they will first be obliged to develop a sound political strategy. It profits us little to spin out beautiful development theories which have no hope of ever being implemented. For us the term "Political Economy," which includes within its scope the political realities of economic relationships, seemed the more accurate one to describe the necessary focus of black economic development.[7]

Nonscientific judgments must be made on what possible social changes are an improvement, on what means are necessary, sufficient, *and* justified.

The interdisciplinary, dynamic, value-laden character of black economics underlies the inclusion in this work of a large policy section (Part 2). This discussion of policy alternatives operating as it does in many aspects of social life, can be understood and properly adjudged only in the context of the ideological considerations treated in the preceding chapter. We have as our objective, then, the integration of ideology, theory, and policy, based upon the comprehensive survey of the anatomy of black differential status which follows.

[7] "Publisher's Preface to the Inaugural Issue," *The Review of Black Political Economy*, Vol. 1, No. 1 (Spring/Summer 1970), iv.

evolution of black poverty

4 evolution of black poverty

INTRODUCTION

It is only a little over 100 years since the end of black chattel slavery in the southern United States. Slavery was not only an alien system for the black population, it was also associated with subhuman social and economic conditions in the strange new culture. Furthermore, class and caste practices and ideologies regarding blacks in both the North and the South permeated the dominant white culture.

After the formal demise of chattel slavery, its heritage was kept very much alive, indeed was nurtured, by the white power structure throughout the country. Despite a small amount of rural–urban migration within the South, the black population was largely trapped in the social and economic prison of southern agrarian peonage for many decades after the Civil War. The handful of slaves and black freedmen who, before the war, were given the chance, already displayed notable capacities as artisans and craftsmen. But after the war those blacks who escaped to the southern cities were systematically prevented, by competing white workers, from learning and pursuing the artisan occupations practiced in the urban areas. The men were confined mainly to manual labor and the women to domestic service. W. E. B. Du Bois, in the passage which follows, outlines brilliantly how and why the wedge was driven between the blacks and the poor whites in the decades after the Civil War.

The southern urban employment pattern, along with ghettoization, was also imposed in the North when South–North migrations became significant, beginning with the turn of the twentieth century. United States agriculture at just this juncture in economic history was beginning to experience its own absolute decline in the total number of persons employed, that number having reached its historic peak in the census of 1910. These reductions, and institutional barriers, meant that the chance to move into northern farming was practically closed for the impoverished black immigrant. Entry into the northern ghetto and into northern unskilled employment was thus the only feasible alternative to remaining a southern sharecropper or laborer.

With all its disadvantages, the northern choice was usually an improvement. It spelled higher money incomes (possibly even real incomes) and a slightly less severe degree of social ostracism. So the migrations continued.

In southern agriculture the slave heritage continued to be nurtured through the sharecropper system. It also persisted in urban environments through segregation, the localization of black businesses in ghettos, the policy of reserving certain (menial) jobs for blacks, and the adherence by whites to the notion of white superiority in all other departments of economic, social, and political life. Whites continued to believe they had a vested interest in the subordination of blacks.

We know from the vicious circle of cumulative causation that the environmental heritage of slavery and its aftermath has fastened disadvantages with respect to preparation for the market economy upon the black population. This historic heritage has been a particularly severe case of the more general tendency for the economic status and distribution of income and wealth of past generations to determine current patterns. Josiah Wedgwood pointed out almost half a century ago, on the basis of his research into the role of inheritance in Britain, that the economic position of a given generation tends to be "predetermined by the economic position of the different members of the family at least *five* generations back." For American blacks, the culturally inherited differential disadvantages in preparation for remunerative economic activity made it all the harder to fight the abiding environmental barriers to material improvement. This is one of the central points in Alan Batchelder's analysis of some of the current effects of *past* discrimination. In his concept of "blasting," we have a fine treatment of the interaction between subjective and environmental factors as a framework for showing the impact of history upon contemporary black differential status.

evolution of black poverty

And yet, as Du Bois reminds us, black people have, in the face of such odds, exhibited an admirable and tenacious determination to throw off the effects of stigma and caste, a determination that has brought them considerable accomplishments compared with their past status. But these accomplishments, he stresses, have not yet begun to "plumb the deeps" of the suppressed black potential.

How did it come about that the great black exodus from southern agriculture was accompanied by the creation of urban ghetto slums in both the South and the North? The answer to this historical question is vital, because the ghetto is the heartland of black society in the United States today and because any basic solution to the problems of black subordination must involve ghetto policy. The answer is advanced in the selection that follows from the *Report of The National Advisory Commission on Civil Disorders*. The *Report* presents in a concise way the major forces at work to generate this particular form of "Apartheid." Those interested in more elaborate treatments will find the literature extensive, one of the best being the discussion of the evolution of the Chicago ghetto in Allan Spear's *Black Chicago*.[1] The ghetto is a unique subculture, and it abides.

As is well known, the incidence of crime in this subculture is widespread with blacks themselves the usual victims. With regard to crime statistics, when dealing with ghetto residents, it should be recognized that laws may well be differentially enforced and statistics differentially reported. Nevertheless, crime as an index of "social pathology" and many other indices show the effects of overcrowding in substandard housing, broken homes, discrimination in the job market, and the resultant poverty.

Significant fiscal problems in connection with the role of government, particularly local government, in sustaining the ghetto are also presented. On the ghetto proper, this chapter contains a statement of unusual clarity and incisiveness by Professor Daniel Fusfeld on the view that the ghetto is a colony of the larger white metropolitan system.

It is the hope of the editors that the reader will find in black history, and particularly in the evolution of black ghetto society, an appropriate framework for comprehending the contemporary

[1] Allan H. Spear, *Black Chicago: The Making of a Negro Ghetto* (Chicago: The University of Chicago Press, 1967).

problem of black subordination and appraising the existing spectrum of policy alternatives. Only through the study of the history of black–white relationships can one understand the depths of disadvantage, discrimination, and prejudice that beset contemporary American society. Only thus can one grasp the enormity of the task that enlightened citizens confront, this time it is hoped with a more serious and determined intent than ever before.

the slave
heritage

discrimination,
past and present

ALAN BATCHELDER

In the United States, whites have had more opportunities than Negroes to participate in economic development. These differences in participation stand out clearly when the American experience is divided into the following three time-space units.

1. *Period One.* The South (1793 to 1940), accumulating physical and human capital slowly, kept most American Negroes in rural areas cut off from access to the rapidly growing physical and human capital of Northern and Western farms and cities.

2. *Period Two.* The South (1940 to date), now rapidly developing, retained most of the American Negro population, but denied it access to the growing physical and human capital of Southern agriculture and manufacturing.

3. *Period Three.* The North and West (1917 to date), experi-

From Alan Batchelder, *The Economics of Poverty* (New York: John Wiley & Sons, 1966), pp. 107–15 *passim*.

evolution of black poverty

encing persistent economic development, received a steadily growing portion of the Negro population of the United States.

Each period deserves detailed consideration.

the south, 1793 to 1940

This was the period between the invention of the cotton gin and the large-scale introduction of tractors, cotton cultivators, and cotton pickers into Southern agriculture. During these years, rapid economic development persisted in agriculture and industry outside the South while change was minimal in Southern agriculture.

The need for skilled labor and the availability of Negro talent provided enough economic incentive to induce antebellum planters to train slaves. . . . Slaves did much of the mechanical, engineering, and bookkeeping work of the old South.

One observer reported that in 1865 more than one-third of North Carolina's Negroes were engaged in mechanical occupations as blacksmiths, gunsmiths, cabinetmakers, shipbuilders, pilots, and things of this kind. This claim may be exaggerated, but Negro craftsmen were so numerous that the plantation owners' practice of supplying slave mechanics to do urban work provoked numerous petitions from white mechanics to the various Southern state legislatures in protest against the Negro competition. These petitions were generally ignored because the legislation requested would have worked to the disadvantage of the planters who controlled the legislatures.

After the Civil War, the planters had to hire their mechanics and thus lost their economic incentive to favor Negroes over whites. Under the banner of white supremacy, white mechanics were at last able to displace Negroes from skilled work and to keep Negroes from the training required by the crafts. Both before and after the war, most Southern Negroes worked in field agriculture. After the war, the crop lien kept Negro farmers perpetually in debt. White sheriffs kept them from leaving the land while in debt. Together, these institutions bound Negroes to the land almost as effectively as slavery had done before the war.

During Reconstruction, public school systems were introduced into most Southern states. The Redemptionists viewed the

Yankee schoolmarms as subversives (to be expelled), and public education (especially in the rural areas) stagnated until the turn of the century. During the twentieth century, public school systems have expanded, but Negroes have been segregated in facilities that have barely qualified for the title, "schools."

The story is told in the official reports of the Mississippi State Department of Education. In 1900, Mississippi school districts spent $8.20 per white child and $2.67 per Negro child for educational costs other than for buildings. For these same purposes, Mississippi in 1940 spent $31.23 per white pupil and $6.69 per Negro pupil. . . .

the south, 1940 to date

During this second time-space unit, the keynote has been economic development. As long as hand labor was required to weed and thin cotton, there was no incentive to replace it in cotton picking or in planting. Beginning in the early 1940's, all stages of cotton culture were mechanized, and livestock and poultry raising supplemented and partly supplanted cotton farming. The new Southern agriculture demanded additional human capital and larger amounts of physical capital per farm.

To obtain the extra land and new equipment to make a go of the new agriculture, farmers needed access to credit. To make effective use of the new equipment, they needed training. Through the Federal Home Board and the system of county agricultural agents, the Federal Government played a primary role in providing credit and instruction to farmers. But the United States Civil Rights Commission found that the Board made loans to whites to buy land and equipment, while making loans to Negroes for food and seed. Loans to whites have permitted increases in the quantity of physical capital per farm. Loans to Negroes have left their capital position unchanged.

There are no statistics showing how willing white Southern bankers have been to lend to Negro farmers for expansion, but the evidence suggests a marked lack of willingness. Between 1930 and 1959, the average size of white Southern farms grew 91% from 130 to 249 acres, while the average Negro farm grew only 21% from 43 to 52 acres. The Civil Rights Commission further found that white agricultural extension agents learned the

evolution of black poverty

new techniques as they evolved and taught them to white farmers, while Negro agents continued to teach the same old techniques of cotton culture and home canning (most Negro extension agents also serve as home demonstration agents to housewives).

Without access to the growing stock of physical and human capital needed in the new agriculture, Negroes found that the larger, efficient white farms were pressing prices down and driving them to the margin on their small, ill-equipped farms. With access to training and credit, whites were in a position to buy the distressed Negro farms and the Negroes moved. . . .

Negroes (and whites) left the farms for Southern cities where the number of manufacturing jobs expanded rapidly. Physical capital piled up in urban areas as factories were built to serve the new Southern markets and to be near newly developed raw-material sources and cheap but unskilled labor. Between 1950 and 1960, there was an increase of 944 thousand jobs in Southern manufacturing. Of these 944 thousand jobs, 12 thousand went to Negro women and none to Negro men. The new physical capital was not to be used by Negroes. . . .

Economic development reached the South after 1940. On farms and in cities, whites had access to the growing stock of physical capital and also to informed agricultural agents, schools, and on-the-job training which created the human capital . . . required to utilize the new physical capital. In contrast, Negroes were permitted limited access to accumulating capital. Whites became increasingly productive, but Negroes, denied access to machines and education, fell behind as Southern public policy widened the gap between the . . . average white and average Negro.

the north and west, 1917 to date

In the third time-space unit, the growing Negro population has had access to more physical capital and better education than has been available in the South. The labor shortages of the two world wars were particularly influential in bringing Negroes into Northern manufacturing activities to work with massive physical capital. In 1949, Northern Negro men enjoyed a median annual income of $2185 compared with a median of only $1033 for Southern Negro men.

discrimination, past and present   **49**

The increasingly frequent recessions and rising unemployment rates of the 1950's damaged the Negro position. In 1949, Northern and Western Negro men had median incomes that were 78% as large as those of white men in those regions. . . . The Northern and Western Negro men were better off than their Southern peers, but were at a severe disadvantage in comparison with Northern and Western white men.

One reason for this disadvantage was that almost one half of the Negroes in the Northern and Western labor force during the 1960's were born in the South where many were educated—or miseducated—in Southern schools. For most graduates of even moderately good public schools, it is extremely difficult to imagine how little education has been provided by the Southern way of life, until they meet someone "educated" on $6.67 a year.

White attitudes toward Negroes derive partly from stereotypes and partly from contact with Negro families with $6.67-a-year educations. Usually these whites will contend that, because the Negroes that they know are productively inferior, *all* Negroes must be similarly inferior. The resulting feeling of superiority induces such whites to discriminate on the basis of color rather than talent. This discrimination, in education and in employment, leads to . . . greater poverty in Negroes, and these results tend to assure these whites that they were right in the first place. . . . Many discriminatory barriers have fallen in recent years, but the effects of past and present discrimination persist not only in inferior educational attainments but also in the "blasting" suffered by Northern and Western as well as by Southern Negro families. Learning begins in the family, but discrimination has blasted the family system of poor Negroes leaving them incapable of emulating white middle-class families. . . . Because of blasting, poor Negro families are likely to perpetuate poverty in their children.

What are the symptoms of blasting? First, poor Negro families are different. Poor urban Negro families—crowded because of relatively high housing costs (10 to 25% higher than for whites in similar quarters) and many children—lack books, pencils, and a safe outdoors to explore. Adults have a small vocabulary and use it with poor diction. . . . Fewer Negro families would be headed by women if there were a decrease in the number of women with children they did not want. As is presently the case, 32% of poor Negro families are headed by women while in many

evolution of black poverty

other families women earn more than men. In most white families, masculinity means being the financial pillar of the family. Poor Negro children daily observe a different system.

Second, the Negro self-image is different. Charles Silberman observed that Negroes "learn in earliest childhood of the stigma attached to color in the United States. . . . Negroes are taught to despise themselves." Asked to choose between white and brown dolls, 60% of 3-year-old Negro children pick white dolls as "the nice ones." . . .

To succeed in our economy, children must believe they can succeed, and then must work and study in pursuit of success. . . . They will not equal whites in the marketplace as long as they reject themselves.

Nor can Negro children succeed while their teachers reject them. And teachers do reject their Negro children. . . . when incumbent teachers in ghetto schools are replaced by teachers who expect the children to learn, the children learn much more than under the kind of teacher attitudes that are typical in the Negro ghetto schools.

back toward slavery

W. E. B. Du BOIS

The political success of the doctrine of racial separation, which overthrew Reconstruction by uniting the planter and the poor white, was far exceeded by its astonishing economic results. The theory of laboring class unity rests upon the assumption that laborers, despite internal jealousies, will unite because of their opposition to exploitation by the capitalists. According to this, even after a part of the poor white laboring class became identified with the planters, and eventually displaced them, their interests would be diametrically opposed to those of the mass of white labor, and of course to those of the black laborers. This

W. E. B. Du Bois. *Black Reconstruction in America, 1860–1880*. [1935] New York: Russell & Russell, 1956, pp. 700–702.

would throw white and black labor into one class, and precipitate a united fight for higher wage and better working conditions.

Most persons do not realize how far this failed to work in the South, and it failed to work because the theory of race was supplemented by a carefully planned and slowly evolved method, which drove such a wedge between the white and black workers that there probably are not today in the world two groups of workers with practically identical interests who hate and fear each other so deeply and persistently and who are kept so far apart that neither sees anything of common interest.

It must be remembered that the white group of laborers, while they received a low wage, were compensated in part by a sort of public and psychological wage. They were given public deference and titles of courtesy because they were white. They were admitted freely with all classes of white people to public functions, public parks, and the best schools. The police were drawn from their ranks, and the courts, dependent upon their votes, treated them with such leniency as to encourage lawlessness. Their vote selected public officials, and while this had small effect upon the economic situation, it had great effect upon their personal treatment and the deference shown them. White schoolhouses were the best in the community, and conspicuously placed, and they cost anywhere from twice to ten times as much per capita as the colored schools. The newspapers specialized on news that flattered the poor whites and almost utterly ignored the Negro except in crime and ridicule.

On the other hand, in the same way, the Negro was subject to public insult; was afraid of mobs; was liable to the jibes of children and the unreasoning fears of white women; and was compelled almost continuously to submit to various badges of inferiority. The result of this was that the wages of both classes could be kept low, the whites fearing to be supplanted by Negro labor, the Negroes always being threatened by the substitution of white labor.

Mob violence and lynching were the inevitable result of the attitude of these two classes and for a time were a sort of permissible Roman holiday for the entertainment of vicious whites. One can see for these reasons why labor organizers and labor agitators made such small headway in the South. They were, for the most part, appealing to laborers who would rather have low

evolution of black poverty

wages upon which they could eke out an existence than see colored labor with a decent wage. White labor saw in every advance of Negroes a threat to their racial prerogatives, so that in many districts Negroes were afraid to build decent homes or dress well, or own carriages, bicycles or automobiles, because of possible retaliation on the part of the whites.

Thus every problem of labor advance in the South was skillfully turned by demagogues into a matter of inter-racial jealousy. Perhaps the most conspicuous proof of this was the Atlanta riot in 1906, which followed Hoke Smith's vicious attempt to become United States Senator on a platform which first attacked corporations and then was suddenly twisted into scandalous traducing of the Negro race.

To this day no casual and unsophisticated reader of the white Southern press could possibly gather that the American Negro masses were anything but degraded, ignorant, inefficient examples of an incurably inferior race.

The result of all this had to be unfortunate for the Negro. He was a caged human being, driven into a curious mental provincialism. An inferiority complex dominated him. He did not believe himself a man like other men. He could not teach his children self-respect. The Negro as a group gradually lost his manners, his courtesy, his lighthearted kindliness. Large numbers sank into apathy and fatalism! There was no chance for the black man; there was no use in striving; ambition was not for Negroes.

The effect of caste on the moral integrity of the Negro race in America has thus been widely disastrous; servility and fawning, gross flattery of white folk and lying to appease and cajole them; failure to achieve dignity and self-respect and moral self-assertion, personal cowardliness and submission to insult and aggression; exaggerated and despicable humility; lack of faith of Negroes in themselves and in other Negroes and in all colored folk; inordinate admiration for the stigmata of success among white folk: wealth and arrogance, cunning dishonesty and assumptions of superiority; the exaltation of laziness and indifference as just as successful as the industry and striving which invites taxation and oppression; dull apathy and cynicism; faith in no future and the habit of moving and wandering in search of justice; a religion of prayer and submission to replace determination and effort.

These are not universal results or else the Negro long since would have dwindled and died in crime and disease. But they are so widespread as to bring inner conflict as baffling as the problems of inter-racial relations, and they hold back the moral grit and organized effort which are the only hope of survival.

On this and in spite of this comes an extraordinary record of accomplishment, a record so contradictory of what one might easily expect that many people and even the Negroes themselves are deceived by it. The real question is not so much what the Negro has done in spite of caste, as what he might have accomplished with reasonable encouragement. He has cut down his illiteracy more than two-thirds in fifty years, but with decent schools it ought to have been cut down 99 per cent. He has accumulated land and property, but has not been able to hold one-tenth of what he has rightly earned. He has achieved success in many lines, as an inventor, scientist, scholar and writer. But most of his ability has been choked in chain-gangs and by open deliberate discrimination and conspiracies of silence. He has made a place for himself in literature and art, but the great deeps of his artistic gifts have never yet been plumbed. And yet, for all that he has accomplished, not only the nation but the South itself claims credit and actually points to it as proof of the wisdom or at least the innocuousness of organized suppression!

the escape from the ghetto: immigrants and blacks

KERNER REPORT

. . . Why has the Negro been unable to escape from poverty and the ghetto like the European immigrants?

The changing nature of the American economy is one major reason. When the European immigrants were arriving in large numbers, America was becoming an urban-industrial society. To

From The National Advisory Commission on Civil Disorders, *Report* (Washington: Government Printing Office, March 1, 1968), pp. 143–45 *passim*.

evolution of black poverty

build its major cities and industries, America needed great pools of unskilled labor. The immigrants provided the labor, gained an economic foothold and thereby enabled their children and grand-children to move up to skilled, white-collar and professional employment.

Since World War II especially, America's urban-industrial society has matured; unskilled labor is far less essential than before, and blue-collar jobs of all kinds are decreasing in number and importance as a source of new employment. The Negroes who migrated to the great urban centers lacked the skills essential to the new economy, and the schools of the ghetto have been unable to provide the education that can qualify them for decent jobs. The Negro migrant, unlike the immigrant, found little opportunity in the city; he had arrived too late, and the unskilled labor he had to offer was no longer needed.

Racial discrimination is undoubtedly the second major reason why the Negro has been unable to escape from poverty. The structure of discrimination has persistently narrowed his opportunities and restricted his prospects. Well before the high tide of immigration from overseas, Negroes were already relegated to the poorly paid, low status occupations. Had it not been for racial discrimination, the North might well have recruited southern Negroes after the Civil War to provide the labor for building the burgeoning urban-industrial economy. Instead, northern employers looked to Europe for their sources of unskilled labor. Upon the arrival of the immigrants, the Negroes were dislodged from the few urban occupations they had dominated. Not until World War II were Negroes generally hired for industrial jobs, and by that time the decline in the need for unskilled labor had already begun. European immigrants, too, suffered from discrimination, but never was it so pervasive. The prejudice against color in America has formed a bar to advancement unlike any other.

Political opportunities also played an important role in enabling the European immigrants to escape from poverty. The immigrants settled for the most part in rapidly growing cities that had powerful and expanding political machines which gave them economic advantages in exchange for political support.

. . . Ethnic groups often dominated one or more of the municipal services—police and fire protection, sanitation and even public education.

By the time the Negroes arrived, the situation had altered dramatically. The great wave of public building had virtually come to an end; reform groups were beginning to attack the political machines; the machines were no longer so powerful or so well equipped to provide jobs and other favors.

Although the political machines retained their hold over the areas settled by Negroes, the scarcity of patronage jobs made them unwilling to share with Negroes the political positions they had created in these neighborhoods. . . .

This pattern exists in many other American cities. Negroes are still underrepresented in city councils and in most city agencies.

Segregation played a role here too. The immigrants and their descendants, who felt threatened by the arrival of the Negro, prevented a Negro-immigrant coalition that might have saved the old political machines. Reform groups, nominally more liberal on the race issue, were often dominated by businessmen and middle-class city residents who usually opposed coalition with any low-income group, white or black.

Cultural factors also made it easier for the immigrants to escape from poverty. They came to America from much poorer societies, with a low standard of living, and they came at a time when job aspirations were low. When most jobs in the American economy were unskilled, they sensed little deprivation in being forced to take the dirty and poorly paid jobs. . . .

Negroes came to the city under quite different circumstances. Generally relegated to jobs that others would not take, they were paid too little to be able to put money in savings for new enterprises. In addition, Negroes lacked the extended family characteristic of certain European groups; each household usually had only one or two breadwinners. Moreover, Negro men had fewer cultural incentives to work in a dirty job for the sake of the family. As a result of slavery and of long periods of male unemployment afterwards, the Negro family structure had become matriarchal; the man played a secondary and marginal role in his family. For many Negro men, then, there were few of the cultural and psychological rewards of family life; they often abandoned their homes because they felt themselves useless to their families.

Although Negro men worked as hard as the immigrants to support their families, their rewards were less. The jobs did not pay enough to enable them to support their families, for prices and

evolution of black poverty

living standards had risen since the immigrants had come, and the entrepreneurial opportunities that had allowed some immigrants to become independent, even rich, had vanished. Above all, Negroes suffered from segregation, which denied them access to the good jobs and the right unions and which deprived them of the opportunity to buy real estate or obtain business loans or move out of the ghetto and bring up their children in middle-class neighborhoods. Immigrants were able to leave their ghettos as soon as they had the money; segregation has denied Negroes the opportunity to live elsewhere.

Finally, nostalgia makes it easy to exaggerate the ease of escape of the white immigrants from the ghettos. When the immigrants were immersed in poverty, they, too, lived in slums, and these neighborhoods exhibited fearfully high rates of alcoholism, desertion, illegitimacy and the other pathologies associated with poverty. Just as some Negro men desert their families when they are unemployed and their wives can get jobs, so did the men of other ethnic groups, even though time and affluence has clouded white memories of the past.

Today, whites tend to contrast their experience with poverty-stricken Negroes. The fact is, among the southern and eastern Europeans who came to America in the last great wave of immigration, those who came already urbanized were the first to escape from poverty. The others who came to America from rural backgrounds, as Negroes did, are only now, after three generations, in the final stages of escaping from poverty. Until the last 10 years or so, most of these were employed in blue-collar jobs, and only a small proportion of their children were able or willing to attend college. In other words, only the third, and in many cases only the fourth, generation has been able to achieve the kind of middle-class income and status that allows it to send its children to college. Because of favorable economic and political conditions, these ethnic groups were able to escape from lower class status to working class and lower middle-class status, but it has taken them three generations.

Negroes have been concentrated in the city for only two generations, and they have been there under much less favorable conditions. Moreover, their escape from poverty has been blocked in part by the resistance of the European ethnic groups; they have been unable to enter some unions and to move into some neighborhoods outside the ghetto because descendants of the

European immigrants who control these unions and neighborhoods have not yet abandoned them for middle-class occupations and areas. . . .

What the American economy of the late 19th and early 20th century was able to do to help the European immigrants escape from poverty is now largely impossible. New methods of escape must be found for the majority of today's poor.

the ghetto

formation of
the black ghettos

KERNER REPORT

. . . the Negro population in America has become more urbanized, and more metropolitan, than the white population. According to Census Bureau estimates, almost 70 percent of all Negroes in 1966 lived in metropolitan areas, compared to 64 percent of all whites. In the South, more than half the Negro population now lives in cities. Rural Negroes outnumber urban Negroes in only four states: Arkansas, Mississippi, North Carolina, and South Carolina.

Basic data concerning Negro urbanization trends indicate that:

1. Almost all Negro population growth is occurring within metropolitan areas, primarily within central cities. From 1950 to 1966, the U.S. Negro population rose 6.5 million. Over 98 percent of that increase took place in metropolitan areas—86 percent within central cities, 12 percent in the urban fringe.

From The National Advisory Commission on Civil Disorders, *Report* (Washington: Government Printing Office, March 1, 1968), pp. 118–20 *passim*.

2. The vast majority of white population growth is occurring in suburban portions of metropolitan areas. From 1950 to 1966, 77.8 percent of the white population increase of 35.6 million took place in the suburbs. Central cities received only 2.5 percent of this total white increase. Since 1960, white central-city population has actually declined by 1.3 million.

3. As a result, central cities are steadily becoming more heavily Negro, while the urban fringes around them remain almost entirely white. The proportion of Negroes in all central cities rose steadily from 12 percent in 1950, to 17 percent in 1960, to 20 percent in 1966. Meanwhile, metropolitan areas outside of central cities remained 95 percent white from 1950 to 1960 and became 96 percent white by 1966.

4. The Negro population is growing faster, both absolutely and relatively, in the larger metropolitan areas than in the smaller ones. From 1950 to 1966, the proportion of nonwhite in the central cities of metropolitan areas with 1 million or more persons doubled, reaching 26 percent, as compared with 20 percent in the central cities of metropolitan areas containing from 250,000 to 1 million persons and 12 percent in the central cities of metropolitan areas containing under 250,000 persons.

5. The 12 largest central cities—New York, Chicago, Los Angeles, Philadelphia, Detroit, Baltimore, Houston, Cleveland, Washington, D.C., St. Louis, Milwaukee, and San Francisco—now contain over two-thirds of the Negro population outside the South and almost one-third of the total in the United States. All these cities have experienced rapid increases in Negro population since 1950. In six—Chicago, Detroit, Cleveland, St. Louis, Milwaukee, and San Francisco—the proportion of Negroes at least doubled. In two others—New York and Los Angeles—it probably doubled. In 1961 seven of these cities are over 30 percent Negro, and one, Washington, D.C., is two-thirds Negro.

The early pattern of Negro settlement within each metropolitan area followed that of immigrant groups. Migrants converged on the older sections of the central city because the lowest cost housing was located there, friends and relatives were likely to be living there, and the older neighborhoods then often had good public transportation.

But the latter phases of Negro settlement and expansion in metropolitan areas diverge sharply from those typical of white immigrants. As the whites were absorbed by the larger society, many left their predominantly ethnic neighborhoods and moved to outlying areas to obtain newer housing and better schools. Some scattered randomly over the suburban area. Others established new ethnic clusters in the suburbs, but even these rarely contained solely members of a single ethnic group. As a result, most middle-class neighborhoods—both in the suburbs and within central cities—have no distinctive ethnic character, except that they are white.

Nowhere has the expansion of America's urban Negro population followed this pattern of dispersal. Thousands of Negro families have attained incomes, living standards, and cultural levels matching or surpassing those of whites who have "up-graded" themselves from distinctly ethnic neighborhoods. Yet most Negro families have remained within predominantly Negro neighborhoods, primarily because they have been effectively excluded from white residential areas.

Their exclusion has been accomplished through various discriminatory practices, some obvious and overt, others subtle and hidden. Deliberate efforts are sometimes made to discourage Negro families from purchasing or renting homes in all-white neighborhoods. Intimidation and threats of violence have ranged from throwing garbage on lawns and making threatening phone calls to burning crosses in yards and even dynamiting property. More often, real estate agents simply refuse to show homes to Negro buyers.

Many middle-class Negro families, therefore, cease looking for homes beyond all-Negro areas or nearby "changing" neighborhoods. For them, trying to move into all-white neighborhoods is not worth the psychological efforts and costs required.

Another form of discrimination just as significant is white withdrawal from, or refusal to enter, neighborhoods where large numbers of Negroes are moving or already residing. Normal population turnover causes about 20 percent of the residents of average U.S. neighborhoods to move out every year because of income changes, job transfers, shifts in life-cycle position or deaths. This normal turnover rate is even higher in apartment

evolution of black poverty

areas. The refusal of whites to move into changing areas when vacancies occur there from normal turnover means that most of these vacancies are eventually occupied by Negroes. An inexorable shift toward heavy Negro occupancy results.

Once this happens, the remaining whites seek to leave, thus confirming the existing belief among whites that complete transformation of a neighborhood is inevitable once Negroes begin to enter. Since the belief itself is one of the major causes of the transformation, it becomes a self-fulfilling prophecy which inhibits the development of racially integrated neighborhoods.

As a result, Negro settlements expand almost entirely through "massive racial transition" at the edges of existing all-Negro neighborhoods, rather than by a gradual dispersion of population throughout the metropolitan area.

Two points are particularly important:

1. "Massive transition" requires no panic or flight by the original white residents of a neighborhoods into which Negroes begin moving. All it requires is the failure or refusal of other whites to fill the vacancies resulting from normal turnover.

2. Thus, efforts to stop massive transition by persuading present white residents to remain will ultimately fail unless whites outside the neighborhood can be persuaded to move in.

It is obviously true that some residential separation of whites and Negroes would occur even without discriminatory practices by whites. This would result from the desires of some Negroes to live in predominantly Negro neighborhoods and from differences in meaningful social variables, such as income and educational levels. But these factors alone would not lead to the almost complete segregation of whites and Negroes which has developed in our metropolitan areas.

The process of racial transition in central-city neighborhoods has been only one factor among many others causing millions of whites to move out of central cities as the Negro populations there expanded. More basic perhaps have been the rising mobility and affluence of middle-class families and the more attractive living conditions—particularly better schools—in the suburbs.

Whatever the reason, the result is clear. In 1950, 45.5 million whites lived in central cities. If this population had grown from

1950 to 1960 at the same rate as the Nation's white population as a whole, it would have increased by 8 million. It actually rose only 2.2 million, indicating an outflow of 5.8 million.

From 1960 to 1966, the white outflow appears to have been even more rapid. White population of central cities declined 1.3 million instead of rising 3.6 million—as it would if it had grown at the same rate as the entire white population. In theory, therefore, 4.9 million whites left central cities during these 6 years.

Statistics for all central cities as a group understate the relationship between Negro population growth and white outflow in individual central cities. The fact is, many cities with relatively few Negroes experienced rapid white-population growth, thereby obscuring the size of white outmigration that took place in cities having large increases in Negro population. For example, from 1950 to 1960, the 10 largest cities in the United States had a total Negro population increase of 1.6 million, or 55 percent, while the white population there declined 1.4 million. If the two cities where the white population increased (Los Angeles and Houston) are excluded, the nonwhite population in the remaining eight rose 1.4 million, whereas their white population declined 2.1 million. If the white population in these cities had increased at only half the rate of the white population in the United States as a whole from 1950 to 1960, it would have risen by 1.4 million. Thus, these eight cities actually experienced a white outmigration of at least 3.5 million, while gaining 1.4 million nonwhites.

The rapid expansion of all-Negro residential areas and large-scale white withdrawal have continued a pattern of residential segregation that has existed in American cities for decades. A recent study[1] reveals that this pattern is present to a high degree in every large city in America. The authors devised an index to measure the degree of residential segregation. The index indicates for each city the percentage of Negroes who would have to move from the blocks where they now live to other blocks in order to provide a perfectly proportional, unsegregated distribution of population.

According to their findings, the average segregation index for 207 of the largest U.S. cities was 86.2 in 1960. This means that an average of over 86 percent of all Negroes would have had to

[1] "Negroes in Cities," Karl and Alma Taeuber, Aldine Publishing Co., Chicago (1965).

evolution of black poverty

change blocks to create an unsegregated population distribution. Southern cities had a higher average index (90.9) than cities in the Northeast (79.2), the North Central (87.7), or the West (79.3). Only eight cities had index values below 70, whereas over 50 had values above 91.7.

The degree of residential segregation for all 207 cities has been relatively stable, averaging 85.2 in 1940, 87.3 in 1950, and 86.2 in 1960. Variations within individual regions were only slightly larger. However, a recent Census Bureau study shows that in most of the 12 large cities where special censuses were taken in the mid-1960's, the proportions of Negroes living in neighborhoods of greatest Negro concentration had increased since 1960.

Residential segregation is generally more prevalent with respect to Negroes than for any other minority group, including Puerto Ricans, Orientals, and Mexican-Americans. Moreover, it varies little between central city and suburb. This nearly universal pattern cannot be explained in terms of economic discrimination against all low-income groups. Analysis of 15 representative cities indicates that white upper- and middle-income households are far more segregated from Negro upper- and middle-income households than from white lower-income households.

In summary, the concentration of Negroes in central cities results from a combination of forces. Some of these forces, such as migration and initial settlement patterns in older neighborhoods, are similar to those which affected previous ethnic minorities. Others—particularly discrimination in employment and segregation in housing and schools—are a result of white attitudes based on race and color. These forces continue to shape the future of the central city.

central city—suburban
fiscal disparities

ADVISORY COMMISSION ON
INTERGOVERNMENTAL RELATIONS

The Commission's detailed analysis of the social, economic and fiscal disparities between the metropolitan central cities and their surrounding suburban communities reveals that: . . .

The large central cities are in the throes of a deepening fiscal crisis. On the one hand, they are confronted with the need to satisfy rapidly growing expenditure requirements triggered by the rising number of "high cost" citizens. On the other hand, their tax resources are growing at a decreasing rate (and in some cases actually declining), a reflection of the *exodus of middle and high income families and business firms from the central city to suburbia.*

A clear disparity in tax burden is evident between central city and outside central city. *Local taxes in the central cities average 7.6 percent of the personal income of their residents; outside the central cities they equal only 5.6 percent of income.* Higher central city taxes are reinforcing the other factors that are pushing upper income families and business firms out of the central city into suburbia.

The central cities increased their relative tax effort during a period when their property tax base either showed a deceleration in the rate of growth, or an absolute decline. The observed changes reflected either increases in property tax rates, introduction of local nonproperty taxes (especially in the case of municipal governments), or, most generally, a combination of the two. The central city tax development contrasts sharply with trends on the outside where high income and a continuation of the growth of the property tax base mitigated tax pressures.

On the educational or "developmental" front, the central

From The Advisory Commission on Intergovernmental Relations, *Fiscal Balance in the American Federal System, Vol. 2: Metropolitan Fiscal Disparities* (Washington: Government Printing Office, October 1967), pp. 5–92 *passim.*

evolution of black poverty

cities are falling farther behind their suburban neighbors with each passing year. In 1957 the per pupil expenditures in the 37 metropolitan areas favored the central city slightly—$312 to $303 for the suburban jurisdictions. By 1965, the suburban jurisdictions had forged far ahead—$574 to $449 for the central cities. This growing disparity between the central city and suburban school districts takes on a more ominous character in light of the fact that the central city school districts must carry a disproportionately heavy share of the educational burden—the task of educating an increasing number of . . . underprivileged children. *Children who need education the most are receiving the least!*

To make matters worse, State aid to school districts actually aggravates this situation by favoring the rural and suburban districts.

On the municipal service or custodial front, the presence of "high cost" citizens, greater population density and the need to service commuters force central cities to spend far more than most of their suburban neighbors for police and fire protection and sanitation services. The 37 largest central cities had a noneducational (municipal) outlay of $232 per capita in 1965— $100 greater than their suburban counterparts. . . .

Table 4-1

Projections to 1975 of Local General Expenditures and Tax Revenues as a Percentage of Income, Central City and Outside Central City Areas in 35 Standard Metropolitan Statistical Areas

	Expenditures		Taxes	
Area	Central City	Outside Central City	Central City	Outside Central City
Los Angeles-Long Beach, California	10.2%	10.2%	6.0%	5.8%
San Bernardino-Riverside-Ontario, California	13.7	14.5	6.0	7.6
San Diego, California	9.4	12.0	4.6	5.3
San Francisco-Oakland, California	11.6	12.2	7.9	6.4
Denver, Colorado	9.3	8.0	6.3	5.2
Miami, Florida	12.9	8.0	6.4	4.9
Tampa-St. Petersburg, Florida	12.5	7.5	5.2	3.6

Table 4-1 continued

Area	Expenditures		Taxes	
	Central City	Outside Central City	Central City	Outside Central City
Atlanta, Georgia	11.7	10.1	4.0	3.6
Chicago, Illinois	8.5	6.3	6.9	2.8
Indianapolis, Indiana	6.6	9.5	5.5	5.5
Louisville, Kentucky-Indiana	8.4	4.8	4.0	2.2
New Orleans, Louisiana	8.0	10.6	3.3	1.7
Baltimore, Maryland	10.8	6.4	4.8	3.2
Boston, Massachusetts	14.8	5.9	7.2	4.4
Detroit, Michigan	9.5	8.0	5.7	4.1
Minneapolis-St. Paul, Minnesota	10.1	10.3	5.5	4.8
Kansas City, Missouri-Kansas	5.1	9.2	3.7	4.6
St. Louis, Missouri-Illinois	11.1	4.5	6.5	2.8
Newark, New Jersey	17.8	7.0	11.2	5.0
Paterson-Clifton-Passaic, New Jersey	9.0	5.6	6.3	4.9
Buffalo, New York	10.9	10.4	5.8	5.3
New York, New York	15.5	8.2	9.6	4.7
Rochester, New York	13.1	9.8	6.0	4.3
Cincinnati, Ohio-Kentucky-Indiana	14.0	4.8	6.2	3.4
Cleveland, Ohio	11.6	6.5	5.9	4.1
Columbus, Ohio	7.7	6.6	4.0	3.9
Dayton, Ohio	12.2	7.2	6.7	4.5
Portland, Oregon-Washington	9.0	7.8	5.8	4.3
Philadelphia, Pennsylvania-New Jersey	8.7	6.1	4.8	3.7
Pittsburgh, Pennsylvania	9.5	6.1	5.5	3.7
Providence, Rhode Island	8.6	5.5	5.1	3.9
Dallas, Texas	5.3	7.7	3.3	2.8
Houston, Texas	6.0	9.2	3.4	4.8
Seattle-Everett, Washington	8.6	15.4	4.1	4.6
Milwaukee, Wisconsin	12.7	8.8	7.2	2.7

Note: Excludes the Washington, D.C. SMSA because of the State-local character of its central city and the San Antonio SMSA because data were not available.
Source: Metropolitan Studies Center, Syracuse University.

Our projections clearly indicate that the observed disparity between central city and surburban areas will not "wash out" over the foreseeable future. There is every reason to expect a persistence of disparities derived from the generally favorable suburban position on both the needs and tax resources fronts (Table 4-1).

evolution of black poverty

These projections also enable us to concentrate on the developing gaps in the tax financing of local public services in the Nation's 36 largest cities—a "minimal" projected tax gap of $2.8 billion or a cumulative ten-year total tax gap of approximately $14 billion. The projected total local tax collections of the major central cities are compared with the amount that would be collected if taxes are to rise only in proportion to the natural increase in the property tax base (that is, with no new taxes or rate increases).

. . . the 1975 estimate of $12.6 billion in tax collections assumes the same average annual growth rate between 1965 and 1975 as was observed for the period 1957–1965. For many of these cities during the second half of the 1957–1965 period the tax base has been increasing at a declining rate, and in some it has actually declined, as compared to the first half. For the entire period, tax rates have had to rise considerably between 1957 and 1965. In no case was there an indicated decline in property tax rates. Our calculations indicate property tax rate increases equivalent to 53 percent in Boston, 50 percent in St. Louis and 42 percent in Detroit. In half of the cities, property tax rates rose 25 percent or more in the eight-year period.

The tax financing "gaps" are minimal for a number of reasons. First, the portion of the 1965–1975 increase that is attributed to the natural growth in the property tax base is undoubtedly overstated in some cities because the computation does not allow for the observed recent decline in the rate of increase in the tax base. Secondly, if the recent trend toward an increasing response to the needs of high-cost citizens in the central cities continues, tax collections will have to grow at an even greater rate than in the past. And finally, our projections made no allowance for needed general improvement in the quality of central city government services.

All of these factors add up to a potentially tremendous tax gap relative to resource growth for these large central cities in particular and for local government generally. Taking account of the three additional factors enumerated above, the annual gap could easily reach $5 to $6 billion by 1975, or a cumulative 10-year total tax gap for the 36 large central cities of $25 to $30 billion. . . .

It is the level at which the gap is bridged that is of crucial importance. If it is to be closed at a high or even an adequate level of governmental service, it will have to be done at enormous cost relative to the community's income and tax base unless many of our central cities are given massive infusions of Federal and State aid, if functions are shifted to the State and Federal levels, or if the cities are given an opportunity to tap an areawide tax base.

Regardless of actions taken by the public sector to control riots, regardless of actions taken by the private sector to protect or increase economic investment and opportunity and regardless of efforts by private and public enterprise together in combating poverty and disease among low income residents of central cities or depressed suburban areas, State, local and Federal legislative action is necessary and urgent to bring fiscal needs and resources of our urban governments into better balance.

the ghetto as
an economic subsystem

DANIEL R. FUSFELD

The ghetto economy differs markedly from the rest of the economic system. It is the home of the bulk of our urban poverty. It is permanently depressed, with unemployment rates normally at the high levels that are characteristic of depressions when they occur in the national economy. It is backward and underdeveloped, lacking the dynamic, progressive changes that bring advancement to the rest of the economy. Its manpower is employed in the low wage sector of the economy, primarily, and provides a pool of low skilled labor for an economy in which this resource is needed less and less. Within the ghetto an irregular economy

Daniel R. Fusfeld, "Welfare Payments in a Ghetto Economy," pp. 13–15. The complete paper appears in Kenneth E. Boulding, Martin Pfaff, and Anita B. Pfaff (eds.), *Transfers in an Urbanized Economy: Theories and Effects of the Grants Economy* (Belmont, California: Wadsworth Publishing Co., 1972). This selection will also appear, in somewhat expanded form, as part of Daniel R. Fusfeld, *The Economics of the Urban and Racial Problem,* to be published by Holt, Rinehart & Winston, Inc., in 1972.

evolution of black poverty

functions, partly legal and partly illegal, which provides many of the services needed by the low income ghetto residents which they cannot afford to pay for in the normal channels of commerce or which the regular economy does not provide at all.[1]

When we look at the relationships between the ghetto and the progressive sector of the economy, two phenomena quickly become evident. First, there is a continuous drain of income and other resources out of the ghetto. Second, there is a continuing accretion of people into it, cast off as unuseable by the progressive sector, which wholly or partially counterbalances those who are able to climb up and out.

The drain of resources includes savings, income, physical capital and human resources. The savings of ghetto residents, small though they may be, are deposited in financial institutions whose loans are made to business firms or mortgage borrowers outside the ghetto, with a much smaller flow of capital into the ghetto for these purposes, leaving a net outflow. The size of the net outflow is unknown, but its presence is acknowledged by those who are familiar with the financial institutions that serve the ghetto.

Income is drained out in more easily observed ways. Products sold in the ghetto and to ghetto residents are produced outside the ghetto. The owners of the retail stores that sell these products and gain the profits live largely outside the ghetto. The same is true of the wholesale and shipping firms, advertising media and other elements of the economy that service retail establishments. A large portion of the employees of ghetto retail firms live outside the ghetto, although this has been less true after the 1967–68 riots than before.

Physical capital flows out of the ghetto largely through failure to replace depreciation of housing and public facilities. The ghetto landlord takes a large portion of his gains in the form of capital withdrawals that come from failure to maintain his property. This drain is large. Typically, 70 to 80 percent of ghetto residents rent their housing (as compared with 22% in the nation as a whole) and rent takes some 35 to 60 percent of family income (as compared with 25 to 30 percent in the economy as a whole). A large portion of those rental payments represent a drain of capi-

[1] For a more detailed description of the ghetto economy, see Daniel R. Fusfeld, "The Economy of the Urban Ghetto" in John P. Crecine and Louis H. Masotti, *Financing the Metropolis: Urban Affairs Annual Review*, Vol. IV (Beverly Hills, Calif.: Sage Publications, 1970).

tal out of housing. Public facilities are subject to the same outward flow, through failure to maintain schools, streets, sidewalks, parks and other public facilities in ghetto areas.

Manpower also leaves, when it can. Many persons move up and out of the urban ghetto through education, skill, initiative and luck. They move out primarily through education and jobs in the high wage sector of the economy, and take with them a large part of the entrepreneurship and skill that any substantial population group generates.

The net result of the drain of income and resources from the urban ghetto is the poor, backward, undeveloped slum that continues to exist in the midst of a growing and progressive society. It is drained of all those resources which might form the base for economic development. When this is added to a weak community structure, inadequate public services, and relatively few professional skills, it is not hard to understand why the urban ghetto has been such an intractable problem.

5

the determinants of income differentials

INTRODUCTION   Because the quality of life available to a family depends so directly on its money income, it is imperative to identify the forces, both economic and institutional, that still keep the black median income at a fraction of the white. In 1969, according to the Census Bureau, black incomes rose faster than did those of whites (12 percent for the former, 9.6 percent for the latter).[1] However, the black median of $5,999 remained well below that for white families ($8,794).

Superficially stated, income received by an individual (or family) is the product of the quantity of resources that he has for sale, their dollar value, and the willingness of employers to use them. The substantive questions are what *determines* his ownership of resources, their quantity and quality, their market value, and the employment opportunities for them. The task of Chapter 5, then, is to survey the determinants of income differentials.

We begin with an overview of recent developments in income

---

[1] The real growth rates are overstated for both groups because of the eroding effects of inflation. In real terms, the average growth rate was 3.7 percent.

differentials as related to employment opportunities in both urban and rural settings and to the effects of changing technology. The book is novel in focusing attention both on the determinants of property ownership as they have evolved historically and on the determinants of individual productivity which begin with prenatal care of the unborn infant and impinge on him throughout childhood, in the home and school. As an adult, the individual faces a market which lacks the attributes of the classical competitive model. He is confronted with discrimination by employers and workers and discrimination in attempts to establish his own business. This chapter closes with an assessment of the quantitative effects of discrimination and a qualitative judgment of the economic, political, and social burdens of racism.

Economics has been notably lax in examining the role of asset ownership as a determinant of income. Lee Soltow shows that if we project the rates at which black Americans have been able to build personal property over the last century that, incredible as it seems, it would be the year 2000 before wealth per black person would attain the dollar amount that the average white held at the end of the Civil War ($3,080). Rectification in the form of reparations or governmental provision of goods and services will long remain a controversial matter in view of this historical deprivation. It is relevant to note that regional income convergence in the case of the South *vis-a-vis* the nation in recent decades has been importantly attributed to Federal government incomes and expenditure policies.

The data do show that in the previous decade the rate of employment gains for blacks outpaced the social average, both in reductions in unemployment and in the quality of the jobs made available. But these average growth rates mask the *widening* gap between employment opportunities for white and black teenagers, as the latter fall farther behind. Growth rates, in turn, have been insufficient to close the levels of unemployment; they remain roughly twice that for blacks as for whites. Dale Hiestand's survey of studies on the consequences of technological change identifies no general racial differential, but such a differential occurs in specific instances, and displacement of labor by machinery remains a threatening possibility. The three articles which follow point to the critical importance of employment opportunities, especially in core cities and rural slums. Lester

Thurow's research[2] validates the charge that the black employee is the "last hired, first fired."

The miniscule ownership of capital by blacks raises the critical role of job opportunities. How well prepared for black workers and how ready is the industrial system to employ them in jobs commensurate with that preparation? The base for productive capacity in human beings is laid long before they enter the job market. Alan Batchelder begins his statement with an examination of the importance of proper medical care for the mother of yet unborn children. "Food, shelter, security and medical care" remain substantive concerns throughout the childhood years.

From his home, itself subjected to differential social pressures dating back to slavery, the black child enters a still segregated school system—one often unprepared as well as unwilling to offer him an education relevant to his contemporary needs. As of 1969, 15 years after the Supreme Court decision to the contrary, 80 percent of the black school population was still attending segregated schools. The results of such discrimination are documented by The Civil Rights Commission and by data correlating educational attainment and later income.

Next we consider the constrained opportunities for education of the black adult in college and on the job, and conclude the "Preparation for Production Income" section with a survey of job attitudes, expectations, and mobility.

Handicapped by past and present institutional discrimination, the black worker enters the job market. Both W. H. Hutt and Alan Batchelder identify the market conditions which, if they existed, would lead to employment and promotion on the basis of given "merit." The failures of the American economy to establish such conditions as well as the institutions that make differential treatment possible are then considered. On the theoretical level, Gary Becker's highly influential *The Economics of Discrimination* (University of Chicago Press, 1957) may be consulted.

Turning to applications, management and union policies are examined. Racial practices of employers on recruitment, hiring, training, and promotion are examined by Vernon M. Briggs, Jr. The attitudes of unions, which are concentrated in industries relying on the blue-collar worker, are reviewed by F. Ray Marshall

[2] See the introduction to Part 2, pages 179–85.

as he examines the formal and informal exclusionary and restriction mechanisms established by them.

Although blacks comprise about 11 percent of the American population, they own and operate less than one percent of the nation's private business firms. Self-employment in this sense is a minor source of income. Eugene P. Foley's views on black business motivation which we have included are only suggestive of the many reasons for the miniscule size of black capitalism considered elsewhere in this work.

We have next sought to quantify the specific causes of earnings differentials; we are particularly concerned with the effect of past and present discrimination on incomes. The more usual treatment has been to subsume such "nonmarket" differentials in unexamined "stochastic parameters."

Finally, motivation for the persistence of white racism is examined in the light of gains to some whites from subordination of blacks on the economic, political, and psychological fronts. While such gains are real, the losses to the total society far exceed the limited individual benefits. As early as 1962, the Council of Economic Advisers estimated as an additional two percent the possible gains in Gross National Product (GNP) from merely using black workers, with their current preparation, as fully as whites with the same occupational distribution. The Census Bureau has estimated that if black potential were as fully developed and as fully used as white potential, the GNP could rise by about 3.5 percent.[3] Considering that the American gross output approximates one trillion dollars yearly, such a loss is of great significance. Such estimates, of course, only begin to evaluate even the economic costs of racism. They ignore the dollar costs of crime, poor health, urban decay, and welfare dependency. Nor do such figures begin to comprehend the political, social, and, ultimately, human costs of racism.[4]

[3] Andrew F. Brimmer, "The Negro in the National Economy," *The American Negro Reference Book,* John P. Davis (ed.) (Englewood Cliffs, New Jersey: Prentice-Hall, Inc.), pp. 271–74, 335–36.

[4] For a survey of the range of costs associated with racism see Barbara Patterson *et al., The Price We Pay* (Atlanta, Georgia: Southern Regional Council and Anti-Defamation League of B'NAI B'RITH, 1964).

recent developments
in income differentials

MANPOWER REPORT OF THE PRESIDENT, 1970

employment and unemployment

Employment gains by Negroes have been more rapid than those by white workers over the past 8 years. Aided by the heavy demand for manpower during these years of economic expansion, Negroes increased their employment by 1.6 million or 23 percent between 1961 and 1969. In contrast, employment of white workers rose by only 8 percent over these 8 years, although in absolute numbers the increase in their employment was, of course, much larger than that for black workers.

Negro men, women, and teenagers all experienced some gains in job opportunities. The employment rise for Negro men was much faster than that for white men between 1961 and 1969 (16 percent compared with 9 percent). However, the employment gains by Negro women merely kept pace with those of white women. And though Negro as well as white teenagers had sharp employment increases, their job gains were barely large enough to take care of the greatly increased number seeking employment and so had little impact on their extremely high unemployment rate.

The average unemployment rate for all Negro workers was reduced by nearly one-half (from 12.4 to 6.4 percent) between 1961 and 1969, reflecting the gains in Negro employment during this period. Here again, the improvement was most marked for Negro men, whose unemployment rate was cut by two-thirds. Among Negro women workers, the reduction in unemployment was smaller, and among teenage girls it was insignificant. The gap in unemployment rates between Negro and white youth actually widened over the 8 years, since unemployment among white teenagers was reduced substantially during this period. (See Table 5-1.)

From The U.S. Department of Labor, *Manpower Report of the President* (Washington: Government Printing Office, 1970), pp. 90–94 *passim*.

Table 5-1

Unemployment Rates for Adults and Teenagers,
by Color, 1961 and 1969

Color, Sex, and Age	1961	1969	Percent Change, 1961–69
White	6.0	3.1	—48.3
Men, 20 years and over	5.1	1.9	—62.7
Women, 20 years and over	5.7	3.4	—40.4
Teenagers, 16 to 19 years	15.3	10.7	—30.1
Boys	15.7	10.1	—35.7
Girls	14.8	11.5	—22.3
Negro and other races	12.4	6.4	—48.4
Men, 20 years and over	11.7	3.7	—68.4
Women, 20 years and over	10.6	5.8	—45.3
Teenagers, 16 to 19 years	27.6	24.0	—13.0
Boys	26.8	21.3	—20.5
Girls	29.2	27.7	— 5.1

occupational advances

The most encouraging aspect of the employment record for
Negroes is their rapid movement into higher level occupations.
More than three-fifths of the increase in Negro employment between 1961 and 1969 was in professional, other white-collar, and
skilled occupations. There was also a large rise in the number of
Negroes in operative jobs. By contrast, in the lowest paid occupations—private household work and farmwork—Negro employment
declined substantially, while the number in nonfarm laborer jobs
remained virtually unchanged. (See Figure 5-1.) . . .

The occupational upgrading of Negro workers has already
given millions of people—workers and their families—a larger
share in the national prosperity. This upgrading also testifies to
the greatly improved climate of opportunity for Negroes in many
fields of public and private employment and so offers hope of
continued rapid progress.

It must be emphasized, however, that occupational parity for
Negroes has not been reached or even approached as yet. Though
the gains by Negro workers have been substantial, especially
in professional, clerical, and skilled occupations, they are still

the determinants of income differentials

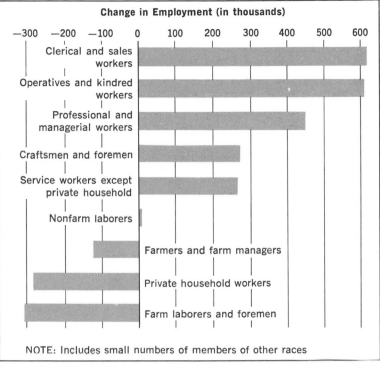

Figure 5-1
Negro Workers Moved into Better Jobs
Between 1961 and 1969

Change in Employment (in thousands)

NOTE: Includes small numbers of members of other races

Source: Department of Labor

seriously underrepresented in these and other relatively high status, highly paid occupations and disproportionately concentrated in unskilled, low-paid laboring and service jobs.

To some extent, these differences reflect educational deficiencies and lack of skill. However, other factors such as inadequate knowledge of better job opportunities and racial discrimination also account for the disparity in employment of Negroes. For example, if at each level of education Negro men had the same opportunities for jobs as whites, the proportion of Negro craftsmen would double, and the percentage of managers and proprietors would triple. On the other hand, the percentage of

recent developments in income differentials   77

Negro men in service jobs would decline by half, and the proportion of nonfarm laborers would be cut by two-thirds. For Negro men in professional and technical jobs, the proportion would remain about the same.

educational gains

Rising levels of education among Negroes were, nevertheless, indispensable to their recent occupational progress, and larger educational gains will be essential to enable greater numbers to enter white-collar and skilled jobs.

The higher educational attainment of young adult Negroes than of middle-aged and older ones is an index of the substantial advances in their schooling during recent decades. According to 1969 data, nearly 3 out of every 5 Negroes 25 to 29 years of age have completed high school, almost twice the proportion among those aged 45 to 54 and four times that for the 55- to 64-year-old group. College education is also much more common among younger than older Negroes, though still achieved by only a small minority. A little over 20 percent of those aged 20 and 21 have completed 1 or more years of college, but in the older age groups the proportion drops progressively (to only 6 percent in the 55- to 64-year-old group). Even these limited gains in college education of Negroes have been important in opening opportunities for them in professional and administrative positions.

The heavy farm-to-city migration of Negroes since World War II has been one of the main reasons for their more extended schooling. They have also been helped and encouraged to stay in school longer by federally aided programs designed to improve the schools, especially in poor school districts, and to reduce dropout rates. However, accomplishments in these directions fall far short of those needed. . . .

. . . educational attainment, as measured by years of schooling, gives no indication of the great differences in the quality of schooling, as measured by achievement tests. A 1965 survey showed that, in the 12th grade, the average Negro youth scores at a ninth-grade level, 3 years behind the average white youth. The gap in school achievement is apparent early and broadens between the sixth and 12th grades. . . .

family income

Reflecting the generally favorable trends in their employment and occupations, the average income of Negroes has risen substantially. Their median family income was nearly $5,600 in 1968, compared with about $4,400 in 1965 (in constant 1968 dollars, adjusted for price increases). This represented a gain in real income of nearly 30 percent in only 3 years and an acceleration over the preceding period. Six years, 1959 to 1965, were previously required for an advance of similar magnitude.

The number and percent of Negroes moving into middle income groups have also increased sharply. Of the 3.3 million Negro families in metropolitan areas in 1968, nearly one-fourth (23 percent) had incomes of $10,000 or more—triple the proportion in 1959. For the 1.3 million Negro families outside these areas, however, incomes as high as this are rare indeed (reported by only 8 percent in 1968).

The Negro-white differential in the proportion of families with incomes of $10,000 or more was about twofold in metropolitan areas in 1968. This represented a substantial improvement since 1959, when the proportion of families at this income level was about four times higher for whites than for Negroes. The differential in family income would be still wider if the average number of wage earners were no larger in Negro than white families. To a far greater extent than white families, Negro households depend on the earnings of one or more workers besides the family head.

Negro families at all income levels have shared in the recent income gains. In fact, in relative terms the income rise has been most rapid for those at the bottom of the income scale. But the dollar rise in incomes has been much greater for the higher income group.

In 1968, the median income for Negro families in the lowest fifth was only $1,723, far below the poverty threshold, though more than double the median for this group in 1959. In contrast, the 1968 median income for the highest fifth was a comfortable $13,000, up by slightly more than 50 percent above the corresponding 1959 figure of $8,483.

Similarly, Negro families have had more rapid percentage gains in income than white families, but this has not been true in terms of purchasing power. The dollar difference in median incomes between white and Negro families in the bottom fifth of the income scale was nearly $1,500 in 1968, compared with about $1,350 in 1959. For families in the highest fifth in income the difference was over $6,300 in 1968, though it had been about $4,500 (in constant 1968 dollars) 9 years before. In the middle-income groups, the differential in dollar income between Negro and white families showed little change; the absolute difference in their purchasing power remains wide.

A complex of economic, educational, and other factors—including discrimination in hiring and promotion—have . . . contributed to these income disparities. . . .

a century of personal wealth accumulation

LEE SOLTOW

. . . Classification of wealth-age gradients by color can lead to exciting clues about economic progress of whites and nonwhites in the United States.

If one is to study the effect of color, he would like to have data extending back at least to the Civil War, the point from which most Negroes could begin participating in accumulation. Fortunately, each individual was asked in the 1870 census of the United States not only his age and color but a declaration of the value of his net wealth in real estate and personal estate. Real estate value was reported wherever it was owned. Personal estate included all bonds, stock, mortgages, notes, livestock, plate, jewels, or furniture, but excluded wearing apparel. . . .

Color as a variable uncovers differences which, when converted to dimensions of age and time, swamp any other variables converted to the same dimensions. Data for whites and non-

From Lee Soltow, "Age and Color in a Century of Personal Wealth Accumulation," paper read at the Workshop in Economic History, University of Chicago, February 7, 1969, pp. 1–28 *passim* (mimeographed).

the determinants of income differentials

whites will be examined for the years 1870, 1953, and 1962. . . .

. . . There are, quite frankly, problems with the nonwhite averages and they must be accepted as possibly having wide percentage measurement and sampling errors. The census enumerators in 1870 were instructed to record individual wealth values only if they exceeded $100 and this was generally the result. It has also been determined that there was an underenumeration of Negroes in the 1870 census.

The nonwhite sample was of size 393; it had an arithmetic mean of $73 with a standard error of $20. For ages 20–29, 30–39, 40–49, 50–59, 60–69, and 70–79, the average wealth values for nonwhites of $16, $53, $55, $232, $227, and $61 were based on samples of size 131, 94, 81, 45, 28, and 7 items. . . .

. . . The one fact of importance is that the overall average of nonwhites was very low as compared to the average for whites. The exponential equations have the [following] results:

Table 5-2
The Average Wealth of White and Nonwhite Males in 1870,
in the United States Classified by Age

Age	Average Wealth		Ratio of White Average
	Whites	Nonwhites	to Nonwhite Average
20–29	$ 793	$ 16	50
30–39	2,068	53	40
40–49	3,746	55	70
50–59	4,345	232	20
60–69	5,364	227 ⎫ 193	20 ⎫ 30
70–79	4,035	61 ⎭	70 ⎭
20 and older	2,661	73	40

Source: The sample of Schedule 1 of the 1870 census.

All, 1870: $W = \$537 \ (1.034)^{age}$
Whites, 1870: $W = \$637 \ (1.032)^{age}$
Nonwhites, 1870: $W = \$ 13 \ (1.036)^{age}$

Some approximations of lags of nonwhites behind whites in the United States in 1870 may be approximated using the above equations. Units of measurement will be age-years or time-years. The wealth value in the equation for whites for a person of age 50 is $W = \$637 \ (1.032)^{50} = \$3,080$. When this value is substituted

a century of personal wealth accumulation   81

in the equation for nonwhites, $3,080 = $13 (1.036)^{age}$, an age figure of 147 years is obtained. This produces a lag of 147 − 50 or roughly 100 years. In what sense can these years be interpreted? They are age-years because calculations have been made using wealth-age growth rates of 3.6 and 3.2 per cent. . . .

John B. Lansing and John Sonquist of the Survey Research Center of the University of Michigan have reported a study of net worth of Negroes in the United States by age class for the years 1953 and 1962. . . .

Table 5-3

Wealth of Negroes in 1953 and 1962 Compared to that of Whites and Nonwhites in 1870 in the United States

Age	Average Wealth of Negro Spending Units, Adjusted to 1957–59 Prices		Average Wealth of Negro Spending Units, Adjusted to 1870 Prices		Average Wealth of White and Nonwhite Males in 1870	
	1953	1962	1953	1962	White	Non-white
23,24	$ 600	$ (700)	$ 300	$ (300)	$ 793	$ 16
33	1,700	1,900	700	800	2,068	55
43	3,100	3,500	1,400	1,500	3,746	55
53	3,700	3,800	1,600	1,700	4,345	232
63	4,900	4,100	2,100	1,800	5,364	227
73	(4,100)	3,400	(1,800)	1,500	4,364	61

Wealth Ratios

Age	Whites in 1870 to Negroes in 1962	Negroes in 1962 to Those in 1870
23,24	2.6	17
33	2.6	15
43	2.5	27
53	2.6	7
63	3.0	8
73	2.9	25

Source: John B. Lansing and John Sonquist, "A Cohort Analysis of Changes in the Distribution of Wealth," Conference on Research in Income and Wealth, March 1967, National Bureau of Economics Research and to be published in Volume 33 of the Series on Income and Wealth. The data for Negroes are the assets minus liabilities of age cohorts from 1929 to 1962 and ages of these cohorts. These cohort data have no averages for the oldest group in 1953 and youngest group in 1962. I have added the . . . values given in parentheses.

the determinants of income differentials

. . . The wealth-age averages have been stated in constant prices using the consumer price index (1870 = 100). The series for 1962 can be seen from Table 5-3 to be remarkably consistent with the white male averages for 1870 and roughly consistent with the nonwhite male averages for 1870.

It must be admitted that comparisons of wealth declarations of today to those a century earlier have major weaknesses. The Survey Research Center microcomponents are spending units and the amounts do not include currency, cash surrender value of insurance policies, value of housefurnishings, interest in pension funds and interest in trust funds and annuities. In the 1870 definition, all were included theoretically, including currency and housefurnishings. The Center's estimate of average net worth in 1962 for whites and nonwhites was $14,600. The Federal Reserve study had an average of $17,100 for 1962. Its measurement included equity in insurance policies, annuities, and retirement plans. One can only speculate about the major issue of human wealth and its effect on century differences. . . .

Generalizations for all of the various averages will now be made using the exponential equations fitted conservatively to age data from 20 to 79. Using dollar wealth adjusted to 1870 prices, these are

		Equation Values of Wealth at Age 50	Equation Values of Age When Wealth is		
			$4,000	$1,000	$200
All families and unrelated individuals in 1963:	$W = \$1,290 \ (1.037)^{age}$	$8,070	31	−7	−51
White adult males in 1870:	$W = \$ \ \ 637 \ (1.032)^{age}$	3,080	58	15	−36
Nonwhite spending units in 1962:	$W = \$ \ \ 270 \ (1.030)^{age}$	1,180	91	44	−10
Nonwhite adult males in 1870:	$W = \$ \ \ \ 13 \ (1.036)^{age}$	78	161	122	77

The great gaps between the levels of the equations are of immense significance. . . . For nonwhites from 1870 to 1962, wealth for the equations at age 50 increased from $78 to $1,180. This yields an average annual per cent of change of 3.0 per cent! This is encouraging since, as the nonwhite rate of improvement, it has been almost three times the 1.1 per cent rate of whites since the Civil War. . . .

The nonwhite level in 1962 was still behind that of whites in 1870. Equation values at age 50 for these levels were $1,180 and $3,080. . . . it would be near the year 2000 before nonwhites would have the level of whites at the end of the Civil War. The reader may think this is preposterous. Recall that the nonwhite mark today still is not that of whites 93 years ago.

The nonwhite level in 1962 is 83 years behind the overall average in the United States in 1963 if we accept the procedure employed in developing the previous point. The wealth of all was 6.8 times that of nonwhites. The equation values at age 50 lead to $8,070 = $1,180 $(1.030)^{88}$. This calculation includes the assumption that the past nonwhite growth rate of 3 per cent will continue.

Even though nonwhites may reach present average levels in 83 years, this is not sufficient since whites will have made further advances. . . .

It has been stated that the nonwhite is 100 years behind the white in average wealth. One can seek solace in one sense. If the past trend were to continue and if the accumulation rate of a nonwhite is 6.4 per cent (as obtained by adding the 3.0 per cent growth rate and 3.4 per cent wealth-age gradient) then a nonwhite of 25 today could accumulate in his lifetime a very respectable amount. It would be equivalent to that of the average person of middle age in 1963. Even this optimistic climb might not satisfy the Negro since it is the standard of nonwhites and whites at a given point of time that interests him. He doesn't wish to remain a generation behind other people.

the determinants of income differentials

technological change
and black employment

DALE L. HIESTAND

Technological change, which is an integral part of the process of economic growth, has often been held responsible for changes in the employment patterns of minority groups. Certainly, to the extent that it affects the over-all industrial and occupational structure, technological change affects the employment opportunities of both white and Negro workers. Does technological change, however, have either a specific or a differential impact on the employment of minorities? Particularly, does technological change in a given industry have an impact on Negro employment in that industry [that is] different from its impact on the employment of white workers? . . .

An underlying assumption of the argument that technological change may have a favorable impact on employment opportunities of minorities is that employers often do not hire members of a minority group because they fear the objections of other employees and of customers. It is contended that many employers believe they could obtain better employees at the prevailing wage rate by employing Negro rather than white workers or women rather than men, but that this would actually add to costs because workers who are necessary to the firm would leave unless they were paid higher wages or because sales would be lost because customers [would] object to or have no confidence in the minority workers. Technological changes, it is further argued, are accompanied by significant alterations in the occupational structure, in the spatial, technological, social, and other relationships between jobs, and in the skill level required in various jobs. With so many institutional relationships changing, the sex and/ or race labels attached to various kinds of work and different jobs may be less firmly fixed in the minds of workers and customers. At such a time employers may be able to shift to available supplies of underutilized minority manpower with little or no objection from others.

An extreme example of the favorable impact of technological

From Dale L. Hiestand, *Economic Growth and Employment Opportunities for Minorities* (New York: Columbia University Press, 1964), pp. 100–107 *passim*.

change on the employment of minorities is one in which the new advance creates entirely new kinds of jobs. A new job may have no definite sex or race label, and employers may be free to fix whatever label gives them the greatest advantage. . . .

The more common argument has been that technological change works against the minority worker, because it creates new kinds of jobs that are attractive to the majority or for which the majority is better equipped in terms of skills or education. The long-run tendency of technological change in this country has been to raise the skill level of the manpower required in various industries, as well as to introduce newer, more complicated techniques into skilled and high level jobs. As a result, it has been said, better educated workers are required, and this gives white workers an advantage over Negroes and men an advantage over women in obtaining new jobs. . . .

To examine adequately all of these assertions would require a full field survey of changes in minority group employment as a consequence of diverse technological changes. But we can obtain some measure of these changes by analyzing the relationship between employment changes and some index of technological change. Specifically, we could interpret technological change in terms of changes in productivity. . . .

The findings are generally the same regardless of the measure of technological change used. The rate of change in productivity in the various industries apparently had little to do with the changes in the employment of Negro men or Negro women in them. Not one of the three measures of productivity used was significantly correlated with either of the two measures of change in Negro male or Negro female employment. . . .

The diverse tendencies that prevailed in the employment of Negroes can be seen in several examples. Productivity increased by 3 percent or more per year in utilities and sanitary services, railroads and railway express, and nonmetals mining. Negro men accounted for 11 and 17 percent of the net growth of employment in the first two industries, respectively, but their number in nonmetals mining declined as the industry total grew. On the other hand, productivity hardly increased in leather and leather goods manufacturing and actually declined in apparel and other fabricated textiles manufacturing. In the former industry Negro men provided 12 percent of the added manpower but only 4 percent in the latter.

These findings are supported by the relationships between changes in employment patterns and technological change as measured by the rate of change in capital per unit of labor input. Here, too, there were no significant correlations in the case of either Negro men or Negro women. The correlations for white men were higher, but still not significant. Percentage changes in the employment of white women were significantly and inversely related to the changes in the capital/labor ratio. Where this ratio increased rapidly, as in tobacco products or apparel manufacturing or in agriculture, the employment of white women increased slowly. At the other extreme were such industries as the manufacturing of furniture and fixtures and local transportation utilities. In these industries the capital/labor ratio lagged as capital input changed little or even declined, but employment, especially the employment of white women, advanced substantially.

The fact that changes in Negro employment and changes in productivity are not correlated may be significant in itself. In some instances productivity changes may lead to increased employment because costs are cut and markets grow, but in other instances it may merely mean labor displacement. If technological change leads to an increase in employment, the employment of minorities will expand, even more rapidly than for whites. On the other hand, if technological change leads to a fairly rapid decline in the over-all employment, the result is likely to be an even more rapid decline of Negro employment. If technological change in a field is merely average, so that its effect on over-all employment is neutral or nearly so, it may be accompanied by a decline in white employment and an increase in Negro employment or a slower rate of decline in white than Negro employment or a slower rate of decline in white than Negro employment, as white workers leave to capture more favorable opportunities in rapidly growing fields. Thus, the impact of technological change on the employment of minorities is no different in character from any other factor making for an expansion or contraction of over-all employment in a field.

unemployment
and
sub-employment

critical significance
of employment

MANPOWER REPORTS OF THE PRESIDENT,
1969 AND 1970

With the gains in employment among Negroes from 1961 onward, their unemployment situation showed corresponding improvement. From 12.4 percent in 1961, the Negro unemployment rate fell below 10 percent in 1964 for the first time in 7 years. By 1968 it had come down to 6.8 percent. Whereas in 1961 nearly 1 million Negroes were unemployed, by 1968 the number had dropped below 600,000.

Long-term unemployment among Negroes was reduced sharply also over the 1961–68 period. In 1961, an average of 350,000 Negro workers—240,000 men and 110,000 women—were unemployed for 15 weeks or longer. By 1968, the numbers had dropped to 40,000 men and 50,000 women. . . .

Unemployment of Negro women aged 20 and over declined less dramatically than that of Negro men, because of the increases in the female labor force during the period. Their unemployment rate nevertheless fell from 10.5 to 6.4 percent, a reduction of 40 percent, compared with 65 percent for Negro men.

Negro teenagers failed to share in this improvement. The number that were unemployed rose by 25 percent, and their unemployment rate remained virtually unchanged and disturbingly high—about 25 percent. In consequence, the gap between the unemployment rates for Negro and white teenagers widened, since the unemployment rate for white youth has decreased substantially since 1961. (See Table 5-4.) . . .

With the lessening unemployment problems in the past few

From The U.S. Department of Labor, *Manpower Report of the President* (Washington: Government Printing Office, January 1969 and March 1970), 1969: pp. 43–48 *passim;* 1970: p. 38.

Table 5-4

Composition of the Civilian Labor Force and Unemployment, 1961 and 1969

(numbers in thousands)

Color, Sex, and Age	1961					1969				
	Civilian Labor Force		Unemployed			Civilian Labor Force		Unemployed		
	Number	Percent Distribution	Number	Percent Distribution	Rate	Number	Percent Distribution	Number	Percent Distribution	Rate
Total	70,459	100.0	4,714	100.0	6.7	80,733	100.0	2,831	100.0	3.5
White	62,654	88.9	3,743	79.4	6.0	71,779	88.9	2,261	79.9	3.1
Men, 20 years and over	39,547	56.1	2,014	42.7	5.1	41,772	51.7	794	28.0	1.9
Women, 20 years and over	18,747	26.6	1,060	22.5	5.7	23,839	29.5	806	28.5	3.4
Teenagers, 16 to 19 years	4,361	6.2	669	14.2	15.3	6,168	7.6	660	23.3	10.7
Negro and other races	7,802	11.1	970	20.6	12.4	8,954	11.1	570	20.1	6.4
Men, 20 years and over	4,313	6.1	504	10.7	11.7	4,579	5.7	168	5.9	3.7
Women, 20 years and over	2,918	4.1	308	6.5	10.6	3,574	4.4	209	7.4	5.8
Teenagers, 16 to 19 years	572	.8	158	3.4	27.6	801	1.0	193	6.8	24.0

Note: Detail may not add to totals due to rounding.

Source: Manpower Report of the President, U.S. Department of Labor, March 1970.

years, the other forms of underutilization of manpower have come into clearer view. . . .

Negroes are more likely to be out of the work force involuntarily than are whites. Relatively more Negroes than whites are forced into this situation by ill health. Many are discouraged by discriminatory hiring practices or, with the addition of even minor handicaps to their already formidable disadvantages, find themselves unable to compete for the limited array of jobs for which they are qualified. The generally low earnings of many Negro families places upon Negro women the burden of adding to the family's income. This creates a situation in which Negro women may urgently want and need a job, even when some impediment prevents them from seeking work. . . .

Nonwhite workers are disproportionately affected by part-time employment. About 500,000 nonwhite workers were on economic part time in 1968; they represented one-fourth of all involuntary part-time workers. The high concentration of nonwhite workers in this category is partly a reflection of their entrapment in lower skilled occupations. More than half of the Negroes (mostly women) regularly working part time for economic reasons were in private household work, where part-time employment is typical.

Having a job—but one without adequate income—can be the most galling of employment problems in an affluent society, and perhaps as destructive of individual and family well-being as unemployment. The jobs now held by millions of workers, however, pay substandard earnings—not enough even to raise the worker and his family above the poverty line. . . .

There are disproportionately large numbers of nonwhite workers and women among the low earners. The large proportion of women in service occupations, especially household employment, is one of the main reasons for their frequently low earnings.

The problems are compounded by the fact that these low-paid workers are often excluded from income protection under workmen's compensation systems. This lack of adequate income protection can make their plight much more severe than statistics on unemployment and family income alone can convey.

Though unemployment and underemployment are clearly national problems, their impact falls unequally on different cities and local areas and affects some sections of some cities much more than others.

the determinants of income differentials

Employment and industrial activity in this country are now highly urbanized—with 2 out of 3 workers employed in 150 major areas. . . .

. . . Among the 150 major labor areas, 51 were listed as areas of "low unemployment" (generally under 3 percent) by the end of 1968. These included a number with large slum neighborhoods, where unemployment and underemployment are known to be high—for example, Chicago, Cleveland, Pittsburgh, and Washington. . . .

While some Negroes moving to the suburbs gain status, with better jobs, higher income, and improved housing, many simply move from a city slum to a suburban slum. They carry with them the disadvantages of their inadequate education and lack of skills and continue to meet the same discrimination they faced when they lived in the city ghettos. . . .

The great majority of urban Negroes, however, are still concentrated in the central cities, and any major effort to solve the employment problems of this group must be focused on the urban cores. . . .

too few jobs in central cities

NATIONAL COMMITTEE AGAINST
DISCRIMINATION IN HOUSING

National unemployment rates do not reveal the extent of job-related problems confronting the masses of Negroes who are concentrated in the nation's urban ghettos. Let us look now at unemployment rates for metropolitan areas and compare them with central city and suburban figures.

In poverty areas, for example, the unemployment rate for non-whites was 9.4 per cent, compared to 6 per cent for whites. An

From The National Committee Against Discrimination in Housing, *The Impact of Housing Patterns on Job Opportunities* (New York: The National Committee Against Discrimination in Housing, 1968), pp. 15–20 *passim*.

Table 5-5

Unemployment in All Standard Metropolitan Statistical Areas*

Nonwhite unemployment across the nation far exceeds white unemployment, whether in poverty areas or not. In poverty areas the actual number of unemployed nonwhites is greater.

	Poverty Sections				Non-poverty Sections			
	Nonwhite Number	Rate	White Number	Rate	Nonwhite Number	Rate	White Number	Rate
Total	280,000	9.4	220,000	6.0	186,000	7.2	1,197,000	3.6
Men	182,000	10.2	148,000	6.3	100,000	6.9	731,000	3.4
Women	98,000	8.1	72,000	5.4	86,000	7.6	466,000	3.9

* March, 1966

Source: Bureau of Labor Statistics Report—**Monthly Labor Review**, Oct., 1966; page 1108, volume 89:10.

explanation is required in the case of this last figure, for the use of the designation "whites" in poverty areas includes, by definition, millions of Mexican-Americans and Puerto Ricans whose unemployment problems are similar to those of Negroes. For this reason, the "white"/"nonwhite" designations do not accurately describe majority/minority employment disparity. Thus, 9.4 understates and 6 per cent overstates minority/majority unemployment in poverty areas. In non-poverty areas, white unemployment was 3.6 per cent; nonwhite, 7.2.

More importantly, within poverty areas the *number* of nonwhites who were unemployed exceeds the *number* of whites who were unemployed, whereas the reverse is true for non-poverty areas. The bulk of the poor and unemployed in the largest SMSA's are Negroes, Mexican-Americans or Puerto Ricans. Negroes comprise from 81 to 96 per cent of the residents of poverty neighborhoods in Cleveland; 60 per cent of the poverty area residents of Oakland; 70 per cent in Boston; 81 per cent in Los Angeles; 65 per cent in San Francisco; 93 per cent in St. Louis.

The unemployment rates for whites and nonwhites in poverty areas and non-poverty areas in the nation's 212 SMSAS, as of March 1966, are shown in Table 5-5.

If unemployment rates for areas of minority concentration within a metropolitan area are compared with unemployment rates for the metropolitan area as a whole (including the poverty districts), considerable insight is gained into the disparity between white and nonwhite unemployment problems. As shown in Table 5-6, this study has tabulated the unemployment rates for ghetto areas in Boston, Cleveland, Detroit, Los Angeles, New York, Philadelphia, St. Louis, San Francisco, Phoenix and San Antonio, and has compared these with unemployment rates for the respective metropolitan areas.

With the exception of San Antonio, each of these slum ghettos has erupted in violence. . . . It is not difficult to see why.

In the Hough and other slum sections of Cleveland, for example, the unemployment rate was 15.6 per cent, compared with an average for the greater Cleveland area of 3.5 per cent. In North St. Louis, where 80 per cent of all Negroes in St. Louis City reside, the unemployment rate was 12.9 per cent versus 4.5 per cent for the St. Louis metropolitan area. In Oakland (San Francisco), the comparable figures are 13 per cent and 5.2 per cent. Indeed, the severe unemployment which the Negro ex-

Table 5-6

Unemployment Rates: Ghetto Areas and
Surrounding Metropolitan Areas

A comparison of unemployment in ghetto areas with metropolitan areas
as a whole during 1966 shows the ghetto rate to be approximately 2
to 4 times the metropolitan area rate.

SMSA	Ghetto Area	Unemployment Rate	
		Ghetto*	SMSA**
Boston	Roxbury	6.9	3.7
Cleveland	Hough and surrounding		
	neighborhood	15.6	3.5
Detroit	Central Woodward	10.1	4.3
Los Angeles	South Los Angeles	12.0	6.0
New York	Harlem	8.1	4.6
	East Harlem	9.0	
	Bedford-Stuyvesant	6.2	
Philadelphia	North Philadelphia	11.0	4.3
Phoenix	Salt River Bed area	13.2	—
St. Louis	North Side	12.9	4.5
San Antonio	East and West Sides	8.1	—
San Francisco-Oakland	Mission-Fillmore	11.1	5.2
	Bayside	13.0	

* as of November 1966
** average for year ending August 1966
Source: 1967 **Manpower Report of the President,** page 75; metropolitan area data
are based on special tabulation of data from the **Current Population Survey.**

periences in the 1960's is comparable to that experienced by the
American public-at-large only in the depth of the Great Depression.

Even these figures do not tell the complete story, for unemployment data constitute an inadequate index to the job-location
problem of many central city residents, especially Negroes. Conventional unemployment data measure only insured unemployment, which presumes a previous and continuing work history.
These data do not reckon with the extraordinarily high non-labor
force participation rates among Negro males, nor with the extent
of involuntary part-time work within the Negro community, nor
with the full-time worker who earns less than minimum subsistence need, nor, finally, with the undercount of adult Negro
males in the census of 1960. This undercount has been variously
estimated to be between 10 and 15 per cent.

To understand these problems more fully, the U.S. Depart-

the determinants of income differentials

ment of Labor undertook a special survey of joblessness and poverty in 14 of the worst ghetto areas of the United States (the Department called them slums). The survey was conducted, in cooperation with state agencies, during November 1966, and the results have recently been made public. It was found, first that Negroes constituted 3 of every 4 unemployed in the areas studied and that their conventional unemployment rate was nearly 10 per cent. Among teenagers, 16 to 19 years old, the average unemployment rate was 28 per cent; the unemployment rate for nonwhite boys in the age group from 14 to 19 was 31 per cent, and for nonwhite girls, 46 per cent.

Secondly, nearly 7 per cent of the residents of the slum ghettos were employed only part time although they would have worked full time if the opportunity to do so was available. (For the nation as a whole the comparable figure was then 2.3 per cent). . . .

Two other survey findings are useful here. An inordinately large number of ghetto residents of working age were not counted in the labor force of these metropolitan areas. Some of these individuals doubtless did not want work, but most have probably given up hope of ever securing a well-paying job. Second, more than 20 per cent of adult men who were likely to be part of the population of these 14 slum areas—given normal distributions of male and female of the population as a whole— were not located by the Department's surveys. When all of these negative factors are taken into account, the unemployment problems of Negroes and of the areas in which they are resident take on even more shocking dimensions.

As a result of these surveys, the Labor Department developed a new technique for measuring unemployment. This new technique is called the sub-employment index, and it covers an entire employment-hardship area. The sub-employment index measures, first, those unemployed workers who are "actively looking for work and unable to find it"; second, those working part-time but seeking full-time jobs; third, heads of households earning less than $60 per week and individuals under 65 earning less than $56 a week in a full-time job; fourth, half the number of non-participants in the male age group 20–64 who are not in the labor force; fifth, a "conservative and carefully considered estimate of the male 'under-count' group." Sub-employment rates for the areas covered by the November 1966 survey are listed in Table 5-7.

too few jobs in central cities

Average sub-employment for all of these cities was an incredible 34.6 per cent. This means that one out of every three residents of these racially- and ethnically-isolated communities who is already a worker or who could become a worker was unemployed, under-employed, or employed at poverty-level wages.

Table 5-7

Sub-employment Rates (November 1966)

SMSA	Ghetto area	Sub-employment Rate
Boston	Roxbury	24%
New Orleans		45%
New York	Harlem	29%
	East Harlem	33%
	Bedford-Stuyvesant	28%
Philadelphia	North Philadelphia	34%
Phoenix	Salt River Bed area	42%
St. Louis	North Side	39%
San Antonio	East and West Sides	47%
San Francisco	Mission-Fillmore	25%

Table 5-8*

Labor Force Participation Rates by Age and Sex, 1969
(Includes armed forces. January–November averages.)

	Men		Women	
	Negro and Other Races	White	Negro and Other Races	White
Total, 16 years and over	78	81	50	42
16 and 17 years	39	50	25	35
18 and 19 years	67	70	46	55
20 to 24 years	88	87	59	57
25 to 34 years	95	97	58	42
35 to 44 years	93	98	59	49
45 to 54 years	89	95	61	53
55 to 64 years	78	84	48	43
65 years and over	26	27	12	10

Source: U. S. Department of Labor, Bureau of Labor Statistics.

* Note: Tables 5-8, 5-9, and 5-10 were selected from a separate source and did not originally appear in the preceding selection by The National Committee Against Discrimination in Housing (eds.).

Table 5-9
Unemployment in Central Cities and Suburbs
of the 20 Largest Metropolitan Areas, 1969
(As ranked in 1960; January–November averages, not seasonally adjusted.)

	Unemployment Rate			Number Unemployed (thousands)	
	Negro and Other Races	White	Ratio: Negro and Other Races to White	Negro and Other Races	White
Central cities	6.3	3.1	2.0	188	277
Adult men	3.9	2.4	1.6	60	121
Adult women	5.3	3.1	1.7	65	98
Teenagers*	26.8	9.8	2.7	63	57
Suburbs	5.3	2.9	1.8	41	418

* Teenagers include persons 16 to 19 years old.
Source: U.S. Department of Labor, Bureau of Labor Statistics.

Table 5-10
Unemployment Rates for Persons 16 and Over,
in Poverty Areas of Six Large Cities, July 1968–June 1969

	Negro and Other Races	White
Unemployment rate for total United States	6.5	3.1
Unemployment rates for poverty areas of:		
Atlanta	9.4	5.3
Chicago	8.8	(*)
Detroit	13.5	9.1
Houston	9.5	5.9
Los Angeles	15.2	6.3
New York City	6.7	6.9

* Base of percentage too small to provide a significant percentage.
Source: U.S. Department of Labor, Bureau of Labor Statistics.

too few jobs in central cities

too few jobs in
rural slums

RUDOLPH A. WHITE

The Mississippi Delta has long been an agricultural center, dominated by cotton produced mainly by Negro hand laborers. Poverty has been widespread: . . . the 1960 census showed that
one-fourth of white families and over four-fifths of Negro families in this region had annual incomes below $3,000.

Any hope that poverty has diminished since 1960 receives little encouragement in some 1967 findings (covering 1966) on
Delta poverty. Almost 4 in every 5 nonwhite families still received incomes below $3,000. . . . Moreover, the gap between
white and Negro incomes has widened, because the number of
white families with poverty-level incomes fell by a larger percentage than the number of Negroes with such incomes.

. . . Since 1960, new crops have appeared in the Delta and
production methods now substitute weed-killing chemicals for
human cottonchoppers and mechanical for human cottonpickers.
This shift has obliterated more than 50,000 agricultural jobs. . . .

The sample survey made in October 1967 showed that the
Delta had a composite unemployment rate of 7.5 percent. Because this rate is based on county-wide relationships, it understates unemployment in the slum areas. The Negro sector,
which somewhat more closely approximates the slum-resident
group, did experience 10 percent unemployment. This level of
unemployment matches that of the worst urban slums, and even
it understates the rates that prevail when cottonpicking is not
available to temporarily reduce the level of unemployment. Although considerable poverty can be attributed to joblessness,
other subemployment elements strongly contribute to poverty
conditions.

Part-time employment in the Delta stood at 6 percent, essentially comparable to the 7 percent in urban slums. The Delta
total is again not restricted to the slum areas only. Nonparticipa-
tion in the labor force of adult males was 10 percent for the
Delta and 11 percent in urban slums, again roughly comparable.

From Rudolph A. White, "Measuring Unemployment and Subemployment
in the Mississippi Delta," *Monthly Labor Review*, Vol. **92**, No. 4, U.S.
Department of Labor (April 1969), 17–23 *passim*.

Male undercount percentages were also comparable, roughly one-fifth of the adult males being undercounted.

It is in the proportions of family incomes below the poverty line that the Delta's comparative disadvantage most sharply shows: Nearly 80 percent of the Delta's Negro families lived in poverty compared to nearly 40 percent in the worst of the urban slums.

preparation
for production
income

determinants of
productive intelligence

ALAN BATCHELDER

As long as the American system distributes output in approximate proportion to productive contribution, the productive contribution of individuals is of primary importance in determining who shall be poor and who shall be nonpoor. The determinants of an individual's potential productive contribution are of two kinds: the physical materials used by him in production, and his productive intelligence. The physical materials derive from the soil and weather, from accumulated technological knowledge, and from accumulated net investment. Productive intelligence derives from heredity and education.

With respect to the materials, it is clear that the more and better the materials a man has, the more he can produce, assuming that he is capable of using the materials. The greater the quantity of land or the more fertile the individual units, the more

From Alan B. Batchelder, *The Economics of Poverty* (New York: John Wiley & Sons, Inc., 1966), pp. 73–76 *passim*.

products a man can grow on it. The more fertilizer a man has, the more he can grow on the land to which the fertilizer is applied. The richer the ore, the more iron he can produce. . . .

Productive intelligence has . . . grown over time as nutrition has improved (for example, fresh fruits and vegetables in winter) and as children have stayed in better and better schools for longer periods—until fully one-fourth of all Americans are at least 21 years old before they leave school. E. F. Denison, America's leading authority on United States economic growth, has attributed 40% of the nation's 1929 to 1957 growth in output per hour to improved productive intelligence.

What is productive intelligence? It is the whole range of human physical and mental abilities valued in the marketplace. Most emphatically, it includes ambition. The determinants of individual productive intelligence may be more conveniently studied if the word "intelligence" is (1) restricted to behavior valued in the marketplace, and (2) subdivided to be applied to three different time periods in each person's life. Doing this, we can distinguish between Intelligence A, the individual's marketable potential at the moment of conception, Intelligence B, the individual's marketable potential at the moment of birth, and Intelligence C, the individual's marketable ability at any point in life after birth. . . .

Intelligence A refers to all kinds of marketable productive potential: ability to count, to persuade, to organize production, to teach, to use a shovel, to write novels, and to assemble transistor radios. The list is very long. We may think of Intelligence A as a single measure comprised of thousands of different kinds of potential ability, or we may conceive of there being many Intelligence A's, one for each kind of ability potential.

For each kind of marketable ability, Intelligence A is the genetic potential at the time of conception. This genetic potential may or may not be realized—that will depend upon events affecting the individual after conception. But the genetic potential, given the present state of biological-medical knowledge, can never be surpassed.

Between the time of conception and the time of birth, a great deal can happen that will lower an individual's potential. The devastating effects upon the baby of German measles in the mother during the second month of pregnancy are well known. . . . During the nine months between conception and birth, the mother's body will do all it can but, sometimes, the mother's body cannot do all that is needed. Malnutrition, incompatible Rh factor combination, and physical mistreatment can cripple the ability of the mother's body to serve the needs of the fetus. . . .

The child's intellectual potential can be eroded by maternal malfunctioning or by the malfunctioning of those attending the delivery. In extreme cases, infants die; in less severe instances, the babies suffer cerebral palsy, mental retardation, epilepsy, or other neurologic disorders. In these cases, Intelligence B and, later, Intelligence C suffer.

The erosion of infants' Intelligence A, caused by incompetence or by inadequate care during [the] obstetrical period, can be avoided by mothers who have access to proper food, shelter, security, and medical care before and during delivery. This evasion is more difficult for poor women. The lower the socioeconomic group of the mother, the further is the Intelligence B of her baby likely to be cut below the baby's Intelligence A and the more likely is the poverty of the parents to be passed on to the children.

After birth, environment begins to operate directly, rather than through the mother, on each person. Intelligence C is the summary combination of environment with heredity. Much of Intelligence C derives from formal schooling: grade school, junior high school, high school, college, and university, for example. But much of Intelligence C comes from the home, relatives, and friends in years before school as well as during the school years. These people can teach the child to be polite or impolite, to be ambitious, complacent, or despairing, to want to be a friar or nun sworn to poverty, or a worthy successor to the father as president of the company, a policeman, or a taunter of police, expert with the switchblade.

The importance of the home can be emphasized by imagining the case of two people beginning with equal Intelligence A but attaining unequal Intelligence C because their families are different. Imagine two male babies with high and equal Intelligence A conceived on the same day in 1946, one to a Negro sharecropper in Sunflower County, Mississippi, the other to a white senior partner in a firm of CPA's and living in Oak Park, Illinois, Grosse Point, Michigan, Shaker Heights, Ohio, Darien, Connecticut, or some other equally comfortable suburb. Trapped in a cotton county with barbarously primitive schools, the Negro boy would be educated quite differently from the white suburbanite. We could safely bet 10,000 to 1 that, despite precisely equal Intelligence A, the two boys would have very dissimilar Intelligence C. The white boy would be superior in nearly all the kinds of Intelligence C that are valued highly in the market.

results of
segregated education

U.S. COMMISSION ON CIVIL RIGHTS

The results of education for all students are influenced by a number of factors, including the students' home backgrounds, the quality of education provided in the schools they attend, and the social class background of their classmates. For Negro students, the racial composition of the schools also is important. Racially isolated schools tend to lower Negro students' achievement and restrict their aspirations. By contrast, Negro children who attend predominantly white schools more often score higher on achievement tests, and develop higher aspirations.

The educational and economic circumstances of a child's family long have been recognized as factors which determine the benefits he derives from his education. Differences in childrens' social and economic backgrounds are strongly related to their achievement in school. The elementary student from a disadvantaged home typically has a lower verbal achievement level than that of a more advantaged student.

. . . From the early grades through high school, a student is directly influenced by his schoolmates. A disadvantaged student in school with a majority of more advantaged students performs at a higher level than a disadvantaged student in school with a majority of disadvantaged students.

This has a special significance for Negro students. Since there

From The U.S. Commission on Civil Rights, *Racial Isolation in the Public Schools: Summary of a Report*, Publication No. 7 (Washington: Government Printing Office, March 1967), pp. 3–5 *passim*.

the determinants of income differentials

are fewer middle-class Negroes, any remedy for social class isolation would entail substantial racial desegregation.

There also is a strong relationship between the attitudes and achievement of Negro students and the racial composition of the schools which they attend. Relatively disadvantaged Negro students perform better when they are in class with a majority of similarly disadvantaged white students than when they are in a class with a majority of equally disadvantaged Negroes. When more advantaged Negro students are in school with similarly advantaged whites they achieve better than those in school with similarly advantaged Negroes. When disadvantaged Negro students are in class with more advantaged whites, their average performance is improved by as much as two grade levels.

There are differences in the quality of education available to Negro and white students in the Nation's metropolitan areas. For example, schools attended by white children often have more library volumes per student, advanced courses, and fewer pupils per teacher than schools attended by Negro children.

Negro students are more likely than whites to have teachers with lower verbal achievement levels, to have substitute teachers, and to have teachers who are dissatisfied with their school assignment. Do these differences in school qualities account for the apparent effect of racial isolation?

The quality of teaching has an important influence on students' achievement. Yet, Negro students in majority-white schools with poorer teachers generally achieve better than similar Negro students in majority-Negro schools with better teachers.

Racially isolated schools are regarded by the community as inferior institutions. Teachers and students in racially isolated schools recognize the stigma of inferiority which is attached to their schools and this has a negative effect on their attitudes and achievement.

The time spent in a given kind of classroom setting has an impact on student attitudes and achievement. The longer Negro students are in racially isolated schools, the greater the negative impact. The longer Negro students are in desegregated schools, the higher their performance.

The cumulative effects of education extend to adult life and account in part for differences in income and occupation. Negro adults who attended desegregated schools are more likely to be holding white collar jobs and to be earning more than otherwise similarly situated Negroes who attended racially isolated schools.

Racial isolation in the schools also fosters attitudes and behavior that perpetuate isolation in other areas of American life. Negro adults who attended racially isolated schools are more likely to develop attitudes that further alienate them from whites. Negro adults who attend racially isolated schools are more likely to have lower self-esteem and to accept the assignment of inferior status.

Attendance by whites at racially isolated schools also tends to reinforce the very attitudes that assign inferior status to Negroes. White adults who attended all-white schools are more apt than other whites to regard Negro institutions as inferior and to resist measures designed to overcome discrimination against Negroes.

black-white schooling and
income differentials

U.S. BUREAU OF THE CENSUS

Table 5-11*

Percent Distribution by Years of School Completed
for Persons 20 Years Old and Over, by Age, 1969

	Less Than 4 Years High School	High School, 4 Years	College, 1 Year or More	Median Years of School Completed
Negro				
20 and 21 years old	42.1	36.6	21.2	12.2
22 to 24 years old	43.9	37.1	19.1	12.2
25 to 29 years old	44.3	40.1	15.7	12.1
30 to 34 years old	49.8	36.7	13.5	12.0
35 to 44 years old	62.8	26.8	10.5	10.6
45 to 54 years old	70.8	18.9	10.3	9.1
55 to 64 years old	85.2	8.7	6.2	7.6
65 to 74 years old	89.7	5.5	4.9	6.1
75 years old and over	92.4	4.1	3.5	5.2
White				
20 and 21 years old	18.1	41.6	40.1	12.8
22 to 24 years old	19.6	44.8	35.7	12.7
25 to 29 years old	23.0	44.8	32.1	12.6
30 to 34 years old	27.3	44.9	27.6	12.5
35 to 44 years old	33.9	41.0	25.1	12.4
45 to 54 years old	40.7	39.3	20.0	12.2
55 to 64 years old	55.2	27.5	17.3	10.9
65 to 74 years old	67.6	18.9	13.4	8.9
75 years old and over	75.1	13.8	11.1	8.5

Source: U.S. Department of Commerce, Bureau of the Census.

* Note: Tables 5-11 and 5-12 were selected from a separate source and did not originally appear in the preceding selection by The U.S. Commission on Civil Rights (eds.).

Table 5-12

Median Income of Men 25 to 54 Years Old,
by Educational Attainment, 1968

	Median Income, 1968		Negro Income as a Percent of White
	Negro	White	
Elementary			
Total	$3,900	$ 5,844	67
Less than 8 years	3,558	5,131	69
8 years	4,499	6,452	70
High school			
Total	5,580	7,852	71
1 to 3 years	5,255	7,229	73
4 years	5,801	8,154	71
College			
1 or more years	7,481	10,149	74

Source: U.S. Department of Commerce, Bureau of the Census.

higher education for blacks

JOHN EGERTON

Desegregation in higher education has received surprisingly little attention in the 15 years since legal segregation in education was outlawed by the U.S. Supreme Court. . . .

But the few statistics available on this subject indicate that desegregation in higher education has been slight—far out of proportion to the ratio of whites to Negroes in the population. . . .

. . . in April of 1968 the *Chronicle of Higher Education* printed the full-time, undergraduate enrollment figures by race (white, Negro and "other") from about 1,400 . . . institutions. . . . According to the *Chronicle,* the Office for Civil Rights reported that a total of 4,764,834 full-time undergraduate students

From John Egerton, *State Universities and Black Americans,* Southern Education Reporting Service (Atlanta; Southern Education Foundation, May 1969), pp. 4–96 *passim.*

the determinants of income differentials

were identified in the survey, and that 245,410 of them—5.15 per cent—were Negroes. About 150,000 of the Negro students were enrolled in previously all-Negro colleges and universities, leaving approximately 95,000—just under 2 per cent of the nationwide total—in the institutions which traditionally have served a predominance of whites.

. . . there is probably no reason to question seriously the overall percentages which showed that five of every 100 college students—and two of every 100 in predominantly white institutions —were Negroes. . . .

In November of 1968, a questionnaire labeled "Survey of Progress in Broadening Educational and Professional Opportunity for American Negroes at State Universities and Land-Grant Colleges, 1968" . . . was mailed to the member institutions of the National Association of State Universities and Land-Grant Colleges. Replies were received from all 100 institutions.

. . . Two institutions—the University of Hawaii and the University of Puerto Rico—answered none of the questions; they replied that they are prohibited by law from collecting statistics by race. . . .

The burden of this report is the information submitted by . . . 80 predominantly white universities. Last fall [1968], their enrollment of full-time and part-time students at all levels totaled almost 2 million—nearly 30 per cent of the estimated 7 million students who enrolled in the nation's 2,500 public and private colleges and universities. . . .

Enough information has been presented by the institutions in the State University Survey to provide a crude benchmark of their involvement in the higher education of black Americans, and from this information some tentative observations and conclusions seem in order:

1. Just under 2 per cent of all the full-time, undergraduate students in the 80 predominantly white state universities and land-grant colleges in this survey are black Americans, and a similar percentage also holds true in the graduate and professional schools of those institutions.
2. Almost half of the black students who are full-time undergraduates in these 80 universities are freshmen, apparently indicating an increase in the institutions' commitment this year to seek out and enroll Negroes.

3. Less than 1 per cent of all persons holding full-time, faculty-rank positions in these institutions are black Americans.

4. It is probable that less than 1 per cent of all degrees awarded by the 80 universities in 1967–68 were presented to Negroes. . . .

The predominantly Negro colleges and universities, . . . still enroll a majority of all Negroes in higher education, and when their numbers are added to those in other colleges and universities, the overall percentage of Negroes in college is improved. The 18 predominantly Negro state universities and land-grant colleges in this survey enroll almost twice as many black students as the 80 majority-white institutions. And, there are indications that Negroes are better represented proportionately in the ranks of part-time undergraduates at some of the 80 universities than they are among full-time students.

But even when all of these circumstances are taken into consideration, the conclusion that black Americans are grossly underrepresented in higher education seems inescapable. In the campus turmoil of the past year, the impression has sometimes been conveyed that a black wave of students has swept into traditionally white higher education, and the starting lineups of many college and university athletic teams tend to confirm that impression in the minds of many people. The statistics in this report contradict that impression, at least as far as the major state universities are concerned. . . .

. . . The annual survey of incoming freshmen conducted by the American Council on Education shows that 5.8 per cent of all freshmen in higher education last fall were Negroes. The reported percentage of black freshmen in public junior colleges was 4.7, in public four-year colleges was 9.8, and in public universities was 3.3. The predominantly Negro institutions are included in these tabulations. The other study, produced by the Ford Foundation, is based on racial enrollment data from a select group of public and private graduate schools of arts and sciences. According to that study, black Americans made up 1.72 per cent of the total enrollment in the graduate schools of arts and sciences in 1967–68, and 0.78 per cent of all the Ph.D.'s awarded by those institutions since 1964 went to Negroes. . . .

The black factor in higher education is growing, and it will continue to grow. Racial equality in American society is not the responsibility of higher education alone, and equality in higher education is not a job just for the state universities and land-grant colleges. But those institutions, because of their history, their traditions, their size and their positions as the leading public institutions in higher education, have a pivotal role to play in the process of racial change. They have come late—and sometimes ill-prepared—to face that responsibility.

education and jobs

MAHLON T. PURYEAR

Discrimination   Discrimination is the most serious and fundamental problem confronting Negroes. This awesome monster crops up in training and education, and plays an important role in turning a poorly prepared product out into the work-a-day world. Most important, poor work backgrounds that result from discrimination make it impossible for Negroes to qualify for many jobs now available or that will appear during the coming years.

Even when there may be no discrimination in a particular job-related situation for a particular Negro, his difficulties in securing advancement or placement stem directly from past discrimination in education and training opportunities. . . .

Training   The net result of discrimination in training opportunities is the present glut of the market with millions of unskilled, unqualified Negro workers and jobseekers.

Lack of vocational and technical skills   Negroes have historically been denied equal opportunities for vocational and technical training. The feeling that Negroes should not be trained

From Mahlon T. Puryear, "Technology and the Negro," in The U.S. National Commission on Technology, Automation, and Economic Progress, *Adjusting to Change*, Appendix, Vol. III (Washington: Government Printing Office, 1966), pp. III 137–39 *passim*.

for jobs unless there were job possibilities has contributed to Negroes being unemployable because they were not given the chance to learn necessary skills. In the South, little or no vocational training was provided in areas other than gardening, cooking, sewing, or other traditional areas of employment. Technical educational opportunities were almost nonexistent until World War II, except in large cities or in the segregated land-grant colleges and other post high school institutions attended by Negroes.

New Negro workers find it difficult to find suitable employment, and the opportunities of older Negro workers are limited because no provisions have been made for them to learn new skills on the job or in organized educational programs. Only in recent years have positive steps been taken to give Negro workers an opportunity to apply for on-the-job training. . . .

Lack of apprenticeship opportunities   Of all training barriers, those in apprenticeship programs have been most unyielding to the Negro's efforts to upgrade his skills. Only recently has noticeable progress been made. The lack of apprenticeship opportunities constitutes one of the greatest tragedies facing Negro youth who wish employment. . . . Another tragic fact must be faced: It is extremely difficult to develop opportunities for apprentices when many skilled craftsmen are on layoff or when there is substantial unemployment.

Inadequate educational and vocational counseling   Many of those counseling Negro youth are either not qualified or do not care about doing a genuine job. They know little or nothing about these youths, their ambitions, their aspirations, or their problems. Many of these counselors have advised Negro youth to accept early work permits or stop their educational programs any time a job became available, and honestly thought they were helping them.

While this situation has prevailed in so-called integrated educational settings, Negro youth in segregated schools with a full complement of Negro teaching personnel have had problems no less frustrating. Here any semblance of guidance and counseling services has been almost completely nonexistent, and the little there is has become the responsibility of teachers whose orientation to the world of work consisted only of what they had read, seen, or heard. Their own lack of experience with business, industry, government, and labor made it impossible for them to do anything resembling a realistic counseling job.

recruiting

Unrealistic recruiting programs   As the number of Negro youth in colleges continues to rise and the quality of their education continues to improve, recruiting on college campuses should become a more fruitful medium for expanding job opportunities. Unfortunately, however, many Negro youths still are not able to move into the broader job market because recruiting and placement services available to them before they leave college are inadequate.

In predominantly Negro colleges, there is a grave shortage of placement services; in predominantly white colleges placement officials continue to be reluctant to believe that recruiters have a genuine interest in interviewing all qualified candidates, regardless of race. The use of interracial teams for visits to all campuses would show Negro and white youth alike that the present world of work can and does make use of the skills of all qualified workers. This would say to Negro youth, "Here is living proof that there are opportunities for you with my company."

Negro college youth do not readily accept mere statements that changes are taking place. They see too few examples of progress and too little evidence that opportunities are opening to them. Their skepticism is the direct outgrowth of the recruiting practices of businesses and firms which continue to overlook the Negro student or graduate as a prospective job applicant.

Lack of cooperation between Negro colleges and employers   Closely related to the problems of recruitment and placement is the lack of mutual information on the part of Negro colleges and industry. This ignorance can be removed only if industry and business offer teachers opportunities to obtain firsthand knowledge of business operations. Such knowledge can then be used to revamp curriculums to meet industry's needs. . . .

Misinformation about Negro jobseekers.   The extent to which misinformation and distorted notions about Negroes and their work habits affect job opportunities can be measured in such phrases as "jobs for Negroes," "white jobs," "Negroes work best at jobs that require muscle and endurance," "Negroes like to work with other Negroes," "white people will not work with Negroes," "Negro men may not work with or around white women," and "Negroes cannot supervise white workers." In many instances, it has been almost impossible to change the attitudes of some employers because of such ingrained notions.

Inability of Negro youth to pass written examinations Negro job applicants fail in alarming numbers to pass written and oral screening examinations. Admittedly, many Negroes have not had a great deal of experience with tests and examinations. However, the major problem appears to be only indirectly related to skills or abilities, and more a matter of attitudes toward tests and the belief that one will not be employed no matter how well one does on such tests. There is also evidence to support the contention that even if a Negro passes the written portion of the test, he is likely to be eliminated in the oral or personal interview. And then, passing the test only means that his name is placed on an eligibility list—then a candidate must wait to be selected over others also on the list. Until discrimination in the testing and selecting process is removed, Negroes will continue to have negative attitudes toward tests and as a result, will perform unsatisfactorily.

advancement on the job

Integrating the work force   The problem of integrating the work force requires the attention of top management and firm plans for implementation of policy at all levels below. Too often policy statements made at the top are considerably watered down by the time they reach the working level, causing many Negroes to lack faith in business, industry, government, and labor. Yet experience has shown that excellent working relationships do not change when well-planned steps are taken to assure Negroes opportunities for promotion and transfer to more responsible jobs.

Lack of opportunities for on-the-job training and retraining Efforts must be made to give underemployed Negroes an opportunity to seek jobs at higher levels, with additional training available in or out of the plant. This is especially needed when a firm opens new plants in the same area and needs additional workers, or when layoffs are probable for employees not trained to more advanced operational techniques.

Special on-the-job training programs, sponsored with Federal funds, are just now beginning to have an impact on training and employment opportunities. Before they are laid off, workers at lower level jobs should be offered training opportunities to increase their skills and maintain seniority rights and other benefits.

job attitudes

MAHLON T. PURYEAR

In higher education, other than in Negro colleges, we have not produced one president of a college or university, not one dean, and very few department heads. There are surprisingly few Negroes holding full professorships in major universities, and this is true despite the fact that Negroes have been graduating from these institutions for more than 100 years.

The opportunity to learn, to acquire meaningful experiences, to explore, to make mistakes and recover from them, to be a part of the whole and not just a segment, to be understood as having desires, aspirations, ambitions, and feelings for America has not typically been the lot of Negro citizens.

Lack of community concern   Motivation and stimulation of Negro youth are major responsibilities of the community at large and cannot be delegated to teachers and professional counselors alone. First, industry, business, government, and labor leaders alike must be made aware of the problem confronting the

From Mahlon T. Puryear, "Technology and the Negro," in The U.S. National Commission on Technology, Automation, and Economic Progress, *Adjusting to Change,* Appendix, Vol. **III** (Washington: Government Printing Office, 1966), pp. **III** 140–41 *passim.*

Negro worker and job-seeker; and, second, positive plans to bring about desired changes in the school and community must be developed and implemented. Counseling and teaching materials at all levels should be redesigned for teachers, counselors, and administrators to depict the true image and worth of the Negro in our economy.

Equally new and dramatic thinking on the part of parents is called for to motivate their children. A parent's own work experiences are reflected in the advice and information he passes on to his children; hence, it becomes doubly important that every effort be made to secure better jobs for adults.

Negroes should participate at all levels of policy-making and policy implementation—planning, advisory, consultation, operation, evaluation, and followup—in overall community programs, as well as those dealing specifically with the Negro and his employment problems.

. . . Some of the problems Negroes face in finding suitable work may be attributed to their failure to take full advantage of available resources. . . . Although many of the State Fair Employment Practices Commissions do not have *real* authority for dealing with the problems they are confronted with, they report that they do not receive enough complaints from persons with genuine cases of discrimination or unequal treatment. . . .

Reluctance to move with plants that relocate in other communities   Despite their widely proclaimed mobility, Negroes are often not mobile, either at time of initial employment or when it is necessary to move with a firm which finds it necessary to relocate. For example, the Mack Truck Division of General Motors Corp. recently moved from its Newark, N.J., operations to Maryland, and not a single Negro worker has accepted a transfer. Despite the fact that many were making more than $125 a week in production shops, they have elected to remain in the Newark area and collect severance pay and unemployment compensation.

Lack of interest in pursuing careers in new areas of work   Negroes shun employment where income is based on commissions; they feel that they are being asked to produce with no guarantee of security or regularity of income. . . .

Attitude of Negroes regarding "prestige" jobs and status

For many years and until very recently, Negroes were builders, chauffeurs, porters, coal shovelers, and nurses. These were the traditional jobs held by Negroes, the parents of today's youth. However, they saw the schoolteacher, the social worker, the preacher, all with personal status, all accepted by the community. These became their symbols of success.

As a result, the Negro told his children about the disadvantages of "hard work," "outdoor jobs," "seasonal work," "serving other people," "working with your hands," being "bossed by white people."

Teachers and administrators had little contact with workers, and unwittingly also helped develop negative attitudes toward manual and technical work. Available vocational programs provided training in limited areas, and technical offerings were virtually nonexistent. Vocational schools were used as dumping grounds for problem children and those who did not do well in English and mathematics.

Consequently Negroes today are not employed in skilled trades. While the need for professional, technical, business, and other white-collar jobs will increase in the years ahead, larger numbers of skilled workers will also be needed. Adults and youth alike would be wise to examine the possibility for achieving success in the skilled trades area.

Difficulty in getting Negroes to believe in changes

Many Negro youth simply do not accept the fact that changes are taking place, and that they are now at long last regarded as worthy of consideration for jobs at all levels in an integrated society. Part of the difficulty can be traced to parents who are still smarting from the evil effects of the situation just a few years ago. However, a really dramatic recruiting program conducted by management, coupled with improved counseling and guidance services at the school level, could change this quite rapidly. Young people do need more information about changes in the world of work and how to fit into this world. Educators and counselors must help youth explore opportunities made available through technological advances.

discrimination in
resource markets

the competitive market
is color blind

W. H. HUTT

. . . When we buy a product in the free market, we do not ask: What was the colour of the person who made it? Nor do we ask about the sex, race, nationality, religion or political opinions of the producer. All we are interested in is whether it is good value for money. Hence it is in the interest of business men (who must try to produce at least cost in anticipation of demand) not only to seek out and employ the least privileged classes (excluded by custom or legislation from more remunerative employments) but actually to educate them for these opportunities by investing in them. . . .

. . . the effective colour bars which have denied economic opportunities and condemned non-Whites to be 'hewers of wood and drawers of water' have all been created in response to demands for state intervention by most political parties (although in some of the most blatant cases, to pressures from those who have claimed to be 'syndicalists' or 'Marxists'). Of course, the extension of state control need not necessarily involve discrimination on the grounds of race, colour, caste or creed; yet in practice it does seem always to discriminate against the politically weak; and by reason of history, the non-Whites have (so far) usually fallen into this class. . . .

. . . The virtues of the free market do not depend upon the virtues of the men at the political top but on the dispersed powers of substitution exercised by men in their role as consumers. In that role, a truly competitive market enables them to exert the energy which enforces the neutrality of business decision-making in respect of race, colour, creed, sex, class, accent, school, or income group. The reader will have noticed that at no

From W. H. Hutt, *The Economics of the Colour Bar: A Study of the Economic Origins and Consequences of Racial Segregation in South Africa* (London: Institute of Economic Affairs, 1964), pp. 173–80 *passim.*

the determinants of income differentials

time have I claimed that the free market which releases the 'liberating force' has been motivated by altruistic sentiment.

For omnipotent representative government (i.e., constitutionally unchecked government, without enforceable rules for making rules) to claim a similar neutrality, we would have to have absolute faith in the virtues of the men who hold, seek or wish to retain power, against the temptations to buy the support of majorities by discriminating against minorities. Virtue may triumph; but in the light of the realities of vote-catching pressures, it demands that the camel shall pass through the eye of a needle.

In a book published nearly 30 years ago, I argued that competition is essentially an equalitarian force.[1] In a country of racially homogeneous population, it tends, unless obstructed by sectionalist law and administration or the use of private coercive power (as by labour unions or business monopolies), to bring about the classless society. In a multi-racial society, it tends, because of the consumers' colour-blindness, to dissolve customs and prejudices which have been restricting the ability of the underprivileged to contribute to, and hence to share in, the common pool of output and income. This is because business decision-makers—'entrepreneurs'—have an immensely powerful incentive to economise for the benefit of their customers, who collectively make up the public. Their success depends upon their acumen and skill in acquiring the resources needed for production at the least cost, and especially in discovering under-utilised resources. . . .

In a truly free enterprise society . . . it is the duty of the state not only to refrain from legislation which raises the income of favoured groups by making certain wanted things scarce, but to prevent private arrangements having the same effect by enforcing laws and procedures which are usually known as anti-monopoly or anti-trust. Indeed, the basic distinction between a competitive enterprise or free market system and a restrictionist system is that, under truly free enterprise, the contrivance of

[1] *Economists and the Public*, 1936, pp. 81–2, 313–15, 319–23. The process of competition may be defined as the substitution, for the consumers' benefit, of the least-cost method of achieving any objective, which includes producing and selling any commodity. This is the most appropriate definition of competition, whatever the institutional arrangements which give rise to that substitution. A competitive system cannot exist unless the state performs its role; but under competitive capitalism the state acts wholly in the collective interest and never in the sectional interest.

scarcity for the private or sectional interest is prohibited, whereas the only limit to the creation of scarcities by 'central planning' is the discontent which may be expressed through the ballot-box or, where free elections are suppressed, through the potential intrigues of groups manœuvring for control of the armed forces and exploiting popular discontent in the process.

In referring to 'truly free enterprise,' I have obviously envisaged a form of society which the course of history has never allowed fully to emerge. In every country of the world, economic self-rule by the people is frustrated to some extent by state intervention to protect sectional interests. By 'economic self-rule by the people,' I simply mean the democratic exercise of consumers' sovereignty. Under a free market system, income receivers as a whole control the economy through the discipline they exercise over decision-makers, through buying or refraining from buying the services and commodities offered in the market. The present is a restrictionist, not an equalitarian or liberal age; and I know of no country in which the state forbids all creation of scarcity, that is, all action for the benefit of at least some politically powerful sections. There is, for instance, no country in the world in which anti-trust legislation, although widely and rightly applied to industrial and commercial activities, has been effectively applied to organised labour and organised agriculture.

In a free market system, however, in which the state has not been prevented (through the political power of sectional groups) from performing its co-ordinating role, the detailed pattern and rate of progress of economic development is set by responsible entrepreneurial planning. The form in which the community's resources are replaced or accumulated is then the result of responsible foresight and decision-making on the part of the business men who seek to avoid 'losses' and to make 'profits' in catering for the freely expressed preferences of the sovereign consumer. . . .

. . . If there is to be a bloodless solution to South Africa's race problems it will, I suggest demand the acceptance of the philosophy of free enterprise, better described as 'liberalism' in its 19th century sense. The ethos of this philosophy is that it denies the right of the state to discriminate. Whilst many laws can be made only by majority decisions, the liberal insists that all the laws so determined must apply to all members of the community in the same sort of way. Under such a precept, as

J. S. Mill acknowledged, the state may legitimately treat classes and races differently if, as a result of history, they happen to be primitive and uneducated. But the precept creates no justification for any *apartheid* ideal. Differentiation is justified only if it is being accompanied by genuine steps to remove the causes of the backwardness which has temporarily justified the differential treatment.

The truth is that parliamentary institutions (not only in South Africa, but in many other countries of the Western world) have been allowed to develop in a manner which the great protagonists of democracy, J. S. Mill, von Humboldt and Tocqueville, would have deplored. Decisions by parliamentary majorities may conflict headlong with the democratic ideal unless the powers of parliament are rigidly limited and defined by powerful tradition or appropriate constitutional checks so as to exclude discriminatory laws. But the so-called democratic world accepted the form of government advocated by the apostles of a free parliamentary system without remembering or understanding the conditions necessary for it to function without injustice or tyranny. In any good society a ruling majority can be allowed no rights (a) to enrich itself at the expense of a minority or an unrepresented class or race; or (b) to attempt to maintain any historically determined status or privilege at the expense of a minority or the unrepresented. The rule of law must be a rule of non-discrimination and a rule, therefore, of limited state intervention in the sphere of markets and free contract.

. . . industrialists and commercial men—for whose policies I have claimed no altruistic motivation—perceived that new and additional products could be brought within the reach of the community's income (hence causing that income to grow) if cheap labour, available through the recruitment and training of non-Whites, was used to the best advantage; that private business firms were always willing to invest in human capital, that is, in the development by training of the industrial capacity of Coloureds, Africans and Indians; that progress has often been obstructed because business managements have not wished to flout influential public opinion or the prejudices of their existing staff, or to fight quixotically against the 'political realities' of their time—the power of the state to make or destroy their fortunes; and finally that, whenever the more enterprising business men have seen some way of evading the legislative obstacles to nonwhite training and employment, they have done so to the benefit of the depressed groups and of the community.

In sharp contrast, the customs, prejudices and inertias which confine the non-Whites in the Republic of South Africa to low-paid work have been perpetuated by state laws and restrictions of organised labour exactly similar to the laws and restrictions that are applauded by people in all political parties who favour state direction. The survival of *apartheid* is, indeed, the survival of a kind of socialism—often altruistically motivated—whilst the dissolution of colour injustice has been continuously assisted by competitive capitalism. . . .

inequality of opportunity in a competitive market

ALAN BATCHELDER

the perfectly functioning market economy

One man's perfection is another man's failure. As used here, "perfect" means that physical capital is privately owned, that education and physical capital are distributed among men in a way that maximizes their efficiency, that no one has monopoly power, that men go to work in the jobs in which they are most productive, and that the output is divided in unqualified accord with the principle "to each according to his contribution to production." This can be called "the perfectly functioning market economy of competitive private enterprise." . . .

The market economy of competitive private enterprise works perfectly when education and training are accessible to those who can use them most productively; when tools, buildings, land, and materials are available to those who can best use them; and when each person knows of all work opportunities and is able to move to one where he is most productive. These conditions are conceivable; they are not attainable. . . .

The perfect market would split the national product in proportion to ownership of Intelligence C [See page 100 for definition] and property: buildings, machinery, materials, land, and intangibles (such as patents and trademarks) used in production. Some persons would begin with more productive property than others because some parents leave larger inheritances than others. To some observers, this inherited-property inequality will appear inequitable. . . .

Perhaps a system would be more equitable if everyone started with the same physical assets and the same Intelligence A [See page 100]. They do not. . . . the perfectly functioning market economy of competitive private enterprise accepts this inequality, uses each person and his assets in proportion to his ability to produce, and divides the output in proportion to the productive contribution of the intelligence and assets of each.

From Alan Batchelder, *The Economics of Poverty* (New York: John Wiley & Sons, Inc., 1966), pp. 76–79 *passim*.

The primary points are: (1) that the perfectly functioning market economy of competitive private enterprise results in income inequality as wide as the inequalities in Intelligence A and physical assets; and (2) that those persons with the least physical assets and the lowest Intelligence A will be left poor by such a system. Among the poor of the United States, there are many who are poor because of inferior inheritance. They would be poor even if the market were perfect in the sense here used. Many of the poor of the United States are poor for other reasons.

management racial practices

VERNON M. BRIGGS, JR.

Of all the social indices used to measure progress toward racial equality, none are as significant as those pertaining to employment. . . . It is apparent, therefore, that an examination of the racial practices of American industry is a timely and vital subject of inquiry. With over 83 percent of the civilian labor force employed in 1968 in the private sector, the responsibility for change in the existing racial employment patterns rests ultimately with nonpublic policies and practices.

The seven industry studies that are the topic of this review are part of the product of a Ford Foundation grant in 1966 to the Industrial Research Unit of the Wharton School of Finance and Commerce of the University of Pennsylvania. . . . The director of the undertaking is Herbert Northrup who is assisted by Richard Rowan. The stated purposes of the project are: (1) to determine why some industries are more hospitable to the employment of blacks than are others; (2) to explain why some companies within the same industry have differing racial patterns; and (3) to propose appropriate policy measures.

. . . Events of the past decade have demonstrated that aggre-

From Vernon M. Briggs, Jr., "The Negro in American Industry: A Review of Seven Studies," *The Journal of Human Resources*, Volume V, Number 3 (© 1970 by the Regents of the University of Wisconsin), 371–81 *passim*.

gate labor market studies are a poor guide to understanding racial employment questions. The concealing nature of broad averages often obfuscates significant considerations. Moreover, the vast differences in the occupational composition of diverse industries mean that policy conclusions based upon global studies are usually meaningless when applied to specific situations. Hence, it has been realized only too slowly that policy-oriented research must depend upon the disclosures of either industry studies or local labor market examinations. . . .

Black militants frequently express the position that black people have been studied long enough. The actual subject of inquiry, they argue, should be whites since they control the power in our society. These studies—although not having such an objective as an avowed goal—are implicit searches into the nature of white power as it has groped with the civil rights explosion. . . .

the automobile industry

It is appropriate that the first study dealt with the automobile industry. Long the bellweather of the private economy, its three major producers ranked as the first, second, and fifth largest manufacturing units in the country in 1966. These firms employed just shy of 1 million employees of whom 13.6 percent were blacks. About one-half of the total employment in the industry is in the blue-collar category of semiskilled operatives (20.2 percent of whom were black in 1966). As a result, the industry has the ability to employ large numbers of poorly educated and inexperienced recruits.

Prior to 1941, substantive black employment occurred only at the Ford Motor Company. . . . Elsewhere in the industry, significant black entry was the product of a marriage of necessity and convenience. That is to say, blacks made their greatest gains during times of tight labor. With blacks migrating out of the South during the war years and settling in northern urban centers, the situation was advantageous for a change from the past.

By 1966, Chrysler had the highest percentage of black employees (23 percent) in the industry, due to its plant concentrations in the inner city of Detroit and its absence of plants in the South; General Motors had the highest absolute number of black employees (56,762); whereas Ford had the best occupational placement record of blacks in craftsmen (6 percent) and office and clerical (7 percent) jobs. In general, however, the occupational patterns for blacks found them in the blue-collar categories of operatives, laborers, and service workers, accounting in 1966 for 92 percent of the black employees. In the skilled trades, blacks held only 3 percent of the craftsmen jobs. As elsewhere, the issue of minority access to apprentice programs has been very difficult—despite the sympathetic attitude of the union leadership. The combination of past (and in some instances present) discrimination and high qualification standards—a high school diploma with a good mechanical and mathematical aptitude—is cited as the roadblock. Likewise, white-collar jobs have afforded little access to blacks who held a scant 4 percent of the office and clerical jobs in 1966. Discriminatory housing and inadequate public transportation systems are cited as the major obstacles to wider black participation. As matters now stand, blacks are overly represented in occupations that are highly vulnerable to technological displacement in an increasingly automated industry.

Events of the late sixties have fostered concern for a racial employment policy. Northrup concludes that the Detroit riot of 1967 shook the industry out of its lethargic state. General Motors, for the first time, agreed to accept job referrals from local poverty and manpower groups; Chrysler "adopted" an inner city high school; and Ford announced its new outreach recruitment policy designed to "screen-in" applicants. The essence of these efforts has been to reverse normal hiring procedures to accommodate increasing numbers of marginal workers. In the process, new issues have arisen for management. The firms report (1) rising incidence of employee discipline, especially with regard to absenteeism, tardiness, gambling, and fighting; (2) adverse effects on production efficiency; and (3) mounting unrest among whites as departments approach an imaginary "tipping point."

the aerospace industry

In sharp contrast to the automobile industry, the aerospace industry is publicly oriented and affords significantly fewer opportunities for unskilled and semiskilled workers. Dependent upon government contracts, it has been forced to be cognizant of government and racial policies. As defined by Northrup, the aerospace industry is the largest employer in the manufacturing sector of the economy. In 1966, 1.3 million employees were on the payroll, almost half (47 percent) of whom were salaried personnel.

Prior to World War II, the industry adhered to a conscious policy of exclusion of blacks. Blacks comprised less than 0.2 percent of the industry's employment in 1940. The major union in the industry, the International Association of Machinists, forbade black members until 1948 and since has seldom exerted pressure for change. It was during World War II, when a number of former automobile plants were converted to aircraft production, that blacks gained a toehold in the industry. Yet at its peak employment period during the war, blacks reached a level of only 4 percent of the work force. . . . By 1966 black employment was 4.8 percent of total employment with 65 percent of the blacks in the operative, laborer, and service categories.

. . . prospects for enlarging the black labor force are not good. The declining number of low skilled jobs has encouraged union resistance to new job seekers, black or white. For the limited number of skilled craftsmen positions, competition is "acute." . . . Another obstacle is location. Although frequently located near high black population clusters, the plants themselves are by necessity located in outlying areas that are distant from city concentrations of blacks. . . . Obviously, with relatively higher educational requisites, societal measures to upgrade the quality and to enhance the retention power of the nation's school system are more important long-run solutions to black employment status than are piecemeal undertakings of the firms themselves.

the steel industry

As for the steel industry, the era of the civil rights movement found the industry in a state of secular employment decline every year between 1957 and 1966. The absolute loss was 48,287 jobs (or 7.7 percent). The full impact of the decline was in the blue-collar ranks as they sustained a reduction of 61,712 jobs (or 12.1 percent); white-collar jobs increased by 11.6 percent. As there are virtually no blacks employed in the white-collar sector (they held only 1.4 percent of these jobs in 1966), blacks have had to fight hard to maintain their original penetration rates. . . . Under such circumstances, the only hope for improving the status of blacks in the steel industry is through upgrading and promotions. White-collar jobs and craftsmen positions would seem to represent the occupations upon which a racial employment policy should focus. Yet the study finds little hope for blacks with regard to entry into either.

. . . Rowan attributes the paucity of blacks in these positions to shortages of qualified blacks (which does not explain why this is more of a problem in the steel than in other industries with higher absolute and relative numbers of blacks in such jobs) and to the distaste that black women have for working in unattractive and isolated offices in or around steel plants (which does not explain why white women will take such jobs). It appears that industry officials do not understand the dimensions of a true corporate racial policy. . . .

In the craftsmen category, the familiar difficulties of blacks with regard to access are rendered more severe by the declining employment picture in other blue-collar positions. Hence, competition between whites and blacks offers small chance for blacks to alter significantly their present percentages. In 1966, blacks were 5.9 percent of the craftsmen in the industry and 5.0 percent of the apprentices.

the hotel industry

The only nonmanufacturing study of the seven under review was of the hotel industry. Due to its growth potential and the fact that it has long been a source of employment for the working poor, its importance to black employment is evident. Since it is an amorphous industry, the authors conducted a 12-city survey in 1967 of 108 hotels which employed 26,595 workers. Blacks comprised 32.4 percent of these employees. Over 87 percent of the blacks were employed in housekeeping, food preparation, and food service. The industry has a small capital investment per worker, has virtually constant productivity rates, and requires little skill for most of its jobs. Almost all but the white-collar workers were union members. Over half of the union-member employees were obtained through a hiring hall arrangement which made union membership a condition of employment (the Taft-Hartley Act notwithstanding). Union policies toward blacks ran the full gamut—from outright restrictionism to positive efforts to attract minority members. Another source of back-of-the-house employees was the state employment service. As most of these jobs are heavily black to begin with, the referrals reinforced the prevailing employment patterns. Although educational attainment is not particularly important as a job qualification, a clean police record is, due to the frequent need to enter the rooms of guests. Low wages contribute to heavy turnover of employees throughout the occupational structure. As a result, it is difficult to attract blacks with the qualifications needed to fill front-of-the-house jobs. Promotions in the industry are usually restricted to departments. Hence opportunities for blacks to advance from departments in which they dominate (such as housekeepers) to those in which they are sparse (such as room clerks or telephone operators) are rare. When blacks are placed in supervisory positions, it was reported, they were resented by both whites and by other blacks. Thus, the Koziaras [see reference section at the end of this selection, page 130] conclude that black employees have limited opportunities to be promoted in occupations in which they dominate and that there are so few blacks in nontraditional occupations that little deviation can be expected from prevailing patterns.

the petroleum industry

The petroleum industry, in contrast to the hotel industry, is highly capital intensive. The extensive introduction of technological advances has virtually eliminated the need for poorly trained and uneducated personnel. In the extraction, refining, and pipeline sectors of the industry, employment has declined sharply. In the refining sector, which is the prime concern of the study by King and Risher [see reference section], employment declined by 58 percent between 1950 and 1966. Moreover, according to the authors, the industry is still "overstaffed" and keeps many employees on its rosters only because of "paternalism." Refinery locations are centered around consumption centers and seaport distribution points. As most of these locations are distant from

management racial practices   127 black population centers, inadequate transportation is again cited as an obstacle to wider minority participation. The significant determinants, however, are the historical pattern of exclusion and the declining number of jobs. Prior to 1940, the only blacks in the industry were in unskilled job classifications. A heritage of segregated local unions cemented the pattern over the years. By the time government prodding for integration had led to their demise, employment had begun to contract. . . . Blacks who were originally hired on the basis of their ability to do laborer work—not because of their potential for promotion— have had difficulty being upgraded to less technologically vulnerable jobs. Of 17 major companies surveyed in 1968, blacks represented only 3.9 percent of their combined work force. In the clerical area there has been a long tradition that these jobs went to relatives of present employees, and as few blacks were employed in the industry to begin with, this past practice severely limited the opportunities for black females to find office jobs. Yet, of the small absolute gains made by blacks between 1966 and 1968 (a net increase of 1,032 positions) in the industry, 73 percent occurred in the clerical sector with black females being the primary beneficiaries. . . .

the rubber tire industry

Although the rubber tire industry is tied closely to developments in the auto industry, the former has never been the significant employer of blacks as has been the latter. Production is highly capital intensive. Output has soared since World War II, while employment has fallen annually except for a few spurts. Total employment declined by 30 percent between 1946 and 1967; blue-collar employment declined by 39 percent. . . . The occupational structure is heavily weighted toward the blue-collar jobs—accounting for 78.1 percent of the jobs in 1966. About one-half of the employees are in the semiskilled operatives classification. Unskilled jobs are few. Wage rates in the industry are far above the average for the manufacturing sector. Prior to World War II, the industry employed almost all white labor, black employees accounting for only 2.1 percent of the work force in 1940. . . .

By 1968, blacks accounted for 8.3 percent of the industry's

employment, with 96 percent of the blacks in blue-collar jobs. Northrup interprets present employment trends as adversely affecting the future for blacks. The jobs in which blacks dominate are the ones that are being automated, the competition for the declining number of positions has led to higher qualification standards being imposed, and the supply of applicants far exceeds the demand for workers so that management has become increasingly selective.

The United Rubber Workers union represents the workers and, although its national policy has been avowedly equalitarian, it has had little impact on the attitudes and practices of the locals. With job security being a crucial consideration, there has been marked opposition by the rank and file to proposals to upgrade blacks or to give special assistance to blacks for apprenticeship positions. Of greater consequence, however, was the union's successful effort to switch from departmental seniority to plantwide seniority in the early 1950s. With employment declining, the older membership wanted security. While it is true that the change did open new occupations to blacks, it has meant that efforts designed to bring more blacks into the industry are often squelched by the first downswing in business activity.

the chemical industry

The chemical industry also has experienced accelerated growth in production. While employment has increased, although at a rate far less than the proportionate increases in output, the percentage of blacks in the industry has declined from 9 percent in 1940 to 6 percent in 1968. The explanation, of course, rests with rising numbers of white-collar jobs and the declining number of blue-collar jobs. Unlike the rubber, steel, and automobile industries, the chemical industry does little training of craftsmen, even though that group is the second largest occupational category in the industry. Rather it seeks to attract its maintenance force in the open market by hiring journeymen from the building trades. As blacks have had difficulty entering these crafts, they have had little opportunity to become journeymen and, in this instance, to become craftsmen in the chemical industry. The prospects for internal advancement of blacks already in the industry are hampered by departmental seniority provisions which lock blacks into traditional occupations. In addition, the locational patterns of chemical facilities—usually in outlying areas—has made access difficult for blacks who live in city ghettos.

. . . the industry has had little to do with on-going federal manpower programs. In spite of the fact that firms have been found "not in compliance" with federal equal employment opportunity edicts, no contract has ever been pulled. Nevertheless Quay [see reference section] feels that federal pressure has been a "prime mover" for social change in an industry that has yet to convince blacks "that justice can be attained within the plant through union and employer action." . . .

These reports indicate that the immediate obstacles to qualitative improvements in black labor market experience are not attitudes per se as they are behavioral practices of corporations and unions. Over the long haul, however, it is apparent that the laws of supply and demand have exerted a greater influence on the quantitative employment patterns of blacks than have the laws of the land. In the wake of rapid technological change, the need to improve the education and skill attainment levels of the black labor force is urgent. It is the underlying theme that is implicit in all of these studies. . . .

Herbert R. Northrup. *The Negro in the Automobile Industry.* Philadelphia: University of Pennsylvania Press, 1968, Pp. vii + 75. $2.50.

Herbert R. Northrup. *The Negro in the Aerospace Industry.* Philadelphia: University of Pennsylvania Press, 1968. Pp. ix + 90. $2.50.

Richard L. Rowan. *The Negro in the Steel Industry.* Philadelphia: University of Pennsylvania Press, 1968. Pp. xi + 148. $3.50.

Edward C. Koziara and Karen S. Koziara. *The Negro in the Hotel Industry.* Philadelphia: University of Pennsylvania Press, 1968. Pp. vii + 74. $2.50.

Carl B. King and Howard W. Risher, Jr. *The Negro in the Petroleum Industry.* Philadelphia: University of Pennsylvania Press, 1969. Pp. viii + 96. $3.50.

Herbert Northrup. *The Negro in the Rubber Tire Industry.* Philadelphia: University of Pennsylvania Press, 1969. Pp. viii + 134. $3.50.

William Howard Quay, Jr. *The Negro in the Chemical Industry.* Philadelphia: University of Pennsylvania Press, 1969. Pp. xi + 110. $3.50.

union racial practices

F. RAY MARSHALL

In discussing union racial practices, we shall emphasize racial exclusion from unions by formal and informal means, segregated local unions, discrimination in the building trades, and the ways unions influence economic opportunities of Negroes. . . .

formal exclusion

The number of national unions with formal racial restrictions has declined significantly in the last 30 years. . . .

The following forces caused unions to abandon exclusion by formal means, or to adopt more subtle forms: Expansion of Negro employment into jurisdictions covered by these unions, especially during World War II; competition between unions for Negro votes in representation elections after the passage of the Railway Labor Act; the embarrassment of exclusionist union leaders at conventions and in the press by criticism from Negro and white union leaders; action by such governmental agencies as the wartime and State FEP committees, especially the creation of the New York State Commission Against Discrimination in 1946; and fear of the loss of exclusive bargaining rights, union shop provisions or other legal privileges under the Railway Labor Act or the Taft-Hartley Act.

informal exclusion

The decline in formal exclusion by international unions does not mean, however, that discrimination declined by the same degree because of local variations from official policies. Unions with formal race bars frequently have accepted Negro members and the locals of some international unions with no formal bars, particularly in the building trades and on the railroads, have excluded Negroes by such informal means as agreements not to

From F. Ray Marshall, "Union Racial Practices," statement before The U.S. Senate, Subcommittee on Labor and Public Welfare, *Hearings*, 88th Congress, Pt. 4, August 6, 7 and September 10, 11, 12, 1963 (Washington: Government Printing Office, 1963), pp. 1192–96 *passim*.

sponsor Negroes for membership; refusal to admit Negroes into apprenticeship programs; refusal to accept applicants from Negroes, or simply ignoring their applications; general "understandings" to vote against Negroes if they were proposed . . . using examinations to refuse Negro journeymen status which either were not given to whites or were rigged so that Negroes could not pass them; and by exerting political pressure on governmental licensing agencies to see to it that Negroes failed the tests. . . .

The evidence seems to support the following conclusions concerning unions that bar Negroes from membership by informal means:

1. Racial exclusion by informal means is not restricted to any particular geographic area. Though restriction is undoubtedly more rigid in the South, unions in the following trades probably have more Negro members in the South than some other places: the trowel trades, longshoremen, teamsters, roofers, hod carriers and common laborers, and hotel and restaurant employees. These trades have been practiced by Negroes in the South because they have been regarded as "Negro work" and because Negroes have sufficient supplies of labor to protect their interests and to protect their employers, who might be boycotted by whites. These occupations also are relatively old and have stable techniques, making it difficult for unions to exclude Negroes by monopolizing the latest technology.

2. While some craft unions have had egalitarian racial policies and some industrial union locals have refused to admit Negroes to membership, as a general rule the unions which practice exclusion are craft organizations. The members of craft locals have the ability to exclude Negroes from membership and from the trade if they can control the labor supply. Industrial unions on the other hand are forced to organize workers hired by the employer, while the craft unions determine in many cases whom he hires. In addition, craft unions at the local level consider it to their advantage to exclude workers, while industrial unions consider it to their advantage to organize extensively.

3. The foregoing factors are not, however, sufficient to identify the general character of excluding unions. Some other fac-

tors include: because of the egalitarian trend in race relations, those unions which are older, other things being equal, seem more likely to exclude than newer unions; in many cases the employer determines the hiring policy; whites are likely to attempt to exclude Negroes from certain status jobs like airline pilots, stock wranglers, locomotive engineers, white-collar and supervisory jobs; and, in some cases, exclusion is directed against all except a particular nationality group. (It has been common practice in the building trades for instance, for locals to be made up entirely of a particular nationality.)

auxiliary and segregated locals

A number of international unions which did not bar Negroes from membership restricted them to auxiliary locals controlled entirely by whites; about the only thing Negro members of these locals were allowed to do was to pay dues. Auxiliary locals were weakened by attacks from the wartime FEPC, court decisions which prohibited the closed shop where auxiliaries existed, NLRB decisions that the auxiliary could not be coupled with the checkoff of union dues, State FEP laws, the Taft-Hartley and Railway Labor Act amendments making the union shop unenforcible if all workers are not admitted on equal terms, and the Landrum-Griffin Act of 1959 which makes it possible for Negro employees to bring action to abolish auxiliary locals. A few auxiliary locals remained in 1959, but had become relatively unimportant by that date. . . .

While it is extremely difficult to generalize about segregated locals, the writer's experiences suggest several broad conclusions:

1. Negroes in the South frequently favor a continuation of segregation because they would usually be in the minority and know that whites might discriminate against them; Negroes have their own buildings and other property, as well as their own officers and representatives, and thus have a vested interest in perpetuating segregation; some Negroes believe they can engage in nonunion matters of interest to Negroes better if they have their own locals.

2. Whether or not Negroes oppose integration depends partly upon the effects of segregation on their economic opportunities. Some unions . . . feel that their economic opportunities would not be improved if they integrated because they have protected territories.

   In other cases, however, Negro workers are extremely unhappy with segregation because they are denied equal job opportunities. . . .
3. The ideological and philosophical positions of Negroes will also influence their attitude toward segregated locals. Some Negro leaders are opposed to segregation on principle and feel that the AFL–CIO should deliver an ultimatum to its segregated locals to integrate or be expelled. On the other hand, a majority of the Negro leaders in segregated unions in the South probably oppose integration. Younger Negro workers are more likely to insist on integration, but older leaders fear Negroes will suffer short run losses from integration.
4. The proportions of Negroes in unions will influence the ability to merge segregated locals. If there are very few Negroes, whites will agree to merge, but if the Negroes are in the majority the whites will frequently oppose integration.
5. Negro resistance to integration has been reduced by special arrangements to make it possible for them to continue to have some control over their affairs when they integrated. . . .

We should note, however, that to say a local is "integrated" might not mean very much. It could mean that one or two Negroes belong to the organization but never participate other than by paying dues. "Integration" might also mean that Negroes are members of the industrial union and if they attend meetings they segregate themselves or are segregated by whites.

control of job opportunities

Craft unions influence job opportunities for Negroes by controlling entry into the labor market through closed-union, closed-shop conditions, job referral systems, apprenticeship programs, and pressure on employers to hire or not to hire Negroes. Indus-

the determinants of income differentials

trial unions affect job opportunities through control of hiring, transfer, promotion, and layoffs. Many employers are convinced that if they transfer Negroes into previously "white" occupations the white workers will strike, and there is sufficient historical precedent to validate this belief, though it is rarely possible for a group of rank and filers to block the employment or upgrading of Negroes without the aid of either the employer or the international.

Finally, unions have positively influenced employment opportunities of minorities by promoting civil rights legislation, including nondiscrimination clauses in contracts and adoption of companywide seniority agreements to make it possible for Negroes to break out of "Negro" jobs.

While our attention has been focused on problems of racial discrimination within unions, we have noted that unions also have contributed to the improvement of the Negro worker's position. In spite of these positive measures, however, racial discrimination is still a serious problem within the labor movement and probably cannot be solved by the unions themselves. This conclusion is based on the belief that those unions and leaders who want to change union racial practices do not have sufficient power to do so.

black business motivation

limitations of the black businessman

EUGENE P. FOLEY

There are myths carried by Negro businessmen and by Negroes in general. The first one has to do with the lack of credit; the second one, with the Jewish merchant; and the third one, with the state of poverty of the Negro community. We investigated these in terms of the Negro entrepreneur in Philadelphia.

In terms of financing, it is true that the Negro businessman has a tough time getting credit, but he does not have any more trouble getting credit than any other small businessman. The Drexel Institute made an actual count of every Negro businessman in Philadelphia. (For those of you who are interested in the field of statistics: in 1960, the Census Bureau counted only about 1,600 self-employed Negro merchants in that city. There actually are about 4,200 Negro businessmen in Philadelphia.) There are no millionaires, but there are about 10 who may have a net worth of approximately $100,000—which, in business circles, does not make them outstandingly successful, but does make them comfortable and secure. Nevertheless, 10 out of 4,200 obviously is not very many. Thus, when we talk about the Negro business community, we are talking about the familiar pattern of retail trades and services—very small businessmen, who in this country just cannot get credit. Sixty per cent of *all* the small businessmen of this type in Philadelphia just do not have any banking relationships.

Banks have branches in the Negro areas of Philadelphia, and they do make loans to Negroes. They make two types of loans: consumer loans and mortgage finance loans. They make them every day and have been for years. But they do not make busi-

From Eugene P. Foley, conference transcript "American Academy," reprinted by permission from *Daedulus,* Journal of The American Academy of Arts and Sciences, Boston, Mass., Vol. **95**, No. 1 (Winter 1966) 425–28 *passim.*

the determinants of income differentials

ness loans to Negroes for the same reason that they do not make them to the same type of white businessmen anywhere else in the city of Philadelphia: business loans are very risky loans. For instance, since World War II, one branch has been making, on the average, fifty consumer loans a month to Negroes; but in its history it has made only two loans to Negro businessmen. I think it is very important to overcome the myth. It is true that Negro businessmen lack credit, but it is not because of a special prejudice peculiar to financial institutions. The banks are in the Negro area to make loans and, therefore, to make money. Very small businessmen—Negro or white—cannot get loans simply because of the risks to the banks.

. . . We took a consumer survey on five different items. We asked eighty-four Negro housewives, in a very small, two- or three-block area in Philadelphia, where they bought these items. Seventy-five Negro housewives shopped exclusively at white grocery stores, and nine shopped exclusively at Negro grocery stores. This was also the case with drug stores. With cosmetics, there was a slight majority for white stores. With dry cleaning, there was a slight majority for Negro stores. With gasoline, there was a considerable majority for white stations.

We asked the women why they shopped in the white store or in the Negro store. The white store was always "lower priced." The Negro store was invariably "more convenient." When we compared the prices of nineteen various grocery items in white and Negro stores in that area, we found that the median prices of most of these articles were actually the same. There were four or five items which were higher priced in white stores, and three or four which were higher priced in Negro stores. This is something I am going to have to look into further. . . . But we have found so far that the median prices in white stores are slightly higher than in Negro stores—contrary to the overwhelming impressions of the Negro housewives in the area. The Jewish merchant is not, in my judgment, an unfair competitor.

With regard to the poverty of the Negro community, we found that, although it is undoubtedly a poor area, there are many white merchants there who are making a very handsome profit.

It seemed that lack of financing, competition from Jewish merchants, and poverty were really not the reasons that there were not more Negro businessmen or that Negro businessmen were not more successful. I decided, therefore, to take a look at the history of Negro business in Philadelphia. It occurred to me that perhaps there was simply a short tradition. However, I found that there was a long tradition of Negro business in Philadelphia—as far as I know, longer than in any other city in the country. We traced Negro business back to 1789. By 1820, there were quite a few Negro businessmen in a small population of Negroes in that city. There were several who were very wealthy and very prominent in the community. Then the European immigration started in the 1820's, and the first riot between immigrants and Negroes occurred in 1829. This rioting occurred every other year or so until the Civil War. (I think most people have forgotten about these riots that occurred in the City of Brotherly Love.) In 1836, Negroes were deprived of the right to vote in Philadelphia. This apparently had its effect, because the number of Negro businesses decreased from 344 in 1838 to 111 in 1849.

One thing to remember is that Negroes in Philadelphia did not live in a ghetto until about the 1890's. They served the general populace; they competed with white merchants. There were good, solid Negro businessmen, including a handful of very successful businessmen, before the Civil War. After the war, the migration northward gradually began; but there were still only 419 Negro businessmen in Philadelphia by 1896. About this time —right around the turn of the century—two things happened. First, there was the great migration; the Southern Negroes came North. The Negroes tended to live in small pockets, and as the migration increased, these pockets grew larger and larger, and a separate retail and service trades' economy gradually developed. Second, the white reaction in the North really set in about that time, and Negroes could no longer use public or commercial accommodations. By 1915, there was really a Negro ghetto. Given the ghetto market, the number of Negro businesses increased to about 1,200. Bear in mind that in 1838 there were 344 and in 1896 there were still only 419. In a matter of less than twenty years, there was a tremendous increase in Negro businesses because the ghetto had become large enough to support a separate economy and because Negroes were denied the privileges of both public accommodations and commercial places in downtown Philadelphia. There was a small rise in the number of Negro businesses during World War I and in the 1920's, a sudden fall, continuing during the Depression (which came first and lasted longest for Negro businesses), another small rise during World

War II, and a steady but not significant rise since World War II.

Why is it that only 10 of the 4,200 Negro businessmen in Philadelphia are significantly successful? We cannot say that the Negro is inherently not capable. When he started on an even keel with the white merchant in the nineteenth century, he was in every business that the white merchant was in, and he was very successful. Furthermore, I am convinced . . . that the Negro is, indeed, capable. . . .

I do not really know why the Negro businessmen are not successful. I think the lack of success probably relates to . . . the feeling of powerlessness. An entrepreneur has to have several qualities: thrift, self-confidence, hope, riskiness. Many Negro businessmen seem to feel "What's the use?" They never really stick with a problem long enough. I think it is the apathy and the tendency to give up so fast—characteristics of all of the social complexes within the Negro community—which probably have had an effect on the Negro as an entrepreneur.

measuring the causes and effects of discrimination

causes of variation in occupational achievement

U.S. DEPARTMENT OF HEALTH, EDUCATION, AND WELFARE

. . . The same data that show abundant opportunity for most Americans also show that Negroes have much less occupational mobility than whites. This can be seen by looking at Table 5-13.

From The U.S. Department of Health, Education, and Welfare, *Toward A Social Report* (Washington: Government Printing Office, 1969), pp. 22–26 *passim*.

Table 5-13

Mobility from Father's Occupation to 1962 Occupation
(Percentage Distributions), by Race, for Civilian Men
25 to 64 Years Old, March 1962

Race and Father's Occupation	1962 Occupation*						Total	
	High White Collar	Lower White Collar	Higher Manual	Lower Manual	Farm	Not in Experienced Civilian Labor Force	Percent	Number (000)
Negro								
Higher white collar	10.4	9.7	19.4	53.0	0.0	7.5	100.0	134
Lower white collar	14.5	9.1	6.0	69.1	0.0	7.3	100.0	55
Higher manual	8.8	6.8	11.2	64.1	2.8	6.4	100.0	251
Lower manual	8.0	7.0	11.5	63.2	1.8	8.4	100.0	973
Farm	3.1	3.0	6.4	59.8	16.2	11.6	100.0	1,389
Not reported	2.4	6.5	11.1	65.9	3.1	11.1	100.0	712
Total, percent	5.2	5.4	9.5	62.2	7.7	10.0	100.0	—
Total, number	182	190	334	2,184	272	352	—	3,514
Non-Negro								
Higher white collar	54.3	15.3	11.5	11.9	1.3	5.6	100.0	5,836
Lower white collar	45.1	18.3	13.5	14.6	1.5	7.1	100.0	2,652
Higher manual	28.1	11.8	27.9	24.0	1.0	7.3	100.0	6,512
Lower manual	21.3	11.5	22.5	36.0	1.7	6.9	100.0	8,798
Farm	16.5	7.0	19.8	28.8	20.4	7.5	100.0	9,991
Not reported	26.0	10.3	21.0	32.5	3.9	6.4	100.0	2,666
Total, percent	28.6	11.3	20.2	26.2	6.8	6.9	100.0	—
Total, number	10,414	4,130	7,359	9,560	2,475	2,517	—	36,455

* Combinations of census major occupation groups. **Higher white collar:** professional and kindred workers, and managers, officials, and proprietors, except farm. **Lower white collar:** sales, clerical, and kindred workers. **Higher manual:** craftsmen, foremen, and kindred workers. **Lower manual:** operatives and kindred workers, service workers, and laborers, except farm. **Farm:** farmers and farm managers, farm laborers and foremen. Classification by "father's occupation" includes some men reporting on the occupation of a family head other than the father.

Source: Unpublished tables, survey of "Occupational Changes in a Generation."

This table shows the occupational distributions of men whose fathers were in the same occupation, and also distinguishes the occupational distributions of Negroes from all of the others surveyed in the study of "Occupational Changes in a Generation."

The table reveals a striking result: Most Negro men, *regardless of their fathers' occupations,* were working at unskilled or semi-skilled jobs. Even if their fathers were in professional, managerial, or proprietary positions, they were usually operatives, service workers, or laborers. Growing up in a family of high socioeconomic status was only a slight advantage for the Negro man. By contrast, the majority of white men with higher white collar backgrounds remained at their father's level and almost half of the white men whose fathers were in clerical or sales work and almost two-fifths of those with a farm or blue collar background moved up into the more prestigious professional and managerial group. But the Negroes from similar origins did not. The Negro man originating at the lower levels is likely to stay there, the white man to move up. The Negro originating at the higher levels is likely to move down; the white man seldom does. The contrast is stark.

. . . Because most Americans can realize their highest ambitions through education, it is often assumed that Negroes can similarly overcome the handicaps of poverty and race. But this has not been so in the past. To be sure, even in minority groups, better educated individuals tend to occupy more desirable occupational positions than do the less educated. Yet the returns on an investment in education are much lower for Negroes than for the general population. Indeed, for a Negro, educational attainment may simply mean exposure to more severe and visible discrimination than is experienced by the dropout or the unschooled.

Thus, in addition to the handicap of being born in a family with few economic or other resources, the average Negro also appears to have less opportunity because of his race alone. Let us examine the relative importance of each of the different types of barriers to success for Negroes.

Table 5-14 shows that the average Negro male completed 2.3 fewer years of school than the average white male, that his occupational score is 23.8 points lower, and that his income is $3,790 lower. Much of the short fall in the relative achievement of Negroes can be attributed to specific causes. One year of the

Table 5-14

Differences in Means Between White (W) and Negro (N) with Respect to Educational Attainment, Occupational Status, and Income

With components of differences generated by cumulative effects in a model of the socioeconomic life cycle, for native men, 25 to 64 years old, with nonfarm background and in the experienced civilian labor force: March 1962.

Years of School Completed	1962 Occupation Score	1961 Income (dollars)	Component*
(W) 11.7 ⎤	(W) 43.5 ⎤	(W) 7,070 ⎤	
⎦ 1.0	⎦ 6.6	⎦ 940	(A) [Family]
10.7 ⎤	36.9 ⎤	6,130 ⎤	
⎦ 0.1	⎦ 0.6	⎦ 70	(B) [Siblings]
10.6 ⎤	36.3 ⎤	6,060 ⎤	
⎦ 1.2	⎦ 4.8	⎦ 520	(C) [Education]
(N) 9.4	31.5 ⎤	5,540 ⎤	
	⎦ 11.8	⎦ 830	(D) [Occupation]
	(N) 19.7	4,710 ⎤	
		⎦ 1,430	(E) [Income]
		(N) 3,280 ⎤	
2.3	23.8	⎦ 3,790	(T) [Total]

* Difference due to:
  (A) Socioeconomic level of family of origin (head's education and occupation).
  (B) Number of siblings, net of family origin level.
  (C) Education, net of siblings and family origin level.
  (D) Occupation, net of education, siblings, and family origin level.
  (E) Income, net of occupation, education, siblings, and family origin level.
  (T) Total difference, (W) minus (N) = sum of components (A) through (E).
Source: O. D. Duncan, "Inheritance of Poverty or Inheritance of Race?" forthcoming.

educational gap arises from the fact that Negroes come from disadvantaged families while an additional 0.1 year is the result of the fact that Negroes tend to be born into larger families where resources must be spread among more children. But even with the allowance of 1.1 years of schooling traceable to these disadvantages, there remains an unexplained gap of 1.2 years. Evidently, this must be caused by something other than the initial socioeconomic differences between blacks and whites. Perhaps it is the Negro's knowledge that he will be discriminated against whatever his education.

If we look at the *occupational gap* of 23.8 points, we see that 6.6 points can be ascribed to initial Negro-white differences in family socioeconomic levels and an additional 0.6 to differences in

the determinants of income differentials

family size. The residual educational gap, already identified, carries over into occupational achievement, lowering the Negro score relative to the white by 4.8 points on the average. There remains a gap, not otherwise accounted for, of 11.8 points. This discrepancy derives from the fact that Negro men with the same schooling and the same family background as a comparable group of white men will have jobs of appreciably lower status. It is surely attributable in part to racial discrimination in hiring, promotion, and other job-related opportunities.

All of the factors mentioned are converted into an *income gap* totaling $3,790. Substantial components of this are due to socio-economic status and family size ($1,010), lower educational attainment ($520), and job discrimination ($830), so that disadvantages detectable at earlier stages clearly have an important impact in lowering Negro income compared to white income. But there remains a gap of $1,430 not otherwise accounted for, suggesting that Negro men, relative to a group of white men of comparable family background, educational attainment, and occupational level, still receive much lower wages and salaries. The specific magnitudes obtained in calculations of this kind are not to be taken as firm estimates. Nevertheless, the substantial discrepancies existing between Negro and white attainment suggest that the Negro has severely limited opportunity, not only because his social and economic background[s] place him at a disadvantage, but also because he faces racial discrimination in the school system and in the job market.

white gains and social costs
from subordination of blacks

U.S. COMMISSION ON CIVIL RIGHTS

Overt racism and institutional subordination provide the following economic benefits to a significant number of whites:

1. Reduction of competition by excluding members of certain groups from access to benefits, privileges, jobs, or other opportunities or markets. The ability to easily identify members of the subordinated group by sight is a key factor linking such reduction of competition to color. An example is the refusal of many hospital medical staffs to accept Negro or Mexican American doctors as staff members.

2. Exploitation of members of the subordinated groups through lower wages, higher prices, higher rents, less desirable credit terms, or poorer working or living conditions than those received by whites. Where racial or color discrimination *per se* is illegal, such exploitation probably cannot be effectively carried out unless the subordinated groups are spatially segregated from the white majority. Then differentials in wages, prices, credit terms, and other policies actually based upon color can be more easily concealed and even rationalized as based upon geographic differences.

3. Avoidance of certain undesirable or "dead-end" jobs (like garbage collection) by creating economically depressed racial or ethnic groups which will be compelled by necessity to carry out those jobs, even though their potential skill levels are equal to those of other groups.

All the political benefits of racism involve receipt by whites of a disproportionate share of the advantages which arise from political control over government. Their share is disproportionate because they prevent nonwhites from receiving what the latter would get if true political equality prevailed. The benefits of political control over government include ability to control government actions and policies as well as jobs. Therefore, political

From The U.S. Commission on Civil Rights, *Racism in America and How to Combat It,* Clearing House Publication, Urban Series No. 1 (Washington: Government Printing Office, January 1970), pp. 6–11 *passim.* The report was prepared by Dr. Anthony Downs.

racism is an extremely important device for maintaining other forms of racism.

The main ways political racism occur are as follows:

1. Manipulation of potential nonwhite voters in order to maintain exclusive white control over an entire governmental structure (such as a county government in the South), or some portion of such a structure (such as a ward in a northern city), which would be controlled by nonwhites if all citizens enjoyed equal voting rights, since nonwhites are a majority of the potential electorate in that area.
2. Manipulation of political district boundaries or governmental structures by whites so as to minimize the ability of nonwhite voters to elect representatives sensitive to their needs. This includes "gerrymandering" congressional districts, creating "at-large" electoral systems in big cities with significant nonwhite minorities, and shifting to metropolitanwide government when nonwhites appear likely to constitute a majority of voters in a central city.
3. Exclusion of nonwhites from a proportionate share—or any share—of government jobs, contracts, and other disbursements through the decisions of white administrative officials.
4. Maintenance of the support of nonwhite voters by either white or nonwhite politicians who fail to provide reciprocal government policy benefits and other advantages to the same degree as for white groups in the electorate. This can occur when nonwhites as a group feel themselves too subordinated in general to demand such benefits, when competitive parties are somehow excluded from effective operation in all non-white areas, or when voters are so poor they can be influenced by small monetary rewards and favors. . . .

Both overt racism and institutional subordination provide the following psychological benefits to many whites in America:

1. Creation of feelings of superiority in comparison to nonwhites. These feelings are extremely widespread among whites, though not always openly expressed or even consciously recognized. . . . all whites who feel the least bit superior to nonwhites as persons—in contrast to believing

they live in *environmental surroundings* superior to those of nonwhites—basically adopt . . . a . . . racist viewpoint. This is true because the obviously inferior economic, political, and social *status* of nonwhites can result from only two factors. Either nonwhites *are* inferior as persons, or white racism has prevented their natural equality with whites from asserting itself in actual attainments during their more than 300 years in America. Therefore, whites who deny that overt racism and institutional subordination are essentially responsible for the currently lower status of nonwhite groups are basically implying that those groups are biologically or otherwise inherently inferior.

2. Suppression in oneself or one's group of certain normal traits which are regarded as undesirable. This is accomplished by projecting an exaggerated image of those traits and "legitimizing" attacks upon them. For example, many American whites unjustly accuse Negroes of laziness, sexual promiscuity, and general irresponsibility. These are exaggerated versions of normal human impulses. But they happen to be the very impulses which the Puritan ethic, long dominant in America, seeks to suppress in favor of extreme industry, sexual purity, and individual self-reliance.

3. Promotion of solidarity and reduced tension among white nationality and social class groups. Racism enables them to focus the inevitable hostilities and antagonisms which arise in modern life upon the subordinated colored groups, and to identify themselves together in contrast to those groups.

4. Avoiding the necessity of adopting difficult or costly policies to solve key social problems by falsely blaming those problems upon "immoral behavior" by members of the subordinated groups. For example, many whites erroneously blame unemployment and high welfare costs upon laziness and sexual promiscuity among Negroes. In reality, more than three-fourths of all unemployed persons are white, most persons on welfare are white, and more than 90 percent of all persons on welfare are incapable of supporting themselves because they are either too old, disabled, children, or mothers who must care for children. By falsely converting these problems into "the results of sin," such scapegoating provides a moral excuse for relatively affluent whites to reduce their economic support for the unem-

ployed and the dependent poor without feeling guilty about doing so.

5. Diverting one's own energies from maximum self-improvement efforts by claiming that white racism makes any significant self-help attempts by colored people ineffective and useless. Such "reverse scapegoating" occurs—often unconsciously—among many minority group members. It is possible only because white racism *does* seriously inhibit—though not entirely nullify—nonwhite self-improvement efforts. This phenomenon can lead to two opposite results: excessive apathy or suicidal violence. Thus, by helping to create such "reverse scapegoating," white racism encourages some nonwhites to exhibit two of the very characteristics—"laziness" and tendencies toward violence—that it often falsely attributes to all nonwhites. . . .

. . . *all Americans—especially whites—[need to be] far more conscious of the widespread existence of racism in all its forms, and the immense costs it imposes on the entire Nation.* Most whites are completely unaware of the many kinds of institutional subordination they themselves support. A crucial task facing those who wish to combat racism is converting this "blindness" into acute consciousness of the many unrecognized ways in which white attitudes, behavior, and institutional structures continue to subordinate minority groups. [These costs include:]

Economic costs, including the loss of national output due to holding minority group members below their maximum productive potential, the loss of markets because the incomes of these groups are kept low by institutional subordination, and large social costs of policies aimed at remedying conditions partly caused by subordination, such as poverty, crime, poor housing, and poor health.

Political costs resulting from tensions in national life caused by unjust subordination of minority groups. These include civil disorders, restrictions of individual freedoms and rights, tendencies toward a weakening of the two-party system, possible rising difficulty in gathering sufficient congressional support for *any* cohesive set of national policies, and decreasing respect for the United States abroad.

Social and human costs caused by the loss of human potential due to institutional subordination, and by the distortion of values in the white majority necessary to sustain such subordination. The first kind of costs includes loss of personal self-respect, weakened family stability, widespread frustration and apathy, frequent resort to narcotics and criminal behavior, and a declining respect for authority among minority groups. The second kind includes excessive narrowness of viewpoint; defensiveness and hostility feelings; resistance to constructive change; lack of human sensitivity; and overly technological (rather than humane) orientation of social policies and activities.

It is impossible to quantify these costs in this analysis. But some future attempts should be made to measure at least the economic costs so as to show what giant losses are involved. For example, in 1965, if Negro families had received the same average income as whites, incomes received by all U.S. families would have been $15.7 billion higher. . . .

The fact that overt racism and institutional subordination produce benefits for many whites does not mean that these benefits outweigh the costs of racism. In the first place, such benefits are wholly illegitimate, since they spring from an unjust subordination of others. Second, creation of these benefits imposes immense costs upon millions of nonwhite Americans. Finally, by preventing nonwhites from developing their maximum productive potential, racism also inhibits them from creating much greater economic, social, and cultural wealth than they do now. This makes all of society poorer than it would be without racism—including the very people who benefit from racist behavior and institutions.

the determinants of income differentials

$$6$$

the black consumer

INTRODUCTION

Institutionalized discrimination serves not only to hinder a black person in earning a living, as we saw in the previous chapter, but it also prevents him from allocating scarce dollars effectively as a consumer. In this chapter we consider the nature of some of these obstacles. The opening discussion by Professor Marcus Alexis points out that, with black unemployment rates at roughly twice that for whites and with the black worker typically "last-hired, first-fired," it would be surprising indeed, if, as consumers, blacks did not reflect these differential risks. Thus, in marked contradiction to the stereotype, for comparable income groups blacks save more than whites and tend to have less debt. While spending more on clothing than whites (with comparable incomes), they spend less for food, housing, medical care, and automobile transportation. The more detailed study by The U.S. Department of Labor which follows, confirms and expands the above results. Restriction in the housing market for blacks is seen as "one of the most serious imbalances of supply and demand in the economy." If the imbalances are serious for whites, they are critical for blacks.

The belief among blacks that they "pay more for less" is generally vindicated in survey findings reported by Phyllis Groom of The Bureau of Labor Statistics. While food prices did not vary significantly by ethnic neighborhoods *when similar store types* were compared, the conclusion is rather empty: the typically lower-priced, larger food chains avoid ghetto locations, leaving the market to smaller, less efficient, and higher-priced independents. The survey research confirms the allegations that meat and produce offered in core areas tend not to be as fresh as elsewhere and that the stores there are "less clean and orderly." In particular, it is shown that, for units of housing of a given quality, blacks pay more.

The next selection considers the important housing situation in some detail. The cliché that black entry destroys housing values is tested against known statistical evidence by George and Eunice Grier. The effect of entry is often *rising* or rapidly fluctuating prices. The meaning of these results, and especially the role of real estate speculation, is considered. There is evidence of "racial panic and the success of sharp operators in exploiting it."

The next selection examines black consumption of health services. Although health levels have improved significantly relative to the past, the racial differential remains a large one. Black citizens continue to have a shorter life expectancy, higher infant and maternal mortality rates, and greater incidence of several major diseases than do whites. Such conditions are reflective of environmental and nutritional deficiencies which lead to lowered disease resistances, of the inadequate availability of medical facilities and personnel to blacks, and of incomes inadequate to permit preventive medical care. As is usual, a general societal problem is exacerbated in its incidence on black Americans.

Black consumers in particular are in revolt against fraudulent selling practices, hidden charges, shoddy merchandise, confiscatory garnishment practices, etc. While legitimate businesses have an interest in curtailing their rivals' sharp practices, the major source of consumer information for blacks could well be knowledgeable members of the black community itself. The concluding selection by D. Parke Gibson offers suggestions for thus bringing the consumer movement to the ghetto.

the black consumer

MARCUS ALEXIS

The "Black Experience"—that totality of environmental effects and internal response common to most blacks—affects the black man's consumption as well as his political and social behavior. Indeed, consumption is in large part a social act. . . .

. . . More than once the American black man has been said to constitute a "Nation Within A Nation." . . .

It is argued that social and economic discrimination have resulted in blacks having patterns of market behavior different from that of whites with equal incomes. Some writers argue that the differences persist even after adjustments have been made for differences in assets, occupation and family responsibilities. . . . [Given] the fact that unemployment rates among blacks average twice the national level in good times and bad and the greater sensitivity of black employment to economic downturns and more lagged response to expansion, there is good reason to expect differences in consumption behavior.

All available evidence consistently points to a higher propensity to save for blacks than for whites at comparable income levels. It follows that if blacks save more than whites at each income level, blacks and whites must differ in the way they allocate their incomes to some classes of consumer goods. More specifically, there must be at least one class of consumer goods for which blacks and whites in the same class spend different amounts.

One of the difficulties involved in [a] discussion of ethnic or cultural differences in expenditures for food is the extent to which such differences represent group preferences for certain classes of foods. Such preferences can affect the expenditure level although there are no differences in quantity of food consumed.

Comparisons of the food expenditures of comparable black and white families in Nashville, Atlanta, Washington, D.C., New York, Detroit, Houston, Memphis and several southern villages

From Marcus Alexis, "Consumption by the Poor," paper presented at the Conference on Research on Urban Poverty held by the Social Science Research Council, the Woodrow Wilson School and the Industrial Relations Section, Princeton University, May 23, 1969, pp. 1–58 *passim* (mimeographed).

reveal that, with few exceptions, food expenditures of white families were considerably higher than the food expenditures of black families. This is in spite of the fact that black families were generally larger than the white families with whom they were compared.

With increases in incomes, however, black families increase their consumption of protein foods more rapidly than do white families. This is very likely traceable to an observed tendency of low income black families to spend less for milk, cream, cheese, vegetables and fruits than white families in the same income class. With increases in their incomes, black families seek to achieve better dietary balance. . . .

The best available evidence indicates that blacks spend more than whites for equal quality housing. However, blacks do not spend a greater proportion of their income for housing than whites in the same income class. This results from the tendency of lower income blacks to have "roomers" and by the upper limitation placed on the quality of housing high income blacks can buy. Thus, upper income blacks spend as much for housing as whites in the same income class, but receive less housing for it. Lower income blacks adjust to the higher cost of housing by sharing quarters.

Expenditures for clothing are an important budget item. Furthermore, there are characteristics of the demand for clothing that suggest that this commodity serves as more than a protective covering for the body.

It is commonly argued that blacks spend more for clothing than do whites. Furthermore, it is said that blacks are not as price conscious as white buyers. The greater emphasis of blacks on clothing is explained by the inability of blacks to purchase some forms of recreation and shelter. Thus, clothing becomes a substitute for inaccessible alternatives. The price behavior proposition is more difficult to understand because of the generally lower incomes of the black population. . . .

As incomes rise, both races increase their consumption of clothing at a faster rate than they increase total consumption. It is also found that wives, without regard to race, increase their expenditures for clothing more rapidly than their husbands when incomes rise.

On the subject of price-consciousness, there is substantial evidence that the alleged lack of concern of black shoppers for price-line merchandise is not representative of their actual behavior.

In fact, the desire of blacks to dress well, and their low incomes act as powerful forces to make blacks price-conscious. In a study of Negro newspapers, it was found that black readers were unhappy not to find price-line advertising. Furthermore, it was pointed out that black readers consulted their local newspapers for such price information. Even more important, a majority of the black consumers in Birmingham, Atlanta and Richmond, questioned about their buying habits, cited price as the most important determinant of the vendor from whom they buy.

. . . While whites justify brand buying as being sophisticated and associate brand with quality, blacks think of it as habitually naive and uneconomical. . . .

The earliest studies of black–white consumption relations, dating back to the early 1930's, reveal lower expenditures for medical care by blacks than by comparable income whites. Also, in each of the Bureau of Labor Statistics postwar studies, including the 1950–51 data, black families have been found to spend less for medical care at all income levels than comparable income white families. . . .

The relationship of non-automobile transportation expenditures and occupation is an excellent example of the effect of social conditions on market behavior. Because so many blacks have been employed in domestic service and domestics have traditionally received part of their wages as carfare, early studies show the percent of incomes paid by low income blacks for non-automobile transportation to be much less than for low income whites.

Since 1940, black employment in the service industries has experienced a secular decline. Consequently, carfare as a part of total compensation has declined in importance. At the same time, there is evidence that the frequency of automobile ownership among black families is lower than among comparable income white families. Thus, one would expect that non-automobile transportation expenditures would be higher for the black than white families in the same income grouping. . . . surveys indicate a consistent tendency for white consumers to spend more for automobile expenses at comparable income levels than black consumers.

. . . There is no available study known to this writer which supports the stereotype of large scale ownership of Cadillac-class automobiles by blacks. Income and possibly restrictive credit practices act as a powerful deterrent to automobile ownership among blacks. . . . When all the data have been digested, the following major findings emerge:

1. Total consumption expenditures of blacks are less than for comparable income whites, or blacks save more out of a given income than do whites with the same incomes.
2. Black consumers spend more for clothing and non-automobile transportation and less for food, housing, medical care and automobile transportation than do comparable whites.
3. There is no consistent racial difference in expenditures for either recreation and leisure or home furnishings and equipment at comparable income levels.

patterns of black consumption

U.S. DEPARTMENT OF LABOR

The Negro urban consumer has about the same spending pattern as the white urban consumer at the same income level. According to the 1960–61 consumer expenditures survey of the Bureau of Labor Statistics, most Negro and white urban consumers fell into a large middle-income group—$3,000 to $7,500. However, almost all of the remaining Negroes had less than $3,000 to spend, whereas the remainder of the whites tended to have $7,500 or more. . . .

The most notable differences between Negro and white consumers were the degrees to which they went into debt, saved,

From The U.S. Department of Labor, Bureau of Labor Statistics, *The Negroes in the United States: Their Economic and Social Situation* (Washington: Government Printing Office, June 1966), pp. 37–40 *passim.* The data from the Survey of Consumer Expenditures, 1960–61 are the most recent data on family income and expenditures. The Department of Labor plans another national survey in 1972–73.

the black consumer

and bought durable goods.[1] Relatively low-income Negroes ($3,000 to $4,999) averaged less debt than white consumers of the same income group. Middle-income Negroes ($5,000–$7,499) averaged larger net increases in savings than middle-income whites. For the same income groups, Negro and white consumers averaged about the same amount of personal insurance, but fewer Negroes than whites, proportionately, bought automobiles or were homeowners (Figures 6-1 and 6-2). These findings may possibly reflect a differential in the availability and cost of credit, regardless of collateral or other assets. They may reflect also family size and responsibility. Negro families, in general, had more persons in the family at each income level than white families. Because they more often have more than one earner, job-related expenses have to be budgeted.

Home ownership presents special problems for Negroes. They generally buy in a highly restricted market. The limitations on Negro home ownership make one of the most serious imbalances of supply and demand in the economy.

The urge toward home ownership is amply demonstrated by

Figure 6-1
Negro Urban Families Showed a Smaller Increase in Debt
and a Greater Increase in Assets Than White Families
in Similar Income Groups in 1960-1961*

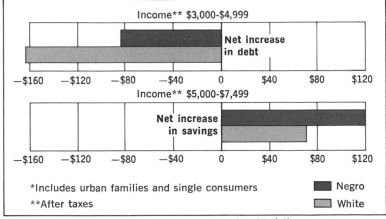

Source: U.S. Department of Labor, Bureau of Labor Statistics

[1] Our emphasis (eds.).

patterns of black consumption   155

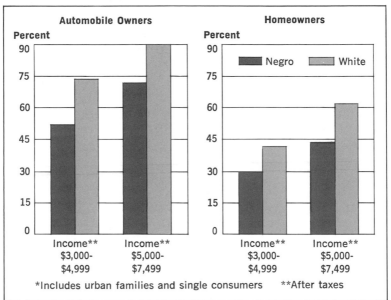

Figure 6-2
Negro Urban Families, in Low as Well as Middle Income Groups,
Were Far Less Likely Than White Families to Own
Automobiles or Homes in 1960-1961*

Source: U.S. Department of Labor, Bureau of Labor Statistics

nonwhite families. Although about half of all nonwhite families were poor in 1960 and many were in very large cities where apartment living is usual, 38 percent were homeowners. This is far lower than the 64 percent for white families. Moreover, about half the nonwhite homeowners owned their houses free and clear, compared with a little more than 40 percent of the white homeowners.

Of the homeowners with mortgages in 1960, the nonwhites were much less likely to have received FHA or VA assistance than the whites or to have bought a new house. In addition, nonwhite homeowners in 1960 were more than twice as likely as white homeowners to be spending 30 percent or more of their income on housing and over three times as likely to be paying over 6 percent interest on a first mortgage (Figures 6-3 and 6-4).

At every income level, relatively more nonwhite than white households occupied substandard housing in 1960 (Figure 6-5). Despite the greater housing need among Negroes, almost 9 in 10

the black consumer

Figure 6-3
Nonwhite Families Were About Half as Likely as
the White To Be Homeowners (1960)

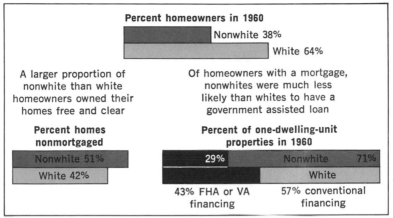

Percent homeowners in 1960

Nonwhite 38%

White 64%

A larger proportion of nonwhite than white homeowners owned their homes free and clear

Of homeowners with a mortgage, nonwhites were much less likely than whites to have a government assisted loan

Percent homes nonmortgaged

Nonwhite 51%

White 42%

Percent of one-dwelling-unit properties in 1960

29%   Nonwhite   71%

White

43% FHA or VA financing

57% conventional financing

Source: U.S. Bureau of the Census

Figure 6-4
Nonwhite Homeowners Were More
Likely Than Others to—

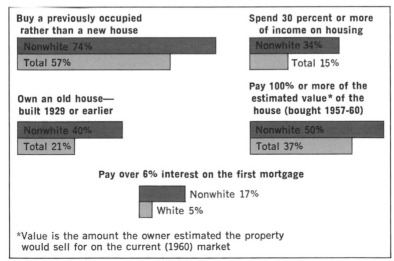

Buy a previously occupied rather than a new house

Nonwhite 74%

Total 57%

Spend 30 percent or more of income on housing

Nonwhite 34%

Total 15%

Own an old house— built 1929 or earlier

Nonwhite 40%

Total 21%

Pay 100% or more of the estimated value* of the house (bought 1957-60)

Nonwhite 50%

Total 37%

Pay over 6% interest on the first mortgage

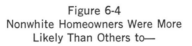

Nonwhite 17%

White 5%

*Value is the amount the owner estimated the property would sell for on the current (1960) market

Source: U.S. Bureau of the Census

patterns of black consumption   157

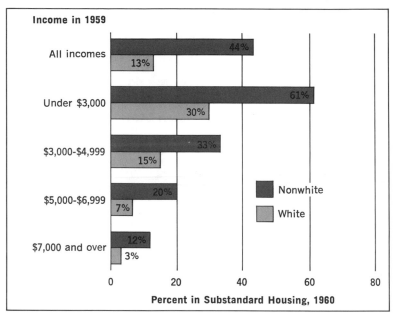

Figure 6-5
At Every Income Level Relatively More Nonwhite Than
White Households Occupied Substandard Housing

Source: U.S. Bureau of the Census

of the 16.8 million housing units added to the "standard housing" supply between 1950 and 1960 went to white occupants. In that period white-occupied substandard units dropped 50 percent, compared to less than 20 percent for nonwhite-occupied substandard units. Nonwhite households occupied a much larger proportion of all substandard housing in 1960 than they did in 1950, although their proportion of the population increased very little during the decade (Figure 6-6). About 40 percent of all nonwhite children in 1960 lived in seriously overcrowded housing and in housing without plumbing (Figure 6-7).

Nonwhite housing is much more likely to be substandard in rural than in urban areas and outside, rather than inside, metropolitan areas (Figure 6-8). Nevertheless, about 40 percent of the housing of nonwhites in the central cities of SMSA's in 1960 was substandard.

the black consumer

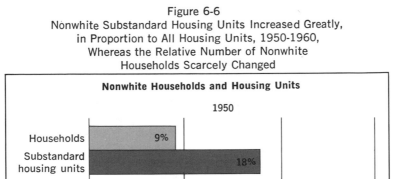

Figure 6-6
Nonwhite Substandard Housing Units Increased Greatly,
in Proportion to All Housing Units, 1950-1960,
Whereas the Relative Number of Nonwhite
Households Scarcely Changed

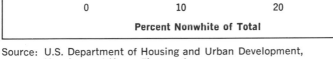

Nonwhite Households and Housing Units

1950

Households — 9%
Substandard housing units — 18%

1960

Households — 10%
Substandard housing units — 27%

0   10   20   30

Percent Nonwhite of Total

Source: U.S. Department of Housing and Urban Development,
Housing and Home Finance Agency

patterns of black consumption   159

Figure 6-7
40 Percent of All Nonwhite Children in 1960 Lived in
Overcrowded Housing or Housing Lacking Some Facilities*

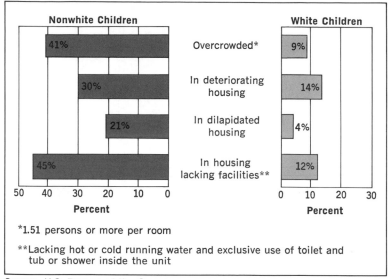

*1.51 persons or more per room

**Lacking hot or cold running water and exclusive use of toilet and
tub or shower inside the unit

Source: U.S. Bureau of the Census

the black consumer

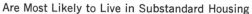
Figure 6-8
Nonwhite Households in Rural Areas and in the South
Are Most Likely to Live in Substandard Housing

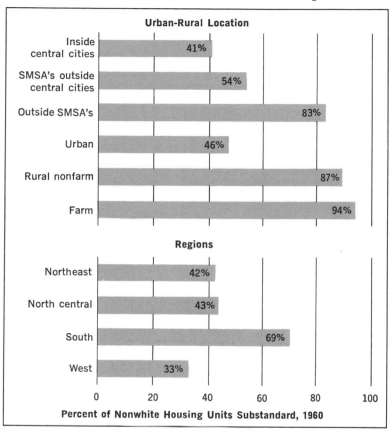

Source: U.S. Bureau of the Census

patterns of black consumption   161

table 6-1

Percent Distribution of Family* Expenditures, by Income and Race, Urban United States, 1950 and 1960–61
(annual average)

Item	1950** Negro	1950** White	1960–61 Negro	1960–61 White
	All Incomes			
Total expenditures for current concumption (average)	$2,614	$3,938	$3,707	$5,609
Percent distribution of total expenditures	100	100	100	100
"Three basic expenses"	62	57	58	52
Food	32	30	25	24
Shelter, fuel, light, refrigeration, and water	16	16	20	18
Clothing, including upkeep	14	11	13	10
All other	38	43	42	48
Household operations and furnishings	11	12	11	11
Medical care	4	5	5	7
Transportation	10	14	12	15
Miscellaneous	13	12	14	15
Family characteristics:				
Size (number of persons)	3.1	3.0	3.2	3.1
Age of family head (years)	45	47	46	48
Percent homeowners	32	50	31	56
Percent automobile owners	25	62	43	76
	Under $2,000		Under $3,000	
Total expenditures for current concumption (average)	$1,373	$1,656	$1,978	$2,192
Percent distribution of total expenditures	100	100	100	100
"Three basic expenses"	70	65	64	63
Food	37	34	29	29
Shelter, fuel, light, refrigeration, and water	21	23	25	27
Clothing, including upkeep	12	8	10	7
All other	30	35	36	37
Household operations and furnishings	11	9	11	9
Medical care	4	6	5	9
Transportation	4	8	6	8
Miscellaneous	11	12	14	11
Family characteristics:				
Size (number of persons)	2.4	1.8	2.4	1.8
Age of family head (years)	49	59	50	61
Percent homeowners	28	41	24	41
Percent automobile owners	8	26	17	31

Item	Money Income After Taxes			
	1950**		1960–61	
	Negro	White	Negro	White
	$2,000 to $5,999		$3,000 to $7,499	
Total expenditures for current concumption (average)	$3,244	$3,838	$4,537	$5,100
Percent distribution of total expenditures	100	100	100	100
"Three basic expenses"	60	57	57	54
Food	31	30	25	25
Shelter, fuel, light, refrigeration, and water	15	16	19	19
Clothing, including upkeep	14	11	13	10
All other	40	43	43	46
Household operations and furnishings	11	11	11	11
Medical care	4	5	5	7
Transportation	11	14	13	15
Miscellaneous	14	13	14	13
Family characteristics:				
Size (number of persons)	3.5	3.2	3.8	3.1
Age of family head (years)	43	43	42	44
Percent homeowners	34	49	33	52
Percent automobile owners	35	68	59	82
	$6,000 and Over		$7,500 and Over	
Total expenditures for current consumption (average)	$6,536	$7,285	$7,983	$8,942
Percent distribution of total expenditures	100	100	100	100
"Three basic expenses"	59	53	53	50
Food	26	26	21	23
Shelter, fuel, light, refrigeration, and water	13	14	16	16
Clothing, including upkeep	20	13	16	11
All other	41	47	47	50
Household operations and furnishings	13	13	13	12
Medical care	3	5	4	6
Transportation	10	15	14	16
Miscellaneous	15	14	16	16
Family characteristics:				
Size (number of persons)	4.8	3.8	4.1	3.9
Age of family head (years)	44	48	44	46
Percent homeowners	48	72	54	75
Percent automobile owners	58	86	88	95

* Including single consumers.
** Alaska and Hawaii not included in 1950. The 1950 income classes were selected to represent approximately equivalent purchasing power of 1960–61 income classes.
Note: Because of rounding, sums of individual items may not equal totals.
Source: U.S. Department of Labor, Bureau of Labor Statistics.

Table 6-2

Savings, Insurance, and Selected Characteristics of Families* in Selected Income Classes, by Region and Race, Urban United States, 1960–61 (annual average)

Item	United States Negro	United States White	Northeast Negro	Northeast White	North-central Negro	North-central White	South Negro	South White	West Negro	West White
	Money Income After Taxes, $3,000 to $4,999									
Savings—net change in assets and debts	−$85	−$163	−$115	−$317	−$39	−$15	−$79	−$125	−$180	−$198
Net change in assets	$74	$129	−$3	−$122	−$212	$304	$261	$313	$94	−$9
Net change in debts	$159	$292	$113	$195	−$173	$320	$340	$438	$275	$188
Personal insurance (including social security)	204	199	194	213	199	205	221	199	148	163
Family characteristics:										
Size (number of persons)	3.6	2.7	3.2	2.6	3.5	2.8	4.0	2.9	3.4	2.5
Age of family head (years)	43	47	40	48	43	47	44	45	42	45
Percent homeowners	29	41	13	36	30	46	38	45	22	36
Percent automobile owners	51	73	34	60	47	76	59	83	72	76

Item	United States		Northeast		North-central		South		West	
	Negro	White	Negro	White	Negro	White	Negro	White	Negro	White
	Money Income After Taxes, $5,000 to $7,499									
Savings—net change in assets and debts	$120	$73	$53	–$14	–$42	$227	$293	$95	$207	–$59
Net change in assets	$504	$568	$177	$454	$550	$562	$564	$631	$1,099	$685
Net change in debts	$384	$495	$124	$468	$591	$334	$271	$536	$892	$744
Personal insurance (including social security)	341	352	288	357	373	355	383	343	305	330
Family characteristics:										
Size (number of persons)	4.0	3.5	3.4	3.4	4.3	3.5	4.4	3.5	3.8	3.4
Age of family head (years)	42	43	43	45	38	42	45	42	38	41
Percent homeowners	42	60	35	52	40	64	57	66	24	59
Percent automobile owners	71	90	59	81	74	91	75	96	89	95

* Including single consumers.

Note: Because of rounding, sums of individual items may not equal totals.

Source: U.S. Department of Labor, Bureau of Labor Statistics.

Table 6-3
Percent of Households Owning Selected Durables,
July 1967 and July 1969

	Negro		White	
	1967	**1969**	**1967**	**1969**
Automobiles:				
One	41.6	40.3	53.5	51.8
Two or more	10.3	12.6	28.8	30.9
One or more recent model				
automobiles*	10.0	11.0	23.2	23.4
Household durables:				
Black and white TV	83.9	81.9	85.8	77.5
Color TV	6.5	12.4	18.7	33.5
Dishwasher	4.0	3.5	15.0	17.4

* In 1967 a 1966 or 1967 model; in 1969 a 1968 or 1969 model.
Source: U.S. Department of Commerce, Bureau of the Census.

prices in black neighborhoods

PHYLLIS GROOM

. . . the Bureau of Labor Statistics was asked to find out
whether merchants charged higher prices in low-income neighborhoods than in better-off areas. . . . this article presents some
of the findings, along with work of the Bureau and others that
bear on the question. In general:

1. For equivalent rents, poor families get poorer housing than
   families with higher incomes.
2. Food prices are associated with the kind of store rather
   than with the geographic area. In buying food, the poor pay
   more if they shop in the small independent stores rather
   than in the large independents and the chain stores, whose

From Phyllis Groom, "Prices in Poor Neighborhoods," *Monthly Labor Review*, U.S. Department of Labor (October 1966), 1085–1090 *passim*.

prices are lower. In poor neighborhoods, small sizes are more popular than the relatively cheaper large sizes.

3. For clothes, appliances, and other items, the survey results are inconclusive. What is confirmed is that the poor do not buy the same items as the better off.

race and housing values

GEORGE GRIER / EUNICE GRIER

Though nonwhite homeowners in general fare considerably better than do nonwhite renters, they also fare considerably less well than white owners. Often the only housing they are allowed to buy is old and in poor condition. Many families undertake extensive repairs and renovations soon after assuming ownership, and the results can be observed in the improved maintenance of many neighborhoods that Negroes have entered in recent years. But some Negro families are forced to pay prices so exorbitant that they have little money left with which to keep up their properties. Moreover, monthly housing costs often are increased by extortionate financing arrangements—such as "lease-purchase" plans or high interest rate second and third mortgages—which Negroes must accept because "reputable" mortgage lending institutions either refuse their business outright or are unwilling to lend money on properties priced at the inflated levels many Negroes must pay. In all too many cases, usurious costs are incurred because the properties available to Negroes are in the hands of speculators who insist on profiting outrageously not merely from the sale itself but from the financing as well.

Exploitation in such a "rigged" market largely accounts for the important finding, in several carefully conducted studies, that Negro entry into a neighborhood does not necessarily send its

Reprinted by permission of Quadrangle Books from *Equality and Beyond: Housing Segregation and the Goals of the Great Society* by George and Eunice Grier, copyright © 1966 by the Anti-Defamation League of B'nai B'rith. (Pp. 33–35 *passim*.)

real estate prices plunging downward; indeed it often causes them to rise instead. The most thorough of these studies, *Property Values and Race,* conducted for the Commission on Race and Housing by the noted economist Luigi Laurenti,[1] surveyed 10,000 transactions in all. The author found that prices rose in 44 percent of cases when Negroes entered, remained stable in another 41 percent, and declined in only 15 percent. These were *long-term* trends, and they were measured *relative to trends in carefully matched neighborhoods which remained all white.*

It does not follow from this that the relatively higher prices of homes in many racially changing neighborhoods benefit the white families who leave them. Rather, the money often goes into the pockets of the speculators who have helped panic the whites into selling for *less* than their homes would bring on a "free" or open market situation. The speculators then proceed to resell the homes to Negroes (often in a matter of days) for *more* than their normal market value.[2]

The Laurenti study found chaotic price fluctuations in many

[1] Luigi Laurenti, *Property Values and Race,* Berkeley, 1960. Laurenti analyzes in depth data specially gathered in Philadelphia, San Francisco, and Oakland, California, during the mid-1950's. He also summarizes the work of other investigators in Chicago, Kansas City, Detroit, and Portland, Oregon. One of the Chicago studies examined was made in 1930. Despite the difference in time and conditions, its conclusions differed surprisingly little from those of other investigations performed a generation later. Since the Laurenti work appeared, additional studies of the property values question have been made in other communities. One of the more notable and recent is Erdman Palmore and John Howe, "Residential Integration and Property Values," *Social Problems,* Summer 1962. While there is a common tendency to believe that one's own community must be unique in its attitudes and behavior with regard to racial matters, the various studies are striking in the similarity of their findings.

[2] Probably the most thorough and telling analysis of the economics involved in racial turnover mediated by real estate speculators was published by the Chicago Commission on Human Relations, a municipal agency, in 1962. In a single block which had changed from all-white to virtually all-Negro, with heavy involvement by speculators, the differential between the price paid by the speculator and that paid by the Negro buyer upon purchase under an installment contract ranged from 35 to 115 percent, with an average of 73 percent. The installment contract itself is a financing device which yields higher than average returns to the entrepreneur, so the profiteering only began with the sale. In Philadelphia, Rapkin and Grigsby found that absentee speculators in a racially changing area more than doubled their investments, on the average, within less than two years. Profits on sales to the first Negro buyer in an area were even higher; thus, the Negro family that "breaks the block" usually pays even more heavily than those who follow. See Chester Rapkin and William Grigsby, *The Demand for Housing in Racially Mixed Areas,* Berkeley, 1960.

the black consumer

of the neighborhoods it investigated—presumptive evidence both of racial panic and the success of sharp operators in exploiting it. Technically speaking, these blockbusters represent an unscrupulous minority of the real estate industry—"outlaws" in a moral if not a legal sense. But their activities would not be profitable if the set of restrictions created by segregation were not accepted by the large majority of builders, brokers, and lenders—not to speak of large segments of the white public as a whole.

By adroitly holding back the Negro market, and permitting its housing needs to be satisfied only on a "waiting list" basis, reputable bankers and members of the building and real estate industries have contributed to the conditions under which their not-so-scrupulous colleagues can flourish. Working in tandem with the speculators, such individuals assiduously guard against the entry of Negroes into solidly white areas of the city. In testimony recently given before the Commissioners of the District of Columbia, the president of the Mortgage Bankers Association of Metropolitan Washington bluntly stated that "applications from minority groups are not generally considered in areas that are not recognized as being racially mixed." A study by the Chicago Commission on Human Relations found that such a policy was pursued by almost all lending sources in that city. Voluminous evidence from both social research surveys and testimony before legislative and executive bodies indicates that the same is true of real estate boards in cities throughout the country.

The profits to be derived from such speculative real estate activities is suggested by a study conducted in Philadelphia. Chester Rapkin and William G. Grigsby, two highly respected real estate economists, found that speculators operating in changing areas double their investments, on the average, in less than two years.

inadequate consumption of
health services

U.S. DEPARTMENT OF HEALTH,
EDUCATION, AND WELFARE
AND U.S. DEPARTMENT OF LABOR

While life expectancy for the newborn has increased significantly since the turn of the century for both white and non-white groups, a wide differential still exists (63.6 years for non-white versus 70.19 years for the white population).

Maternal mortality rates among non-white mothers are approximately four times those among white mothers (in 1965, 90.2

Figure 6-9
Expectation of Life at Birth: 1920 to 1967

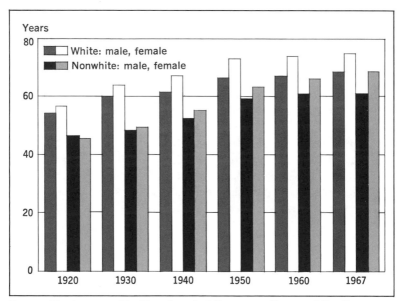

Source: Chart prepared by Department of Commerce, Bureau of the Census.
Data from Dept. of Health, Education, and Welfare, Public Health Service.

From The U.S. Department of Health, Education, and Welfare, Office of the Assistant Secretary for Program Coordination, Program Analysis, *Delivery of Health Services for the Poor* (Washington: Government Printing Office, 1967), pp. 3–32 *passim*.

the black consumer

and 22.4 maternal deaths per 100,000 live births, respectively).
In infant mortality, a similar trend exists (21.5 deaths per 1,000
live births among white infants compared to 40.3 among nonwhite infants).

High differentials in non-white versus white mortality are
found for tuberculosis, influenza and pneumonia, vascular lesions
affecting the central nervous system, and death due to homicide.
For each of these, the ratios are greater than 2 to 1. There is also
a higher non-white mortality from cancer of the cervix, a neo-
plasm almost entirely curable with early diagnosis and treatment.

Children under age 15 average two physician visits per year in
families with incomes under $2,000 compared to 4.4 in families
with incomes over $7,000.

In families with incomes under $4,000, 22 percent have never
seen a dentist as compared to 7.2 percent in families with incomes over $10,000.

Table 6-4

Maternal and Infant Mortality Rates, 1940, 1950, and 1960–1967
(per 1,000 live births)

| | Maternal | | Infant | | | |
| | | | Less Than 1 Month Old | | 1 Month to 1 Year Old | |
	Negro and Other Races	White	Negro and Other Races	White	Negro and Other Races	White
1940	7.6	3.2	39.7	27.2	34.1	16.0
1950	2.2	0.6	27.5	19.4	17.0	7.4
1960	1.0	0.3	26.9	17.2	16.4	5.7
1961	1.0	0.2	26.2	16.9	14.5	5.5
1962	1.0	0.2	26.1	16.9	15.3	5.5
1963	1.0	0.2	26.1	16.7	15.4	5.5
1964	0.9	0.2	26.5	16.2	14.6	5.4
1965	0.8	0.2	25.4	16.1	14.9	5.4
1966	0.7	0.2	24.8	15.6	14.0	5.0
1967	0.7	0.2	23.8*	15.0*	12.1**	4.7**

* Figures are for infants less than 28 days old.
** Figures are for infants 28 days to 1 year old.
Source: U.S. Department of Health, Education, and Welfare.

Note: Table 6-4, and Tables 6-5 and 6-6 which follow, did not originally appear
in this selection by The U.S. Department of Health, Education, and Welfare. They
are taken from pp. 65, 66, and 67, respectively, of **The Social and Economic
Status of Negroes in the United States 1969,** Report No. 375, Current Population Reports, Series P-23, No. 29, U.S. Department of Labor, Bureau of Labor
Statistics (Washington: Government Printing Office, 1969).

inadequate consumption of health services   171

Table 6-5

Percent of Population With One or More Physician or
Dental Visits for Selected Income Groups, July 1966–June 1967

| | Family Income | | | |
| | $3,000 to $4,999 | | $7,000 to $9,999 | |
	Negro and Other Races	White	Negro and Other Races	White
Percent with one or more visits to				
Physician	59.3	66.4	64.4	70.3
Dentist*	20.0	31.0	33.0	52.0
Percent of all visits to physicians made in				
Physician's office	51.4	73.5	64.3	73.2
Hospital clinic	30.4	9.5	22.4	6.7
Other (mainly by telephone)	18.2	17.0	13.3	20.1

* Dentist visits based on data for fiscal year July 1963–June 1964 (latest available) and for family income $2,000 to $3,999 and $7,000 to $9,999.
Source: U.S. Department of Health, Education, and Welfare.

22.5 percent of non-white children age one to four have had *no* DPT immunization compared to 8.6 percent of white children.

The following are a few salient reasons for the poor health status of the low income population:

1. The current "system" in which the poor receive health services perpetuates fragmented emergency-oriented medical care which is often relatively inaccessible in terms of time and location.

2. Despite recent legislation, inability to pay for services remains an important barrier to the poor's quest for health care.

3. Medical facilities and health manpower are particularly scarce in areas with a high concentration of poor.

4. Environmental and nutritional deficiencies . . . lead to lowered host resistance and greater exposure to health hazards. . . .

While it is difficult to get reliable statistics on subtle discriminatory practices, it is clear that racial discrimination interferes with the delivery of adequate medical care, particularly in

the black consumer

the South, but also in the North. The situation improved somewhat with the requirement that providers of service under Medicare comply with civil rights regulations. The result has been that many younger Negroes, as well as the old, are being served in facilities previously closed to them. However, in areas where a dual hospital system existed, many facilities have been unable to change their "white only" image and subsequently are under-utilized by Negroes. Three hundred hospitals in the South are still not in compliance with civil rights regulations. In addition, Negro physicians are often denied staff privileges in the better hospitals.

Table 6-6

Days of Disability Per Person Per Year, July 1965–June 1967,
and Percent of Population with Activity Limitations
Resulting from Chronic Illnesses

| | All Income Groups | |
	Negro and Other Races	White
Restricted-activity days*	16.5	15.4
Bed-disability days	7.1	5.8
Work-loss days**	6.8	5.4
School-loss days†	4.2	5.3
Percent of persons with chronic conditions and activity limitations	11.2	11.5

* For all types of illnesses, including chronic conditions, adjusted for age differences in the white population and that of Negro and other races.
** Includes persons 17 years of age and over currently employed.
† Includes children 6–16 years of age (data not age-adjusted).
Source: U.S. Department of Health, Education, and Welfare.

consumer education

D. PARKE GIBSON

Customer practices toward Negro consumers, as well as other low-income groups, have helped to shape a distrust toward retailers and manufacturers in the Negro market. The Negro consumer has long known that he pays a "color tax" in higher prices for food and other consumer products and in installment credit charges.

The increasing unrest toward these practices could have repercussions in the Negro market. The growing frustration of the Negro to higher prices for substandard goods and services could result in far more "consumer explosions" than have been witnessed in the past.

Consumer protection to combat sharp selling practices, excessive charges, poor-quality merchandise, abuse of credit regulations, and improvement of garnishment laws would contribute substantially to an improved climate among Negro consumers toward business, even though such protection may have to come from the government.

A 1967 Congressional subcommittee which investigated consumer problems in New York City and St. Louis learned what many Negroes and low-income consumers knew—that the poor are often charged more for groceries and often get worse goods and services than shoppers in suburbs and middle-class city neighborhoods. The subcommittee learned that people in the slums spend up to 33 percent of their income on food as compared to 23 percent of all Americans.

In New York City subcommittee members went to a supermarket where packaged goods were mismarked, frozen foods were half thawed, and the manager admitted that after two days on the shelf, packaged meat was taken back to the butcher's block, repackaged, relabeled, and a new date placed on the package.

Practices such as these have led to the destruction of those outlets considered to have "unfair" practices toward Negroes during racial unrest in major cities. Other tactics have been developed as well, including the practice of selective patronage,

From D. Parke Gibson, *The $30 Billion Negro* (New York: The Macmillan Company, 1969), pp. 141–45 *passim*.

the black consumer

shopping in predominantly white shopping centers, and building of Negro-controlled cooperatives.

The Negro national community offers an excellent opportunity for consumer education through consumer information. Very little has been done by business and industry to inform and educate Negro consumers. Even the planned efforts of major organizations in the Negro community are far from establishing enough consumer educational programs, which are vitally needed. Those firms that develop efforts to inform and educate the Negro as a consumer could expect benefits to accrue to them over and beyond what a normal advertising and marketing program might bring. . . .

There has been some activity among business firms, trade associations, and Negro organizations to do some of the work that is needed in the area of consumer education. . . .

The Harlem Consumers Council, a consumer-education unit operating in New York, developed a brochure advising *How to Say NO to a Door-to-Door Salesman*. A number of copies were distributed in Harlem, and the effort was brought to the attention of the Advertising Women of New York. . . .

The National Livestock and Meat Board has had a Negro home economist in its Homemakers Service Department for a number of years. She carries on an active consumer information and education program in predominantly Negro high schools and colleges. The home economist gives meat-cookery demonstrations and advises on the selection, care, cooking, and serving of meat. During summer months she advises individuals in school lunch programs on cooking meat in quantity.

The Negro Business and Professional Women's Clubs, with some six thousand members in an estimated seventy-five local senior and junior clubs throughout the United States, has consumer education as one of its national projects. Seminars, workshops, films, and materials are used locally for members and the community. Subjects discussed have included packaging, consumer frauds, what to look out for, and similar topics. . . .

policy
alternatives

strategies to attack
black poverty

LESTER THUROW

Aggregate economic policies to increase the use of economic resources are important instruments in reducing both poverty and discrimination. As fiscal and monetary measures raise the level of aggregate demand for goods and services, job opportunities for the disadvantaged expand, labor mobility increases, families are attracted into the labor force, and Negro incomes rise relative to white incomes. Reducing unemployment by 1 percentage point would reduce the number of persons in poverty by 1.25 million; the long-run effects of higher resource utilization would be even greater.

Economists traditionally pay homage to the concept of a balanced labor market in which the demand for labor is equal to the labor supply. In such a market, however, there are no economic pressures leading to change. If changes in the distribution of income are to occur, a labor shortage rather than a balanced market is required to make a real dent in poverty.

Tight labor markets would increase both white and black incomes, but the favorable effects would be greater for blacks. In a loose labor market (7 percent unemployed), the nonwhite median family income is 50 percent of white incomes; in a tight market (3 percent unemployed), it rises in the short run to 60 percent of white incomes. In the long run, the effects might be even greater. Although a 10 percentage point change in relative incomes does not eliminate all income differences, it represents a great improvement, especially when compared with the impact of other policy instruments for altering income distribution.

Tight labor markets have beneficial qualitative effects as well as quantitative ones. Shortages of skilled workers encourage businesses to enlarge their training programs. Restrictive union practices may decline when workers are less fearful of competition for a limited number of jobs. As the probability of finding a desired job increases, individuals have more incentive to develop

From Lester Thurow, *Poverty in Black and White: Highlights of Poverty and Discrimination,* Brookings Research Report 100 (Washington: The Brookings Institution, 1969), pp. 4–9. Copyright © 1969 by The Brookings Institution, 1775 Massachusetts Ave., N.W., Washington, D.C. 20036.

skills and knowledge and become more willing to complete government training programs. Such improvements would be especially helpful to Negroes.

As a practical policy instrument, creating tighter labor markets presents several other advantages. Aggregate economic policies are impersonal. They can be carried out without recruiting a bureaucracy of administrators, trainers, teachers, and social workers. They do not require state and local cooperation. They do not interfere with personal choice. They can be implemented quickly and cheaply, and they can take effect in a short time.

Unbalanced labor markets are not, of course, without disadvantages. They are accompanied by inflation; but to support a policy of balanced labor markets for the sake of price stability means reducing the relative gains in employment for blacks and for whites, and a cut in their incomes.

Any increased use of economic resources alone cannot eliminate either poverty or discrimination. Other changes are needed as well, but they may require tight labor markets as a precondition. Hence, a low unemployment rate should be an important target for the war on poverty and discrimination.

Human capital   (individual skills and knowledge) is a major determinant of the distribution of income. Individuals with little education, training, and skill have low marginal productivities and earn low incomes. The productivity approach to the elimination of poverty is aimed at improving the quantity and quality of human capital.

The poor and the blacks underinvest in their own human capital for good reasons. The returns to education and experience are much lower for blacks than for whites. Blacks, and especially those in the South, receive fewer benefits from job experience. Lower wages for the same work, less on-the-job training, and a lack of adequate physical capital with which to work are a partial explanation. The result is a large gap in human capital resources between the rich and the poor, between whites and blacks.

More important than the returns to either education or training are the interactions among training, education, physical capital, and technical progress. Programs to increase education and training must be carefully coordinated if either type of program is to result in increased incomes. The joint effects of having both

strategies to attack black poverty

education and training are, on the average, four times as large as the sum of their separate effects.

Programs to alter the quantity, quality, or price of human capital can significantly reduce the problems of poverty and low incomes of blacks, although they cannot solve them. Given the general characteristics of the poor, remedial programs should be designed to raise everyone in the labor force to at least eighth-grade standards of literacy. The social benefits from such a program would be large; even from a narrower economic point of view, the benefits would be sizable. Without this level of education, training has little payoff. Programs to bring the working population up to this standard must focus on adult education, but this area is where the least effort has been made. Something must be done for those who are now in the working population and who are going to be in the labor force for the next thirty years.

Raising functional literacy to eighth- or tenth-grade standards may be an important factor in raising incomes, but it will not be successful unless it is combined with training opportunities and job opportunities. As long as there is discrimination, more education produces few benefits for blacks. For them the principal need is for more on-the-job learning. A large part of the difference between white and black incomes is explained by differences in the returns to on-the-job experience, from which blacks receive much less value. Thus, a major part of the task of increasing human capital among the poor must be achieved in the private sector of the economy. Government can provide significant incentives for private actions, but government education programs will have small returns unless the private job market can be opened at the same time.

The mobility of labor   also affects the distribution of income. With imperfect labor markets, competitive pressures do not equalize incomes for individuals with the same education, training, and experience. Those who work with little physical capital or in technically backward areas receive low incomes, while persons in areas with high capital–labor ratios and high technical efficiency earn large incomes. The impact of such market imperfections is particularly hard on black workers.

A major part of the effort to eliminate low incomes among both whites and blacks must be directed toward improving labor mobility. Improvement can be achieved directly, by providing better labor market information and incentives for mobility, or indirectly, by encouraging industrial firms to move into Negro areas.

Discrimination   in all its forms must be eliminated if poverty is to be eliminated. Each type of discrimination makes it easier to enforce and perpetuate the others. Together they reduce black political power and the possibility of acting to end discriminatory practices.

Although the total output of the economy could be raised by eliminating discrimination, the practice does produce large economic gains for specific whites. Consequently there are important vested economic interests supporting discrimination, and programs to eliminate it must take them into account. Eliminating discrimination in government at all levels may be one of the most effective means of tempering resistance to the elimination of discrimination and of breaking down the monopoly powers of whites.

guaranteed employment

Families and individuals cannot benefit from programs to raise their earning power if they are outside the labor force. Perhaps no one in such a family can take advantage of education, training, or better job opportunities in order to earn an acceptable income. Some persons, because of age, lack of education and training, poor work habits, or a deprived prior existence, cannot be brought up to acceptable levels of productivity. If they can no longer be trained or educated, the errors of the past are irreversible.

There are two ways of providing income for these people. The first is to guarantee them jobs and sheltered employment. The second is to provide them with direct income transfers.

Wages for guaranteed jobs would be set according to the desired distribution of income rather than the productivity of the worker. Thus the job would be partly a work-creation program and partly an income transfer program. In many cases it might

strategies to attack black poverty

be easier to create jobs that fit the capabilities of the worker than to develop his skills to fit available jobs. Subsidies could be given to private employers to hire specific categories of workers, or the government could become the employer of last resort for those whose productivity was not high enough to be attractive to private industry or public agencies.

Given the obstacles to subsidizing private industry and competing with employed workers, the National Commission on Technology, Automation, and Economic Progress has suggested that guaranteed jobs be created in public services or private nonprofit institutions. Finding useful jobs with low skill requirements would not be difficult in public services. Millions of jobs could be found in schools, hospitals, conservation programs, natural beautification, and city sanitation. Wages would probably exceed the workers' productivity, but needed services would be provided and the real cost would be much lower than that of a straight income transfer. Perhaps the major benefit of guaranteed employment, however, would not be the lower real costs but the resultant self-respect of the worker.

There are three major objections to guaranteed jobs: (1) employed workers might feel threatened by subsidized workers; (2) guarantees might create a class of dead-end jobs that were unacceptable to the poor and stigmatized by the affluent; and (3) public institutions require a stable labor force if they are to be efficient.

The first objection might be met by requiring that the jobs be used to expand public services and not to cut labor costs. On the other hand, there is no certain way of knowing how many people would have been hired if the guaranteed jobs had not existed.

Opposition on the second score might be reduced if guaranteed jobs were coordinated with efforts to increase workers' productivity by creating associated training programs for those who wish to use them. Programs such as the Neighborhood Youth Corps use guaranteed jobs to attract individuals into training programs, to provide some training, and to serve as an income transfer mechanism. This feature should be retained in any national system of guaranteed employment.

The third objection cannot be overcome in any way. Society must simply decide whether the benefits of guaranteed employment exceed the costs of inefficiency imposed on public institutions.

income support

If poverty is to be eliminated and not merely reduced, some system of direct income transfers must also be brought into play. Many people cannot enter the productive economy, others can be brought in only at prohibitive cost, and society may wish to encourage still others to stay out. Consequently, some form of guaranteed annual income is essential.

Provided that income transfers were limited to people who cannot work, they would present few economic problems; income would simply be transferred to these households. But difficulties could be created by spillover effects on other persons. For example, participants in guaranteed job programs or on-the-job training might be encouraged to drop out. Experience suggests, too, that incentives to work are reduced when direct income transfers are combined with high marginal tax rates. Proposals such as the negative income tax are intended to reduce this adverse effect of public assistance, which in effect has been "taxed" at a rate of 100 percent—that is, payments stop when the recipient gets a job. To lower this "tax" would increase the incentive to work, since less leisure time would have to be sacrificed to earn a given income. In designing direct income transfer programs, society must decide how it is going to balance the incentive effects of lower marginal tax rates against the need to help those who cannot enter the labor force.

Along with its potential benefits, a negative income tax would create one other problem. A marginal tax rate of less than 100 percent would mean that some people who are above the poverty line would have to receive aid if no one were to be left below the poverty line. The problem becomes less significant if one recalls that a band—not a specific line—really separates the poor from the nonpoor, and that definitions of poverty might be based on relative rather than absolute incomes.

Quantitatively, direct income transfers have approximately the same effects on the incomes of both whites and blacks; without them, poverty can be eliminated in neither community. Guaranteed jobs, however, would have a much greater relative effect on black incomes. Most white workers earn incomes above the levels proposed under guaranteed jobs; most black workers do not. Eliminating the lower end of both the white and black income distribution would substantially close the gap between them.

Examination of the problems and opportunities presented by both guaranteed jobs and direct income transfers shows the need for integrating productivity programs, guaranteed job programs, and direct income transfers. All three are necessary; each can function more effectively if the others are present, but each might be relatively ineffective if the others were not well coordinated with it.

By the same token, reducing the income gap between rich and poor and closing the income gap between black and white are related problems. To solve either problem would bring improvement in the other, but no set of programs can reach a solution unless it recognizes the interaction between poverty and discrimination. Programs to eliminate poverty will not work for blacks unless they work to reduce racial discrimination. Programs to put an end to racial inequality will not work unless they act on the causes of poverty, which afflict black and white alike.

7

the choices
before us

INTRODUCTION

Lester Thurow has argued that the removal of differential black poverty requires a simultaneous, multi-pronged attack within a framework of tight labor markets throughout the economy. Such a multifaceted policy approach is implied in our theme that black differential status emanates from a vicious circle of interrelated causes. The Black Caucus, the twelve black members of The U.S. House of Representatives, presented more detailed, specific recommendations, similar to Thurow's, to the president in March of 1971. Their economic proposals introduce this chapter. Here and in the policy chapters that follow we present alternative viewpoints on the options indicated by both Thurow and the Black Caucus. The choices discussed usually would require full employment as a necessary condition for their success.

But there is more to policy than the substance of programs. If policy discussion is to be more than an intellectual game, it is necessary also for advocates to choose the effective organizational strategy to further given policy objectives. In the brief selection that immediately follows the recommendations of the Black Caucus, Kenneth B. Clark spells out the main types of strategy open to those who would pursue various programs to reduce or eliminate black–white differentials. Trienah Meyers, on the other hand, emphasizes purely programmatic matters. She also invokes the vicious circle framework to stress the need for simultaneous

186

action on three mutually reinforcing fronts—educational, economic, and motivational. However, neither her educational nor motivational category deals with the task of dispelling white racist psychology, and this vital aspect of policy—the eradication of such racist psychology—is therefore emphasized in the following discussion by Anthony Downs. But white racism has a long history and, as a general category, it can be made to bear the responsibility for accumulated costs of discrimination over many generations. Such a notion underlies in large part the proposals for reparations to be paid by the whites to the Blacks for these costs. Reparations is a highly controversial issue, the pros and cons of which are given in the final selections by Whitney M. Young, Jr. and Kyle Haselden.

recommendations to president nixon

CONGRESSIONAL BLACK CAUCUS

We sought this meeting, Mr. President, out of a deep conviction that large numbers of citizens are being subjected to intense hardship, are denied their basic rights, and are suffering irreparable harm as a result of current policies.

. . . Most of the districts that we represent are predominantly black, though our constituencies also include whites, Spanish-speaking, Indians, Japanese-Americans, and Chinese-Americans, some suburbanites as well as residents of the central cities, poor, middle income, and even some well-to-do Americans.

But our concerns and obligations as Members of Congress do not stop at the boundaries of our districts; our concerns are national and international in scope. We are petitioned daily by citizens living hundreds of miles from our districts who look on us as Congressmen-at-large for black people and poor people in the United States. Even though we think first of those we

From *The Congressional Record*, Vol. 117, No. 45 (March 30, 1971), pp. H2190–H2194 *passim*.

were directly elected to serve, we cannot, in good conscience think *only* of them—for what affects one black community, one poor community, one urban community, affects all. . . .

Since you assumed office, we have spent billions on war, while over 2 million Americans have been added to the ranks of unemployed, and 2.5 million more are now on ever-mounting relief rolls. Inflation is reducing our standard of living, and most cities face bankruptcy. The racist policies of public and private U.S. institutions insure that blacks and other oppressed peoples suffer much more than others, whether in good times or bad. Economic recovery—not now in sight—cannot possibly secure rights and opportunities that millions of citizens never had. In our view, the quest for economic stability cannot be separated from the basic need for a redistribution of wealth and income, so that there is no longer destitution amid opulence. Nor can we easily repair the damage done to our children by inferior schools, hunger, and ill-health. . . .

The recommendations which follow represent our own deep concerns and the expressed concerns of organizations and individuals from all over the country. We have not attempted to rank them in any order of priority. We feel that they are all essential to the long overdue task of making America one nation. We do not claim that they represent a comprehensive agenda of needs and remedial actions. We do not believe that they represent more than merely a good beginning. . . .

Recommendations

A. Economic Security and Economic Development

1. Manpower and Employment Rights

RECOMMENDATION 1: Within the framework of a comprehensive manpower planning program, this Administration should provide permanent job creation programs—with jobs in the public sector targeted to the areas of persistent unemployment and underemployment without regard to national employment rates. These jobs must be useful and desirable and have adequate wages and supportive services. Present manpower programs fail to deal adequately with the gaps between national rates and the critically higher jobless rates for blacks and other minorities in urban and rural ghettos.

RECOMMENDATION 2: A federal job creation program in the public service fields must be adopted. Such a program should initially provide a minimum of 500,000 productive jobs during the first six months of operation, and 600,000 in the second six months in this one program alone, with additional jobs in other programs to meet the unemployment crisis.

RECOMMENDATION 3: A minimum of 1 million NYC jobs should be provided for in-school youth during the summer. Present planning in this area is totally inadequate. The jobs should be provided by the federal government with no local matching fund requirement and should be for 10–32 hour weeks at not less than $1.60 an hour. This program must be understood to be no substitute for the needs addressed in Recommendation 1.

RECOMMENDATION 4: Basic changes must be made in federal recruitment, testing, and promotion policies and day-to-day administration to insure blacks and other oppressed minority peoples equal results to whites in the middle and upper levels of federal employment.

RECOMMENDATION 5: Executive Order 11246 must be enforced, requiring affirmative action by government contractors and subcontractors to provide equal employment opportunities and to extend the requirement of goals and timetables for achievement to all government contractors and subcontractors.

RECOMMENDATION 6: We call for vigorous support for expansion of the Civil Rights Act of 1964 to provide cease and desist power to the Equal Employment Opportunity Commission, coverage of employers of eight or more persons, and to eliminate the present exemption of state and local governments, and educational institutions.

RECOMMENDATION 7: At a time when blacks are fighting and dying in disproportionate numbers in Indochina, we urge the White House to initiate a thorough investigation of the status of blacks and other minorities in the Veterans Administration—90 per cent of whose black classified employees are in grades GS-8 or below. The investigation and the remedial action which must follow should include not only equal employment opportunity within the Veterans Administration, but should focus on closing the critically wide gap between the needs of black veterans and the inadequate and uncoordinated existing programs of the Veterans Administration, the Department of Labor, Housing and Urban Development, and other federal agencies.

2. Welfare Reform

RECOMMENDATION 1: We recommend that the present welfare system be replaced by a guaranteed adequate income system. We oppose any welfare reform which fails to establish a satisfactory timetable for reaching a guaranteed adequate income system of a minimum of $6,500 a year for a family of four from cash assistance, wages or both.

RECOMMENDATION 2: Any federalization of existing welfare programs must have as an ultimate objective the realization of individual economic self-sufficiency. The federalized programs should guarantee the standardization of eligibility requirements, the establishment of adequate payment standards, the elimination of abusive and degrading administrative practices, and the provision of suitable work opportunities which maximize individual freedom of choice and self-respect.

RECOMMENDATION 3: Until a fully operational cash assistance program is established, we urge you, Mr. President, to direct the appropriate federal agencies to overhaul the food assistance delivery system, so that the minimum standards and goals of existing legislation can be guaranteed. Further, the necessary budgetary revisions (or supplemental budget requests) should be made so that the needs of all children eligible for free or reduced-price school breakfast or lunch programs by 1972 are met.

3. Federal Assistance to State and Local Government

The Caucus recognizes that the concept of revenue sharing is already operative and that the issue is really one of block grants versus categorical grants. The federal government has been sharing federally-collected tax money revenue with states, cities, counties, and individuals for the past forty years. The Caucus would, however, support a form of federal assistance to state and local governments with the following provisions:

1. Assurance that the funds will be spent in ways or in the amounts that will benefit the poor and the minorities who are least able to prevail in the inevitable contests at the local level that are bound to be waged over such expenditures.
2. Allowance for the participation of neighborhood and other community units in planning and in the decisions about how funds will be spent.

the choices before us

3. Enforcement of civil rights laws with respect to the expenditure of federal funds.

4. Incentives for states to shift from forms of taxation that fall most heavily on low-income families to more progressive income taxes.

RECOMMENDATION 1: Immediate, short-term financial assistance should be afforded local communities by releasing frozen funds for development projects, closing the growing authorization/appropriations gap, and by expeditiously proposing and strongly supporting an emergency public service employment bill.

RECOMMENDATION 2: We strongly recommend that the program of welfare nationalization and reform called for in Recommendations 1 and 2 under Welfare Reform should not be considered as an alternative to the Administration's general "revenue-sharing" proposal.

RECOMMENDATION 3: The population-based distribution formula in the Administration's "revenue-sharing" bill must be altered to more accurately target the funds to places of maximum need. Specifically, we would recommend that one per cent (1%) of the individual tax base be distributed to all categorized welfare disbursing units on a basis reflecting the proportion of national welfare costs paid by that unit during 1970, providing that the unit maintains its 1970 welfare effort.

RECOMMENDATION 4: The distribution apparatus of the present proposal for "revenue-sharing" must be changed to funnel more funds to major urban centers, i.e., .5% of the individual tax base be distributed to all local units not sharing in Recommendation 3 above and which have a population of 50,000 or more.

RECOMMENDATION 5: The civil rights guidelines set forth in the Administration's "revenue-sharing" package must be greatly strengthened, particularly in regard to equal employment hiring, and an effective compliance program.

RECOMMENDATION 6: Although we support general "revenue-sharing" to states and localities, under the conditions set forth above, to assist in the provision of basic services, we are opposed to the apparent abandonment of national leadership in such areas as education, housing, etc. that would result from proposed program "revenue-sharing." While states and localities can be given more flexibility in administering federal grants, national priorities requiring accountability for delivering services to those most in need of them must be maintained.

4. Minority Economic Development

RECOMMENDATION 1: An independent agency should be organized as a non-profit quasi-public, publicly-funded development bank for consolidation of present programs intended to assist minority business, and should receive an initial annual appropriation of 1 billion dollars. This agency should be under the direction of a board with broadly representative minority membership.

RECOMMENDATION 2: A federally-financed guarantee organization similar to the Federal National Mortgage Association should be created to insure securities and obligations of community development corporations—firms providing employment for and owned by residents of low-income areas.

RECOMMENDATION 3: In addition to increased federal support and employment of direct set-aside programs for all procurement, we urge you to support the enactment of legislation requiring that contractors working on federally-assisted and financed projects, set aside a specified percentage of their subcontract work for minority firms.

RECOMMENDATION 4: Federal management and technical assistance should be increased and made more broadly available to minority trade associations, development corporations, and other organizations of minority businessmen, with assistance provided more as an aid than as an audit.

RECOMMENDATION 5: Funding for Community Development Corporations should be increased to at least 50 million dollars for the development of community-based minority business ownership.

RECOMMENDATION 6: The Federal Deposit Insurance Corporation should be authorized and directed, by specific legislation, to use some of its assets to provide technical assistance to minority banks. No federal or quasi-federal agency presently provides technical assistance to these institutions, with the result that other kinds of programs (such as the $100 million deposit program) are less effective than they would be otherwise.

5. Poverty Programming

RECOMMENDATION 1: We urge the Administration to abandon any plans—now or two years hence—which will weaken the programs now under the aegis of the Office of Economic Opportunity and submerge them in existing agencies or in a broader plan for government reorganization. We believe that converting the Office of Economic Opportunity to a research and evaluation organization will deprive the poor of an advocate agency in Washington. Further, we recommend the restoration of the $116 million by which the Economic Opportunity Act was reduced in the fiscal year 1972, and a substantial increase in anti-poverty funds for the following fiscal year, and the elimination of the matching requirement which makes it impossible for some communities to participate in the program.

RECOMMENDATION 2: We support the continued existence and expansion of the OEO legal services. [We] urge that new guidelines be drawn and new legislation be proposed which would limit the power of state and local authorities to intervene politically in the operation of these programs. Should this prove infeasible, we recommend that every low income American citizen be guaranteed access to free, quality legal assistance through the establishment of a National Services Corporation.

B. Community and Human Development

1. Education

RECOMMENDATION 1: We urge you, Mr. President, to initiate (and/or support) such child development legislation and to require the promulgation of such administrative regulations for existing child development programs, which incorporate the following principles:

a) significant expansion of child development services;
b) development rather than custodial programming;
c) child development services provided as a right rather than as mandatory eligibility requirements;
d) encouragement of educational innovation and reform;
e) the validity of programs designed by and in accordance with the special needs of minority groups; and
f) consumer control.

In conjunction with the support of minority business enterprises, special assistance should be provided to minorities for the development of day care and other child development programs. The grant system should be adopted, as opposed to the voucher system. Further, the federal government should issue grant and/ or loan funds directly to day care institutions.

RECOMMENDATION 2: We recommend a strong program which enforces the priorities established by Congress under Title I of the Elementary and Secondary Education Act of 1965. In addition we recommend that this title be full funded in advance so that educational systems may plan a continuing program of high quality as was true during the time of the Morrill Land Grant Act of 100 years ago.

RECOMMENDATION 3: We specifically urge that the Administration abandon its plans to consolidate federal education legislation into a program of block grants.

RECOMMENDATION 4: We urge this Administration to support pending legislation that is designed to provide quality integrated education so that the concept of equal educational opportunity will become a reality for blacks and others among the oppressed in the country.

RECOMMENDATION 5: We support and call on the Administration to make real its own announced commitment to universal literacy for every American in this decade.

Because illiteracy will be even more crippling for our citizens in the 1970's and 1980's than at any previous time in our history, we urge that the Administration revive and strongly fund and support a national "Right to Read" program like that originally proposed by your own first Commissioner of Education.

RECOMMENDATION 6: We specifically urge that the federal government increase substantially its financial support for predominantly black institutions of higher education in order to insure their growth and expansion. For immediate relief of black colleges we recommend the full funding of $91 million authorized in the Developing Institutions Program of Title III of the Higher Education Act of 1965, and the elimination of the matching fund requirement.

RECOMMENDATION 7: We recommend, Mr. President, that you arrange to convene a meeting of the officials of black institutions of higher education with the heads of major federal agencies and departments such as the National Science Foundation, Department of Labor, Department of Agriculture, HUD, and HEW, to consider how black colleges may have greater access to the funds, programs and technical assistance of those agencies.

RECOMMENDATION 8: While we would support a request for a 70 percent increase in student aids in grant and work study over the previous fiscal year, we would strongly request reconsideration of the change in formula which reduces from approximately $1,800 to $1,000 the amount of grant and work study funds. A high proportion of black students now attending or hoping to enter our colleges would not be able to sustain the financial burden of the loans now being proposed. We would support the proposed increase in the availability of subsidized grants to students whose family incomes are less than $10,000 per annum. We would recommend, however (1) that existing grant and loan programs for student financial assistance be continued at least at current levels until the proposed programs become operational; (2) [that] the ceiling in terms of family income be raised to $15,000 per annum; and (3) that interest rates on the available loans be stabilized.

Student financial aid for most black students must assume little or no family financial aid. They need money for almost all their costs. We therefore believe that the major emphasis should be placed on grants rather than loans in supporting their education.

RECOMMENDATION 9: We recommend that the Administration give strong support to the establishment and maintenance of community colleges. We ask you to direct the Department of Health, Education and Welfare, the Department of Labor, and the Office of Economic Opportunity to work with the appropriate public officials and private citizens to restructure vocational, technical, and post-secondary education for the 70's and 80's. A critical aspect of this mission must be making certain that community colleges do not become dumping grounds for the children of the poor and near-poor. We are concerned that community colleges develop into one of the strongest ,and most flexible links in the continuing education in which millions of our people must be involved at various stages in their lives if they are not to be crippled by dead-ends or unmarketable skills, or by undeveloped capacities as citizens and human beings.

2. Housing and Urban Development

RECOMMENDATION 1: We call for the immediate release of supplemental FY 1971 funds of $150 million for public housing. This can be accomplished immediately by Presidential action.

RECOMMENDATION 2: We recommend the implementation of the Uniform Relocation Act to insure an adequate stock of low and moderate income housing for displaced persons. Immediate action by the President could achieve the implementation.

RECOMMENDATION 3: We urge you to support legislation to amend the Housing Act so that urban renewal money may be used for housing development projects other than new construction.

RECOMMENDATION 4: The Department of Housing and Urban Development should institute and enforce a uniform policy of site selection applicable to all of its departmental programs. The current regulations of the Department of Housing and Urban Development affecting site selections apply only to low rent housing. All other Housing and Urban Development programs, including Sections 235 and 236, should be brought under this policy to insure that they expand opportunities for black citizens and avoid reinforcement of segregation. Immediate action in this area is possible.

RECOMMENDATION 5: We strongly urge the amendment of Executive Order 11512 (1970) concerning the selection of sites for federal installations, in accordance with the U.S. Commission on Civil Rights' recommendation on "Federal Installations and Equal Housing Opportunity" to assure that communities are, in fact, open to all economic and racial groups as a condition of eligibility for location of federal installations.

RECOMMENDATION 6: Tax legislation providing favorable treatment of investment in new and rehabilitated housing should be broadened to provide identical preference to investment in any inner-city real property development, sponsored or substantially-owned by a community development corporation or other organization of minority or low-income citizens.

Mr. President:

As we indicated earlier, we have not at this time placed before you the full range of concerns which we and those we represent believe to be subject to amelioration by the federal government of which you are the duly elected head. We look forward to the opportunity to work cooperatively with you and other representatives of your Administration on the issues we have laid before

the choices before us

you today, and on others which we hope to consider with you in the future.

Respectfully submitted,

THE CONGRESSIONAL BLACK CAUCUS

Charles C. Diggs, Jr.,
Chairman
Michigan

Augustus F. Hawkins,
Vice-Chairman
California

Charles B. Rangel,
Secretary
New York

Shirley Chisholm
New York

William L. Clay
Missouri

Louis Stokes
Ohio

George W. Collins
Illinois

John Conyers, Jr.
Michigan

Ronald V. Dellums
California

Ralph H. Metcalfe
Illinois

Parren Mitchell
Maryland

Robert N. C. Nix
Pennsylvania

strategy alternatives: a spectrum of policy options

KENNETH B. CLARK

Various groups in Negro society have chosen, or moved unconsciously into, civil rights strategy positions which seem of sufficient consistency of character to justify an attempt to identify and classify them, with the usual injunction advisable in establishing all such categories; namely, that few individuals or groups fit precisely into any.

There is *the strategy of prayer,* applied for generations in the past, a strategy which relied on divine intervention. This strategy was doomed as a social instrument whatever it has meant in terms of individual solace because it was ineffective in producing direct evidence of social change. And solace itself may be inappropriate in the face of sustained injustice.

There is *the strategy of isolation* employed by the very few

From pp. 220–21 in *Dark Ghetto* by Kenneth B. Clark. Copyright © 1965 by Kenneth B. Clark. Reprinted by permission of Harper & Row, Publishers, Inc. (Also published in London by Victor Gollancz Ltd.)

aristocratic or wealthy Negroes who choose to live apart from the aspirations and despair of middle- and lower-class Negroes, secure as possible behind their wall of privilege, electing conspicuous consumption instead of responsibility in an abdication of leadership.

There is *the strategy of accommodation,* practiced for generations by those in the Negro middle class whose aspirations could only be achieved by adaptation to white middle-class mores: the Puritan ethic of thrift, cleanliness, education, hard work, rigorously proper sexual mores. A sense of guilt about their own flight from the ghetto and their own personal success has now led many of these persons to a closer identification with the struggling Negro masses.

There is *the strategy of despair* of the Negro rural and urban masses. Despair does not seem properly identified as strategy and yet, in a real sense, it is; for to abandon hope—to withdraw—in the presence of oppression is to adjust to and accept the condition.

There is *the strategy of alienation* advocated by the Communists in the 1930s, who tried in vain to convince Negroes that a separate black republic was the answer to American racism. The Black Muslims and the Black Nationalists today follow the same strategy based on hatred of the enemy and pride in group identity. Like the Communists, the Muslims, too, advocate rigorous group discipline, ascetic self-control, unquestioning devotion to dogmatic ideology, defense of violence, and the unquestioned leadership of authority. This strategy of alienation is, in a sense, the most desperate of all, for those who follow it admit their total loss of confidence in the possibilities of democracy.

There is *the strategy of law and maneuver,* the technique of the NAACP and National Urban League who work within the existing systems of constitutional society and democratic capitalism, achieving significant gains by patient hard work, and by tough, relentless pressure on the groups that hold political and economic power, working with whites where practical. Such groups have often run the risk of being labeled "Uncle Tom" for proceeding at a pace too slow and complicated for the younger, militant civil rights leaders. They have, nevertheless, been effective, content with results even at the risk of poor public relations.

There is *the strategy of direct encounter,* the action patterns of the student sit-ins, the picket lines, and the boycotts, the strategy of CORE, SNCC. This strategy dramatizes flagrant injustices, involves individuals directly, and demands that individuals take sides. This strategy does not effect social change directly, but it impels the mobilization of social power to facilitate or to resist the desired change.

There is, finally, *the strategy of truth,* the method of the intellectual who has sought, through academic research, through drama, writing, and speaking to motivate others to achieve social change by the power of eloquent expressions, a fusion of reason and feeling. Theirs has been the belief that men's minds and hearts can be reached and that truth has the power to transform society. The strategy of truth is the most abstract and nebulous of all, and often seems the least effective; there is much evidence that truth fails when selfish power is threatened by it—or fails, as one must believe, in the short run. Nevertheless, the search for truth, while impotent without implementation in action, undergirds every other strategy in behalf of constructive social change. None could proceed toward democratic ends without it.

the vicious circle
and poverty

TRIENAH MEYERS

The extra costs of being poor . . . are not only economic—they are also psychological, educational, and physical. Clearly these are not independent costs. In fact, there is almost insidious interrelationship creating an entrapment that might lead one to conclude that the *only* means of reducing the costs of being poor is to be rich. The recommendation made at the White House Conference for a $5,500 annual minimum income for a family

From Trienah Meyers, "The Extra Cost of Being Poor," talk at The National Agricultural Outlook Conference, Washington, D.C., February 18, 1970, pp. 8–10 *passim* (multilithed).

of four was a thought in that direction—but that alone will not solve many of the problems . . . even if such federal expenditures were feasible.

When one looks in depth at the nature of the costs of being poor and looks across the effectiveness and ineffectiveness of poverty programs of the past couple of years, the importance of the three separate types of leverage comes more clearly into focus.

The first and most far-reaching is *educational* leverage. Education has long-term effects. It also has a multiplier effect. Aides in the nutrition education program have observed this multiplier effect of education among homemakers—they find that what was discussed in one household, about low-cost meals, sometimes is known to the lady down the block before the aide arrives at that home. Certainly education is generational within the family. What the mother learns about food preparation is learned by her children through example. The converse is undoubtedly true. What children learn in 4-H and in school is carried home and can influence parents. The same is true of all other facets of education of the poor. To educate one person in Marengo County, Alabama beyond the fourth grade enhances the probability that several others will aspire to more than a fourth grade education. And, although the delivery costs of education are high, the maintenance costs are close to zero dollars. Once the concepts are incorporated by the learner, she or he has them at their disposal from that time on.

The second approach is through *economic* leverage. Economic leverage has potential for what we might call positive regenerative feedback. That is, each dollar added to a poor person's income can reduce the added costs of being poor. The Food Stamp Program provides some of this type of leverage. Much more of this type of assistance is needed.

The third type of leverage is *psychological* or motivational in character. We have seen some of this kind of leverage coming into play in the recent nutrition conference, and more widely in the community action agencies throughout the country. The poor are becoming their own voice and the sound is penetrating the barriers of stereotyping, moralizing, and philosophizing that have separated the other two-thirds of the Nation from them. Just to be heard is motivating. . . .

. . . any one of these three approaches, used alone, won't work.

Certainly the leverage gained by the three in unison will be far greater than the sum of the three used independently. Together they tend to nurture one another, to have a synergetic effort. Or, to put it in the language of the poor, that would really BANG it.

white racism

U.S. COMMISSION ON CIVIL RIGHTS

Racism in America is extremely complex and deep-rooted. Consequently, only an equally complex and profound set of actions can possibly eliminate or counteract it effectively. Summarized under nine basic headings, each of the kinds of actions involved describes a basic strategy which aims at one or both of two essential objectives: *changing the behavior of whites* so they will no longer consciously or unconsciously support racism; and *increasing the capabilities of nonwhite groups* so they can overcome the handicaps racism imposes.

The nine basic strategies can be briefly summarized as follows:

1. *Make all Americans—especially whites—far more conscious of the widespread existence of racism in all its forms, and the immense costs it imposes on the entire Nation.* . . .

   The process of education necessary to change white perceptions will never work if it consists mainly of some people "lecturing" others. Rather, it must involve intense participation by two types of people. First, various groups of whites must thoroughly examine their own behavior in order to uncover all the subtle and unconscious forms of racism embedded in it. This should be done by teachers concerning schools, by property managers and realtors concerning real estate practices, by personnel directors concerning employment practices, etc.

From The U.S. Commission on Civil Rights, *Racism in America and How to Combat It,* Clearing House Publication, Urban Series No. 1 (Washington: Government Printing Office, January 1970), pp. 6–11 *passim.* The report was prepared by Dr. Anthony Downs.

Second, whites must overcome their habitual exclusion of Negroes and other minority group members in this process of self-examination. Whites, themselves, are not likely to discover all the forms of subordination they impose on others without the help of the latter. . . . unless white self-examination incorporates significant contributions from nonwhites, it will embody a form of racism in itself.

2. *Build up the capabilities of minority group members, and greatly strengthen their opportunities and power to exercise those capabilities, especially regarding public and private activities that directly affect them.* . . .

Four key observations are relevant to this strategy:

a. *An essential ingredient is expressing strong political support for key national policies concerning housing, education, civil rights, employment, welfare programs, tax reforms, and other measures with antiracist effects.* . . .

b. *In primarily Negro areas, the strategy is closely related to the concepts of "Black Power" and "Black Nationalism," but it need not involve support of geographic separatism.* Undoubtedly, one effective way to build up capabilities quickly among the most deprived members of the black population, and to enhance the self-respect of the already capable members, is for Negroes to dominate most public and private activities in predominantly Negro neighborhoods. This includes the design as well as the execution of such programs. . . .

c. *One important device for developing Negro and other minority group business capabilities is the "third-party contract" for providing both public and private services.* For instance, if expanded government services concerning neighborhood maintenance were to be carried out, the local government could contract that function in mainly Negro areas to a Negro-owned and operated firm organized for that purpose, rather than enlarging the government itself. . . .

d. *One of the objectives of this basic strategy is to equip Negroes and other minority group leaders with much greater bargaining power in dealing with whites.* This would enable such leaders to more successfully persuade whites to carry out some of the institutional and be-

the choices before us

havioral changes necessary to eliminate racism. For example, a Negro mayor of a large city who can form a coalition with Negro councilmen to control property tax rates is in a strong position to influence white-dominated employers there to alter discriminatory hiring practices. . . .

3. *Develop legislative and other programs which simultaneously provide benefits for significant parts of the white majority and for deprived or other members of nonwhite minority groups, so it will be in the immediate self-interest of the former to support programs which aid the latter.* Publicly supported programs which benefit the most deprived persons in society, regardless of color, often have difficulty obtaining vital white middle class support. An example is the Federal anti-poverty program. Such programs provide benefits for a minority of the population by imposing taxes or inflation on the remaining majority. In reality, there are significant long-run benefits to the majority in thus aiding the minority. . . .

There are two important qualifications to this strategy. First, such programs will not improve the *relative* position of the minority groups concerned unless they provide larger benefits to those groups than to members of the middle class majority they also aid. . . .

This leads to the second qualification: it is virtually impossible to create programs which provide *net* benefits both to most severely deprived people and to most of the middle class white majority. Any program which redistributes income to poor people must cause a net loss to some other group. The only group with enough total income to support a meaningful redistribution of this kind is the middle-income majority. So no program can cause *net* redistribution favoring all of the lowest-income group and all of the middle-income group simultaneously. . . . Such "program packages" can be designed or promoted in ways that soften their negative impact upon those who bear it. For instance, they could be financed out of the "automatic" increase in Federal income tax receipts which occurs because of economic growth without any increase in tax rates. . . .

4. *Insure that minority group members are in a position to contribute to the design, execution, and evaluation of all*

*major social policies and programs. This will improve the
quality of such policies and programs by introducing a certain sensitivity to human values which is too often lacking
in the overly technology-oriented behavior of the white
majority. . . .*

An example may help clarify this reasoning. For two decades, many urban highways were constructed through low-
income neighborhoods, thus forcing thousands of poor
families to move. No compensation was paid to those up-
rooted unless they owned their own houses, and even then
it was grossly inadequate. No relocation services were provided; no alternative housing was built to make up for the
destruction of thousands of units in the midst of a shortage
of housing for poor people; and little thought was given to
the losses caused by destroying local schools, stores, parks,
and even whole neighborhoods. This striking insensitivity to
the problems of poor people—most of whom were "outside
the system"—resulted from the almost completely technological orientation of the highway engineers responsible for
building roads. They were concerned solely with moving
traffic from point to point in the technically most efficient
manner. . . .

. . . So in 1968, Federal policies regarding highway construction were changed to include much more adequate
compensation to displaced owners *and* renters, and the provision of relocation assistance and perhaps even new housing. This is a clear example of heightened sensitivity to
human needs partly counteracting an overly technological-
oriented social policy. . . .

5. *Influence local, State, and national policies and programs—
both public and private—so they have certain characteristics
which will reduce their possible racist effects.* Two such
characteristics have already been discussed: heightened
sensitivity to human values, and "gap-closing" improvement
of the most deprived or subordinate groups relative to
others benefited by the same policies. Others include:

a. *Avoidance of any action or arrangement that unneces-
sarily produces, sustains, or emphasizes derogatory or
stigmatizing forms of differentiation.* . . .

c. *Use of a metropolitan areawide geographic focus when-ever possible.* . . .

6. *Create recognition among all Americans that overcoming the burdens of racism will cost a great deal of money, time, effort, and institutional change; but that this cost is a worth-while investment in the future which both society as a whole and individual taxpayers can bear without undue strain.* . . .

7. *Search out and develop alliances of nonwhites and whites organized to obtain common practical goals, particularly in combating racism.* . . .

8. *Create many more positively oriented contacts between whites and Negroes and other minority group members— including personal contacts, intergroup contacts, and those occurring through mass media.* . . .

9. *Open up many more opportunities for minority group members in now predominantly white organizations (such as businesses), areas (such as suburban neighborhoods), or in-stitutions (such as public schools)*, and encourage other ar-rangements where members of different groups work, live, or act together. This *strategy of integration* is implicit in many of the eight others. . . .

The nine strategies described above are not mutually exclu-sive; nor do they exhaust all the possible ways to combat racism. Yet they encompass the key approaches that must be carried out over the next few years—and decades—if racism is to be reduced to an insignificant factor in America.

Americans seeking to combat racism should understand [that it] . . . is the product of more than 300 years of systematic subordination of Indians and Negroes by the white majority, plus later subordination of still other groups. The racist attitudes, behavior patterns, institutional structures, and cultural heritage built up over these three centuries are profoundly embedded in our society. They cannot be eradicated overnight, or in just a few years. Therefore, effectively combating racism will require con-tinuous and prolonged persistence by both whites and Negroes. They must be deeply committed—indeed, dedicated—to this goal.

reparations:
pro and con

for reparations

WHITNEY M. YOUNG, JR.

Recently, the National Urban League has attracted nationwide attention with its proposal for a temporary "more-than-equal" program of aid for Negro citizens. In the current drive for civil rights, with its demonstrations, marches and sit-ins, this proposal has confused many white Americans. They ask: Is the Negro not to be satisfied by equality alone? Or, is he seeking, not equality, but preference? In the face of these questions, our history should teach us that what the Urban League proposes is not only directly in the American tradition, but has the arguments of racial justice, economic practicality and morality—secular as well as religious—behind it.

On an economic level, the hard but simple fact—borne out by comparative statistics on unemployment, income, mortality rates, substandard housing and education—is that the past of the Negro exists in the present. Citizens everywhere must realize that the effects of over 300 years of oppression cannot be obliterated by doing business as usual. They must know, too, that in today's complex, technological society, a strong back and a will to succeed are no longer sufficient to break the bonds of deprivation, as was the case with minority groups in the past. For, in addition to the ordinary forces affecting one's way of life, the Negro's struggle into America's mainstream has been thwarted by the barriers of discrimination and denial based on the color of his skin. . . .

To overcome these conditions the National Urban League declares that the nation must undertake an immediate, dramatic and tangible "crash program"—a domestic Marshall Plan—to close this intolerable economic, social and educational gap, which

From Whitney M. Young, Jr. and Kyle Haselden, "Should There Be 'Compensation' for Negroes?", *The New York Times* (October 6, 1963), Section VI, p. 43. © 1963 by The New York Times Company. Reprinted by permission.

the choices before us

separates the vast majority of Negro citizens from other Americans. Unless this is done, the results of the current heroic efforts in the civil-rights movement will be truly an illusion, and the struggle will continue, with perhaps tragic consequences.

In its plea for such a domestic Marshall Plan, the Urban League is asking for a special effort, not for special privileges. This effort has been described as "preferential treatment," "indemnification," "special consideration," "compensatory activity." These are "scare" phrases that obscure the meaning of the proposal and go against the grain of our native sense of fair play.

We prefer that our recommendations be seen as necessary and just corrective measures that must be taken if equal opportunity is to have meaning. They are necessary, because only by such means can the majority of Negro citizens be prepared to assume the increased responsibilities that they will face in a more integrated society. They are just, because such an effort alone can repair the devastation wrought by generations of injustice, neglect, discrimination and indifference, based on race.

To put it another way, the scales of equal opportunity are now heavily weighted against the Negro and cannot be corrected in today's technological society simply by applying equal weights. For more than 300 years the white American has received special consideration, or "preferential treatment," if you will, over the Negro. What we ask now is that for a brief period there be a deliberate and massive effort to include the Negro citizen in the mainstream of American life. Furthermore, we are not asking for equal time; a major effort, honestly applied, need last only some 10 years. This crash program must be a cooperative effort by all agencies, institutions and individuals, public and private.

The elements of the crash program, or domestic Marshall Plan, would include:

Education   For the deprived child—Negro as well as white —provision for first-class schools, with the most modern facilities and the best and most experienced teachers. These are necessary to help him realize his potential and prepare him to take advantage of greater educational opportunity. Necessary also is intensified remedial instruction in the lower grades for culturally deprived and retarded pupils. Schools and colleges must find new ways to seek out Negro youths with undeveloped talents. Similarly adult education programs must be expanded and geared to the needs of citizens lacking the basic literary and technical skills.

Employment   A planned effort to place *qualified* Negroes in all categories of employment, at all levels of responsibility. This would mean that employers would consciously seek to hire qualified Negro citizens and would intensify apprenticeship and training programs to prepare new Negro employees and upgrade those already employed. Labor unions, too, must make a conscientious effort to include Negroes in their membership and training programs.

Further, where Negroes have not been employed in the past at all levels, it is essential that there be conscious preferment to help them catch up. This does not mean the establishment of a quota system—an idea shunned by responsible Negro organizations and leaders. But, because we are faced with the hypocrisy of "tokenism," where the presence of two or three Negro employees is passed off as integration, we are forced, during the transitional stages, to discuss numbers and categories. We demand, in all fairness, that the Negro not be expected to bear the brunt of unemployment.

Housing   Racial ghettos eliminated by providing genuine housing opportunities on the basis of need and financial ability. Programs of redevelopment and relocation, planned to provide both low-income housing and a racial diversity, are needed throughout our communities. This will require the active participation of real estate brokers as well as homeowners.

Health and welfare   Public and private agencies seeking to provide the best personnel and facilities in low-income neighborhoods, and increased counseling services to troubled families. Here, particularly, the churches and schools must combine efforts to help Negro families develop a deeper sense of parental and community responsibility.

Finally, qualified Negro citizens should be sought and named to public and private boards and commissions, particularly those which shape employment, housing, education, and health and welfare policies. In achieving this objective, we would develop strong, responsible leadership within the Negro community. Also, we would prompt private foundations, business and government to reassess the extent and aims of their financial contributions to established Negro leadership and organizations.

The program outlined here has a simple, practical aim: to provide the Negro citizen with the leadership, education, jobs and motivation that will permit him to help himself. . . .

against reparations

KYLE HASELDEN

Compensation must be rejected as an equalizer of competition between Negroes and whites for several reasons, all of which rest on the grounds to which the Negro appeals in his demand for freedom and equality.

First, compensation for Negroes is a subtle but pernicious form of racism. It requires that men be dealt with by society on the basis of race and color rather than on the basis of their humanity. It would therefore as a public policy legalize, deepen and perpetuate the abominable racial cleavage which has ostracized and crippled the American Negro. Racism, whoever may be its temporary beneficiary, should be eliminated from the social order, not confirmed by it.

Second, preferential economic status for Negroes would penalize the living in a futile attempt to collect a debt owed by the dead. The 20th-century white man is no more to blame for the fact that his ancestors bought and held slaves than are 20th-century Negroes for the fact that some of their ancestors captured and sold slaves. This is the ironic tragedy of exploitation. It leaves with the descendants of the exploiters a guilt they cannot cancel and with the descendants of the exploited a debt they cannot collect.

Third, a scheme which gives Negroes preference in employment and a premium in salary would bestow on Negroes the

From Whitney M. Young, Jr. and Kyle Haselden, "Should There Be 'Compensation' for Negroes?", *The New York Times,* October 6, 1963, Section VI, p. 43. © 1963 by The New York Times Company. Reprinted by permission.

debilitating social status which has for centuries cursed the initiative and enterprise of the white man in the South. Preferred status for the Negro, however much society may owe him a debt, will inevitably destroy in him the initiative and enterprise required of a minority people in a highly competitive society. Slavery corrupts ambition and self-reliance; so, too, does patronizing social status.

Fourth, compensation for Negroes would be unfair to other minorities handicapped by their history or by rapid social and industrial change: Puerto Ricans, Mexican-Americans, migrants of all races, Indians, coal miners and others. Negroes are entirely right in demanding that they be hired, paid and promoted on their merit and in boycotting those enterprises which discriminate on a racial basis. But they are not right in demanding an artificial scheme which is unworkable, racist, destructive of initiative and unfair to other struggling Americans.

8

preparation
for production
income

INTRODUCTION

As we have seen in Part 1, the same society that has required more of blacks than whites for any given job has provided less job preparation, whether in formal education or on-the-job training, for blacks. Thus current discrimination in the job market is compounded by past discrimination in education (and elsewhere), and current failures in education will yield a differential burden to black workers in the future, even if institutional barriers in job markets continue to be destroyed.

This chapter accordingly examines the massive reorientations required in the educational system. "Culturally deprived" children, as any children, can and do learn *if they are taught*. The existing vicious circle of educational inefficiency is created by adults, not by children, and can be broken only by bringing predominantly black schools to standard levels of excellence and relevance. A more controversial suggestion is that, whether as a prelude to full integration or a goal in itself, educational quality may involve as much a reallocation of resources as a commitment of additional resources to the schools.

The superintendent of schools in Berkeley, California, Dr. Neil Sullivan, points to *de facto* segregation as the single most important reason for the poor education afforded blacks. He proposes a philosophical base for action. The two following articles examine access to higher education in preparation for professional and managerial roles, and the availability of on-the-job training in "blue-collar" jobs, both with policy suggestions.

The discriminatory determinants of income differentials discussed in Part 1 and especially in Chapter 5 not only doom the individual to less than his or her potential productivity and income, but have "spillover" effects as well. As a result, society foregoes products which it could have and, meanwhile, must bear additional public aid expenses. Furthermore, society bears "negative externalities": an underprepared youth, out of work, is predictably inclined to turn to crime and other antisocial activity. The extent of this relationship is measured by Phillips, Votey, and Maxwell, who conclude that "a successful attack on rising crime rates must consider the problems facing young people. In particular the attack should concentrate on improving educational opportunities as well as labor market conditions."

basic criteria for
school desegregation

NEIL V. SULLIVAN

Educational leaders, particularly in the cities, are increasingly coming to recognize *de facto* segregation as the most pressing problem with which they must come to grips today. This recognition is in itself progress. Until recently educators generally felt that segregation was not their problem—that their problem was simply to provide the curriculum required for whatever students happened to show up at a given school. There remains today a powerful rear guard of school officials who are still fighting that battle. However, they are now finding themselves forced to get into the subject of racial competition of schools whether they think it belongs in their domain or not. . . .

From Neil V. Sullivan, "Desegregation Techniques," paper prepared for The U.S. Commission on Civil Rights in *Racial Isolation in the Public Schools, Vol. 2* (Washington: Government Printing Office, 1967), pp. 285–87.

Although cities will vary in the way in which they attack the problem and in the details of the solutions they develop, their approaches must meet certain criteria if their solutions are to be genuine. These criteria include the following:

1. Segregation must in fact be ended. This point should be self-evident. However, in too many cases the so-called solutions developed represent token gestures toward racial balance but do not wipe out *de facto* segregation. It may not be possible to wipe out *de facto* segregation totally overnight, but a community must accept the fact that tensions will continue and the problem will not be solved until this result has finally been achieved.

2. Desegregation must be combined with a general program of educational improvement. It is not enough simply to mix youngsters, many of whom come from a background of educational deprivation. These children must be given special help to overcome this deficit and to succeed in the new environment. Also large segments of our communities, unconvinced of the educational necessity for integration, must be shown that the new program is in the best interests of all children.

3. The "solution" to *de facto* segregation must involve the *total* community. No area of the city must be made to feel that it is being picked on or sacrificed to solve a total community problem. The experience of my own city [Berkeley, Calif.] is an example. A proposal made by a citizens' committee to achieve desegregation by redistricting junior high school boundaries met with a storm of protest in one area of the community that felt it was being sacrificed to solve a city-wide problem. When, in the course of community deliberation, another plan was substituted, providing an even greater degree of integration and involving *all* areas of the city, the community accepted the proposal. This criteria also means that Negroes cannot be asked to bear the total brunt of the drawbacks (e.g. long distance travel) accompanying desegregation. *De facto* segregation is a community-wide problem and must be solved on a community-wide basis.

4. Educators in working toward the solution of *de facto* segregation must act in good faith, and build the confidence of the community in that good faith. Unless such confidence

is built securely, educators risk being considered antagonists and too often are denied the time and community cooperation needed to prepare programs for solving the problems.

access to higher education

MANPOWER REPORT OF THE PRESIDENT, 1970

The major barrier to further growth in employment of Negroes in professional and managerial occupations is the limited number with sufficient education. In 1968, fewer than half a million Negroes had 4 or more years of college education; in 1969, the figure was probably a little higher. The gap between Negroes and whites in the proportion with at least 4 years of college was actually wider in 1968 than in 1960. Though gains in college education were substantial among Negroes during this period, they were larger among whites. (See Figure 8-1.)

The extremely small proportion of Negroes who have completed 5 or more years of college is of great significance from the viewpoint of their professional preparation. In 1968, only about 1 out of every 100 Negroes aged 25 or over had as much education as this, compared with 4 out of every 100 whites. Moreover, of the relatively few Negroes with postgraduate training, a high proportion probably are teachers with master's degrees in education.

It is apparent that action to expand Negro college education —and thereby enable increasing numbers to qualify for professional and other high-level jobs—should proceed in two major directions. It should be aimed, on the one hand, at enabling and motivating more Negro youth to enter and complete college and, on the other, at rapid enlargement in the numbers of Negroes obtaining doctoral degrees or other specifically professional training in a wide range of high-demand fields.

Assistance to all Negro youth in preparing for medicine and

From The U.S. Department of Labor, *Manpower Report of the President, 1970* (Washington: Government Printing Office, March 1970), pp. 184–85.

preparation for production income

Figure 8-1
Proportion of Negroes Who Are College Graduates Is Increasing
but Remains Much Lower Than for Whites

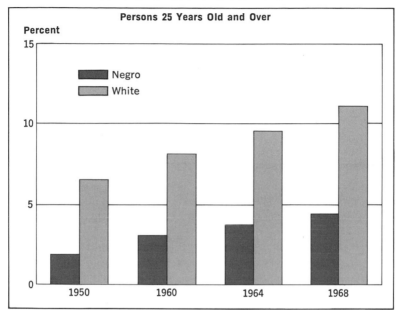

Source: Department of Labor, based on data from
the Department of Commerce

dentistry is a particularly urgent need. One reason why Negroes suffer so severely from the lack of medical care is the very small number of Negro physicians and dentists. Recent reports indicate that only 2 percent of all physicians and only 2.4 percent of all medical school students are Negroes. Furthermore, fewer than 2 percent of all dental students are Negroes, and the number of Negro dentists has actually been declining over the past 30 years. The situation is likely to deteriorate further unless positive remedial action is taken, since students may be less willing to make the sacrifices involved in preparing for these professions when alternative professional opportunities are available.

Programs aimed at raising the educational sights of able youth from poor families have had demonstrated success. For example, the Upward Bound Program, established and supported under the Economic Opportunity Act, aided 24,000 poor high school students during fiscal 1969, of whom half were Negroes. A high proportion of Upward Bound students have entered and stayed

access to higher education   215

in college. However, the number of young people whom it has been possible to help through this program, with the limited budgetary resources available, has been very small relative to the total need. It has been estimated that perhaps 600,000 youth, the majority Negroes, would qualify for aid under the program.

The establishment of community colleges in more local areas will also be an important means of increasing college enrollments of poor Negro youth, as will the availability of financial assistance to the students. In addition, strong support should be given both to the efforts of white institutions to enroll more Negroes and to those of the predominantly Negro institutions to improve the quality and range of their educational offerings. The latter institutions will certainly be called on to play a continuing major role in higher education of Negroes. They need more funds for faculty salaries, libraries, laboratories, and other facilities and equipment if they are to make hoped-for progress in equipping Negro youth for the opportunities now open to them.

expanding on-the-job training

WILLIAM L. HENDERSON / LARRY C. LEDEBUR

. . . job placement and training for the hard-core unemployed ghetto resident remains a problem of major proportions. Creating employment opportunities and placing ghetto residents in jobs is viewed as a viable approach, and several Negro organizations, large corporations, and numerous federal agencies[1] have been directing their energies to this end.

The Urban League is one of the few national civil rights

From William L. Henderson and Larry C. Ledebur, "The Viable Alternative for Black Economic Development," *Public Policy*, Vol. **XVIII**, No. 3 (Spring 1970), 430–32 *passim*.

[1] Government programs such as CEP, CAMPS, Model Cities, Neighborhood Youth Corps, New Careers, and MDTA attempt to improve the employment and potential employability of minorities and seek to indoctrinate young ghetto residents as to the values of work. For discussion of the format and structure of these programs, see *The Manpower Report of the President* (transmitted to the Congress April 1968; Washington, D.C.: Government Printing Office), pp. 193 ff. . . .

preparation for production income

organizations that has a program of job placement and employment opportunities. The Urban League, during the past half-decade, has assumed the primary obligation for planning on-the-job training programs funded by the Department of Labor, which are implemented by Urban League affiliates. Among economic programs, the Urban League's activities are unique because of the large number of people participating. Over 40,000 people have taken advantage of its job placement services, and in 1966 4000 received training and job placement.

Emphasis on job placement and skills training dominates the programs of many other Negro organizations, but they tend to be local in scope. Opportunities Industrialization Centers, established in 81 cities, are locally owned and black managed. The OIC approach is based on self-help and self-motivation in the training of adults in saleable skills to meet the needs of local industry. After giving training, the OIC aids in job placement by emphasizing the individual needs of the trainee and the employer. A high rate of job placement for graduates is characteristic of this program. The OIC training and other programs are financed by private sector grants—bank loans, local contributions, and foundation support—and are not dependent on government support. In the five Philadelphia OICs more than 8000 people have been placed in jobs.

. . . 70,000 people are participating in a program that can train a worker for about one-third the cost of government job-training programs. The OIC is firmly established as a viable skill training and job placement format.

The most vigorous participants in the job placement efforts to improve the economic lot of Negroes belong to the private sector.[2] Corporations in several urban areas have joined together in

[2] A business-oriented position on the importance and role of the private sector in the jobs approach is illustrated by the following recommendation by the Chamber of Commerce of the United States:
> Solutions to the problem of chronically unemployed workers should give priority to programs that offer basic education and training in skills leading to jobs in the competitive labor market. Emphasis should be placed upon upgrading the ability of these workers. Administrative improvement in government manpower programs should be undertaken particularly so as to coordinate and rationalize efforts at the local level. Government programs should be refocused increasingly toward helping the hard core unemployed. Massive federally financed employment programs in public and nonprofit jobs should be avoided. Such programs could lead to the development of a locked-in class of workers unprepared for the transition to regular jobs.

consortiums to bring the jobless into contact with jobs. In other areas, individual corporations have inaugurated efforts to hire the hard-core unemployed.

The consortium approach is typified by Cleveland's AIM-JOBS, which has helped over 600 applicants to find jobs. The St. Louis Work Opportunities Unlimited has worked with over 6500 people; more than 5000 have been aided in either prejob training or on-the-job counseling by the Boston Community Development Corporation. The Detroit Committee and the Los Angeles Management Council have been successful in similar efforts.

education and jobs, or crime

LLAD PHILLIPS /
HAROLD L. VOTEY, JR. / DAROLD MAXWELL

The prominent role of youth in the worsening crime situation suggests that the young suffer particularly from a disadvantaged social or economic position in society. . . . In the labor market young people have higher unemployment rates and lower participation rates than their elders. During much of the period from 1952 through 1967 labor market conditions were deteriorating for youths, particularly nonwhites. If we regard economic crime as a possible alternative to income earned by honest pursuits we would expect to find a disadvantaged economic position in the labor market associated with a greater tendency to commit economic crimes. . . .

. . . At the present, the model has been estimated for four felonies: auto theft, larceny, burglary, and robbery. Since males account for the great majority of all arrests, only male labor force data was included in the model. . . . The empirical estimation of this model demonstrates that the trends in arrest rates for 18

From Llad Phillips, Harold L. Votey, Jr., and Darold Maxwell, "Labor Market Conditions and Economic Crimes: An Econometric Study," pp. 2–29 *passim* (unpublished paper).

preparation for production income

and 19 year olds can be explained in terms of changing labor market conditions. Thus, we can conclude that for this age group, the population is not becoming more criminal, but that conditions which generate crime are becoming more accute. Of particular interest is the finding that unemployment rates increase arrest rates similarly for white and nonwhite, but . . . the latter have much higher unemployment rates and have experienced a greater increase in unemployment rates since 1952. The relationships linking participation rates and arrest rates are especially significant. We find a different pattern for whites and nonwhites, even though the participation rates for both groups were falling during this period. A decrease in the labor force participation rates for white youths decreases arrest rates. We believe this is due to the fact that a large proportion of white youths outside the labor force are in school preparing for a productive and legitimate career. In contrast, an increase in the labor force participation rate for nonwhite youths decreases arrest rates. We suggest that this may be caused by a large fraction of nonwhite youths outside the labor force who are discouraged with legitimate society because of both inadequate labor market and educational opportunities. We propose that our findings indicate that a successful attack on rising crime rates must consider the problems facing young people. In particular the attack should concentrate on improving educational opportunities as well as labor market conditions.

9

discrimination in resource markets

INTRODUCTION   Employer and employee attitudes, as expressed in policies of recruitment, hiring standards, job placement, and advancement procedures, are all critical either to society's full utilization of its manpower potential or to its failure to do so. The lead article which follows considers the potential impact of voluntary employer policies on equal employment opportunities based on the actual experiences of 20 highly varied companies. Significantly, the companies with the greatest amounts of experience found that black workers, given the opportunity, performed on the same level as other employees.

White employee intransigence to the entry of black workers into many labor markets is documented in a large and growing literature, especially with respect to union attitudes. We have selected a brief case study in the construction trades as indicative of some policy directions. Increased militancy among civil rights leaders in this area is aimed at enlarging the measure of their control over union hiring and training practices, the keys to major advancement.

Regrettably the voluntary liquidation of discriminatory policies has come slowly. If such changes are to be properly accelerated while the basic institutions of society are maintained, the laws of society *must be enforced.* Otherwise, it matters little that civil

220

rights laws are on the books in virtually every area of federal jurisdiction, and increasingly so at state and local levels. The policies to implement laws are crucial, and suggestions to that end are discussed in the concluding section, "Federal Policy and Job Discrimination."

A continuing failure of society to obey its own stated policies on civil rights invites the alternative to the above: violent upheaval.

employer job policies

U.S. DEPARTMENT OF LABOR

This monograph tells about the problems—real and imagined—faced by 20 companies when they voluntarily embarked upon programs for equal employment opportunity and how they attempted to solve them. . . .

The 20 companies covered a wide range of industry: Heavy and light manufacturing, public utilities, service, retail and wholesale trade, transportation and distribution. The smallest company was a tool and die shop with fewer than 50 workers. At the other extreme, two manufacturing plants had more than 5,000 workers each. . . . The work force ranged from overwhelmingly female to overwhelmingly male, from predominantly semiskilled to predominantly technical and professional. . . .

. . . managers reported some progress toward establishing and maintaining equal employment opportunities. Those who had the most experience with Negro employees reported that they found them to be average workers, neither significantly better nor significantly worse than comparable groups of white workers. . . .

To overcome the obstacles to an effective program of equal

From The U.S. Department of Labor, Manpower Administration, *Finding Jobs for Negroes: A Kit of Ideas for Management,* Manpower/Automation Research, Monograph No. 9 (Washington: Government Printing Office, November 1968), pp. 1–13 *passim.* The monograph is based upon a contract research study by Louis A. Ferman, Institute of Labor and Industrial Relations, University of Michigan and Wayne State University.

employment opportunity, one or another—and sometimes most—of the companies took action that touched all phases of employment within the company. Naturally, major emphasis was placed on recruitment.

   Realistic recruiting   Active recruitment efforts were usually tailored to the size of anticipated Negro employment, the jobs for which Negroes were sought, the number of Negroes already employed, the jobs held by these Negroes, the availability of Negro applicants through traditional sources, and employment conditions in the area. However, they had one thing in common: The companies emphasized the cultivation of new sources of minority group applicants.
   Use of the mass media was common. Typical practices were:

1. Including the slogan "Equal Opportunity Employer" in employment advertisements and notices.
2. Advertising jobs in publications read by minority groups.
3. Publicizing recruitment efforts in company publications and in trade and association journals.

But the employers stated that these impersonal techniques, while useful, were only complements to direct and personal contacts with individuals and associations that were actually in touch with minority group members.
   Several companies encouraged their executives to serve on commissions, special committees, and boards of agencies that dealt with minority group problems. But such activities generally represented only the first stage of developing contacts with the Negro community.
   Some companies sponsored or cosponsored community programs more directly linked to the recruitment of minority group workers. Some of these were long-range programs—high school "career days"; tours of company facilities; work-experience programs after school hours; and job orientation and placement programs, conducted by such agencies as the Urban League.
   A number of companies attempted to form close personal relationships with key members of the Negro community—ministers, teachers, scout leaders, directors of settlement houses, welfare workers, and recreational workers, for example. Such contacts yielded many applicants who could not be reached

through traditional job referral channels, especially for nonprofessional and nontechnical jobs. . . .

The companies most often used specialized Negro agencies for recruitment—for example, the Urban League's regional skill banks, which serve both Negro job applicants and companies seeking Negro workers. The companies also made intensive use of predominantly Negro high schools and southern Negro colleges as sources of recruitment. Direct applications were less important sources of Negro than of white workers. . . .

The more successful recruiting techniques involved a combination of agency and company efforts rather than the company's going it alone. . . .

In addition, unconscious as well as conscious discrimination patterns in recruitment need to be identified and eliminated. The unconscious ones are often defended on the basis of "organizational efficiency." The location of such barriers and action to eliminate them may be as efficacious in the long run as any other actions.

Hiring standards   Many of the companies involved reported that a reexamination of interviewing and testing practices, and particularly their role in placement and promotion opportunities, was necessary to open employment doors to many Negroes hitherto barred. As a rule, managers felt that test scores should not be the sole basis for hiring. In the hiring of clerical and technical workers, a number of companies gave preferential treatment to Negro job applicants whose test scores were comparable to those of white applicants. Reexamination of interviewing practices led, in different companies, to:

1. Educational programs for plant managers, interviewers, and vocational counselors on the issue of minority group discrimination.
2. The development of an audit system that, for example, required interviewers to report in writing on their contacts with Negro applicants, indicating the Negro's qualifications, the jobs for which he was considered, and, if he was rejected, the reasons for rejection.
3. The use of techniques such as asking the Negro applicant to come back several times to give the interviewer a better

picture of his abilities and interviewing by a Negro–white team.

. . . Some Negro applicants were given special job preparation and helped to learn social skills for the job, or to obtain transportation, special tools, or medical treatment. Occasionally, extended followup services—psychological, medical, or vocational —were also provided. . . .

Job placement All of the executives in the study agreed that the first Negro employee should not be chosen at random, but there were contradictory opinions about the ideal characteristics of the first one. Most believed that he should have superior qualifications, but several contended that hiring a Negro who was overqualified would create morale problems among white workers and make it difficult for Negroes employed later to match his performance.

Similar differences of opinion existed on where to place the first Negro employee. Some believed he should be in a highly visible job, while others regarded this practice as tokenism. There was general agreement, however, that he should not be placed in a department where there were few chances for promotion, because of the resulting competition among workers. The executives also agreed that the first Negro employee should be assigned to a supervisor with prestige among his subordinates and a successful record of handling interpersonal relations. They also pointed out that a supervisor with high work standards would control behavior by white workers that threatened those standards and would quickly integrate the Negro into a functioning role in the group.

Whether white workers should be given any special preparation prior to the hiring of the first Negro was another point of disagreement among the executives in the study. Twelve of them felt that such a practice could generate sensitivity to the "special event" of Negro employment. Two companies, on the other hand, did have special orientation programs to acquaint white workers with company policy on equal employment opportunity and to ascertain which employees might offer resistance. These sessions were not designed as an attempt to win popular approval for the employment of Negroes; rather, they stressed firmness in applica-

discrimination in resource markets

tion of the policy and the requirement that all workers comply with it. . . .

. . . Although initial procedures were modified as Negro employment increased, placements of Negroes continued to be made —for example, opening up departments where no Negroes were employed or following the buddy system of placing two or more Negroes in a department.

Promotion and upgrading   Negroes' opportunities for promotion or upgrading depend primarily upon the supervisor's recommendation. They may, however, also be influenced by low turnover rates, higher educational requirements for jobs above the entry level, traditions or union contractual provisions for separate lines of promotion, dual standards for Negro and white promotions, and the Negro's own reluctance to bid for better jobs.

Company practices to stimulate Negro promotions included counseling and training, a review of promotion policies, a search for eligible Negro employees, and the development of auditing and educational techniques to reduce the biases of the supervisors.

A particularly effective technique was review of the personnel files of minority group employees to see if any qualified for higher level jobs and an interview with each one about qualifications and interests that might not be recorded in the official file. New data were sent to the employees' supervisors, and a followup was made to see what action had resulted. Counseling was used to increase the flow of information about job and training opportunities, and help overcome Negro employees' reluctance to bid for these opportunities.

Reexamination of the seniority system and lines of job progression sometimes disclosed that Negro workers were "frozen" in certain departments and thereby excluded from promotion or upgrading. Companies in the study had negotiated union contract revisions which called for merging segregated operations, eliminating dual seniority and progression lines, basing eligibility for training and promotions on merit instead of seniority and experience, and modifying the apprenticeship system.

One company was offering tuition-free night classes for workers who lacked a high school diploma, which was required for jobs above the entry level. . . .

Preferential treatment as a policy to increase Negro promotions was uniformly opposed, as was the lowering of standards for certain jobs.

Opportunities for training   If employees are to qualify for better jobs, they often need training to supplement and strengthen their skills. . . .

More than any other feature of the work situation, the lack of exposure to informal job learning was described with bitterness and frustration by the unskilled Negro employees, who saw it as a reflection of interpersonal relations at work. The fact that management spokesmen were unaware that Negroes were virtually excluded from informal job learning suggests that such de facto discrimination may be well insulated from earnest attempts to equalize opportunities. . . .

In formal training programs, the supervisor is usually the gatekeeper to opportunity, since selection for training depends heavily on his recommendation, although seniority may also count. To guard against supervisory bias, four of the companies had set up checking procedures to see if qualified Negroes were being referred for training. In one, the supervisor was required to justify in writing any failure to refer a qualified Negro.

Four companies had also taken special measures to overcome an apparent unwillingness of Negroes to bid for training opportunities. Essentially, these were counseling programs designed to inform Negroes of their eligibility for training, to discuss the opportunities with them, and to encourage them to undertake training.

Several companies had developed formal training programs to compensate for the lack of specialized training among Negro job applicants. . . . The experience of these companies indicates that the best compensatory training programs are coupled with related work for which the employee is adequately paid and last no longer than necessary to bring the worker to some minimum skill level. . . .

Other areas of change   In the companies studied, action for equal opportunity sometimes extended to practices less directly related to employment.

. . . Experiences such as these were unique. There was, however, one area of concerted action: Any segregated facilities and

discrimination in resource markets

sponsorship of segregated social activities for employees were eliminated—with little fanfare, quickly, and completely.

bucking big labor in
construction—a case study

THOMAS J. BRAY

The construction industry has become an increasingly visible target for civil rights groups in recent years as more and more money has been poured into the cities—including the ghettos—under such programs as public housing, urban renewal and Model Cities. "It's impossible to imagine that blacks will continue to stand on the sidelines while lily-white unions come into these areas and take home all the pay," NAACP executive director Roy Wilkins said recently.

Though . . . demonstrations in Pittsburgh, Chicago and elsewhere have focused on private building projects, the primary emphasis in the past has been on government-financed construction. The reason: Laws and statutes governing hiring procedures under contracts involving Federal, state and local money are much clearer than on privately financed projects.

Under Federal contract compliance laws, for example, the Government is empowered to cut off funds on any contract where officials consider equal employment opportunity laws to have been breached. And in a landmark decision in May 1967, a Federal district court in Columbus, Ohio, directed state officials to insure that equal opportunities for minority workers are provided before entering into public works contracts.

Other laws go even further. Under Model Cities legislation, for example, authorities not only are required to observe existing anti-discrimination statutes but also are directed to provide "maximum opportunities for employing residents of the area (designated for Model Cities funds) in all phases of the program." . . .

From Thomas J. Bray, "Negro Drive for Jobs in Construction Unions Is Gaining Momentum," *The Wall Street Journal* (September 26, 1969), p. **10.**

There are strategy differences in the Negro ranks. Some moderate blacks fear that tackling the unions head-on may lead to a battle that can't be won. For one thing, the very shortage of skilled workers would help protect these men from much of the civil rights pressure; if work is shut down in one area, most craftsmen can find it elsewhere with a minimum of difficulty. It's already common practice for unions to call in craftsmen from as far away as 200 miles to work on building projects.

Moderates also fear that a powerful backlash could develop if the jobs issue is pushed too fast and too hard. The unions, after all, aren't exactly newcomers to the arts of organizing and demonstrating. . . .

. . . civil rights leaders involved show little sign of slackening their efforts. If anything, their stance is becoming more militant. In Chicago . . . the black coalition rejected an offer by unions and contractors to provide up to 4,000 construction jobs within a year if the economy remains strong. The coalition has been asking for 10,000 jobs. Other demands: That Negroes with four years experience be made foremen on construction in black communities and that the union hiring hall system of assigning jobs be abolished.

Civil rights leaders also have become increasingly critical of the so-called Philadelphia Plan, a complicated arrangement worked out by Federal officials, unions and contractors that sets "goals" for hiring minority workers. Union leaders also have attacked the Philadelphia Plan, on the ground that it establishes illegal hiring "quotas." . . .

"It's a step in the right direction," concedes the NAACP's Mr. Hill, who is generally acknowledged to be one of the main driving forces behind the attacks on the building trades, "but it doesn't get at the roots of the problem. First of all, the plan would require constant Government enforcement and scrutiny. Secondly, if a contractor merely signs a statement that he has made a sincere effort to find Negroes, he's home free. It's a prime example of paper compliance."

Thus, in addition to demanding more jobs, it has become increasingly clear that the real goal of Negro protest groups is to gain some measure of control over union hiring and training practices. Under the present system, contractors nominally share responsibilities for hiring workers and apprenticing them. But in practice contractors exercise little real power in hiring.

When a contractor needs a work force, he calls the union for referrals. First call goes to union members who have been certified as competent by the unions themselves. Indeed, a union "book," or journeyman's card, gives a craftsman almost unlimited mobility to work anywhere in the U.S. Without the card, he may still be able to find a substantial amount of work, but usually only for a fraction of union wages and seldom on prime projects.

This system affects all would-be building tradesmen, of course. Whites as well as blacks can find it difficult to obtain a union card. The International Brotherhood of Electrical Workers in Pittsburgh, for example, has 1,000 members—the same number it had 25 years ago.

But when unions do decide to take in new members, there is little question that whites stand a better chance than blacks. For one thing, most building craft unions are extremely clannish. Memberships often are handed down from generation to generation, or at least reserved for members of common ancestry.

In addition, Civil rights leaders argue that apprenticeship standards are unduly tough. Apprentices must be between 18 and 26 years of age, have a high school education, work at half salary and be willing to undergo three to five years of training. "It's a little unreal," says Pittsburgh's Mr. Smith. "You can get a Ph.D. from Harvard in less time than you can get a painter's book."

federal policy and job discrimination

RICHARD P. NATHAN

Seven major types of actions by which policy implementation in the field of equal employment opportunity can be strengthened and improved are discussed below. They are: presidential com-

From Richard P. Nathan, *Jobs and Civil Rights*, prepared for the U.S. Commission on Civil Rights by The Brookings Institution (Washington: Government Printing Office, April 1969), pp. 222–64 *passim*.

mitment, enforcement, interpretation, strategy, procedures, resources, and reorganization. These seven categories are closely interrelated. . . . This analytical framework is used because of its usefulness in summarizing measures which could be taken to increase the effectiveness of the equal job programs and activities of the Federal Government and because of its broader implications for the study of policy implementation as a political process. . . .

Among the areas in which strong presidential commitment could be expected to increase the effectiveness of the government's equal job policies, the area which stands out is contract compliance. The contract compliance program has enormous potential, but this potential can be realized under present conditions only if there is communicated throughout government a sense of presidential priority. . . .

The government's training programs for the disadvantaged have fared better lately as far as presidential commitment is concerned, the most recent illustration being the establishment of the new JOBS (Job Opportunities in the Business Sector) program. President Johnson sent a special manpower message to the Congress on the JOBS program and established the National Alliance of Businessmen under Henry Ford II to administer the program for industry. In other manpower policy areas, notably with reference to the state employment services, efforts to provide special aids for the disadvantaged have been slow to take hold. It is clear that more presidential muscle, as well as other steps, would be required to redirect the entrenched bureaucracies of [the] U.S. Employment Service and many state employment service agencies. . . .

A second means of strengthening policy implementation, closely related to the first, involves stronger enforcement, here defined to mean the more forceful application of sanctions and penalties. Again, the contract compliance program offers the clearest example, although an essentially negative one from the point of increasing results under the equal employment opportunity programs of the Federal government. . . .

To date, no major contract held by a major employer has been cancelled as provided under Executive Order 11246, although there have been recent signs of progress. Penalties have been applied or threatened on an *ad hoc* basis by several contracting agencies. The use of sanctions, however, must be made more

discrimination in resource markets

systematic and thus more predictable if the contract compliance program is to succeed in achieving its stated objectives.

The same problem, weak enforcement, applies to several of the manpower programs. Apprenticeship training programs have not been de-registered on civil rights grounds as threatened in the middle of 1967, although admittedly this is a limited sanction. Likewise, the U.S. Employment Service (USES) has not on a systematic basis withheld or reduced budget items for state employment services as a means of enforcing civil rights regulations in a program area in which resistance to change—any change—is very strong.

The EEOC [Equal Employment Opportunities Commission], on the other hand, offers an interesting case of what might be called the vigorous enforcement of non-sanctions. The Commission has weak enforcement powers, i.e., "informal methods of conference, conciliation, and persuasion" and referral to the Attorney General. Yet, it has tended to find reasonable cause on a liberal basis, that is, moving ahead on all cases in which there is ground for the supposition that a violation . . . may have occurred. . . .

Interpretation of basic policy statements by the responsible program administrators is an instrument which can be used to strengthen policy implementation. . . .

On substantive matters, this report at several points details an unwillingness to come to grips with politically sensitive issues in the interpretation of major policies. . . . Although it may be true in some circumstances that a discreet vagueness in the interpretation of controversial policies can make it easier to put them into effect, this idea has quite clearly been carried too far under the government's major programs for achieving equality of opportunity in private employment. . . . In the case of the contract compliance program, the recent new emphasis on pre-award reviews is an illustration of a new strategy which has proven effective. It concentrates resources on opportunities to affect contractor operations at a time when the government's leverage is likely to be greatest. . . .

Decisions on the procedures through which a given policy is translated into operational terms can also have an impact on policy implementation. Although, for these decisions to have an important and lasting effect on major policies, they ordinarily must be tied to other decisions interpreting policy in such a way as to permit or facilitate the adoption of new and stronger administrative processes. . . . It is recommended that the OFCC [Office of Federal Contract Compliance] adopt new enforcement procedures under which targets or objectives for the employment of minorities by government contractors would be used on a systematic basis. Contractors who fail either of two tests, (1) to meet their objectives [in] the employment of minorities or (2) to implement specific affirmative action measures detailed in a post-review agreement, would automatically be subject to hearings. . . .

. . . Because of the controversial nature of the equal job programs and the relatively low visibility of many budget processes, there have been a number of instances in which the opponents of equal job programs have been able to undercut their effectiveness through the budget process. The 1968 reduction of 50 percent by the Congress in the President's request for increased funds for the EEOC is a case in point. The contract compliance program has at various times been under major attack by strategically placed members of Congress in a position to hold up appropriations on a program-wide basis.

Although resources is treated here as a separate instrument through which program effectiveness can be increased, almost all of the proposals advanced in this report could not be put into effect unless some additional resources were made available or transferred out of related programs. . . . reorganization is the only one of the seven options which *as a general rule* does not involve increased expenditures.

Reorganization can make equal job programs more prominent and can increase their productivity by enabling them to relate to each other more systematically. . . .

. . . Today, experience has accumulated and techniques have been developed to the point where policy leaders are in a position to improve substantially the implementation of the policies of the Federal Government for reducing inequalities in the labor market. It is an opportunity that should not be missed.

10 housing and jobs

INTRODUCTION

In this chapter we are mainly concerned with one vital aspect of the housing problem: what to do about the locational fact that black residential segregation in the ghetto, together with the overwhelming concentration of job growth outside of the ghetto, subjects black Americans to serious communication, information, and cost barriers. These barriers accentuate black unemployment, undermine job incentives, and destroy occupational aspirations.

Proposals to attack these problems of housing–employment separation proceed in terms of either residential dispersion by the black population throughout the metropolitan area or the location of more economic activities in the ghetto, or a mixture of these two policies. Experience already accumulated in Boston, for example, shows that cheap bussing as an alternative under the present spatial segregation would probably not bring together black job-seekers and suburban job opportunities because of, among other reasons, scheduling problems and the need for heavy subsidies. In the first selection which follows, therefore, The National Committee against Discrimination in Housing emphasizes that, in the typical cases of New York City and Newark, New Jersey, housing and, consequently, jobs in the suburbs must be made available to low-income minorities presently ghetto-bound. In asserting that such housing must be publicly subsidized, the Committee is joined by many other students of the problem, such as Chester Hartman of Harvard's Joint Center for Urban Studies. Hartman stresses his conviction that a sufficient number of jobs cannot be expected to be brought into the ghetto because private corporate enterprise does not have the will to invest in ghetto industry in the face of the economic risks, the lack of communication, and likely stockholder opposition. Thus, while most jobs are still in the central cities, job growth will continue to be concentrated outside the core cities.

The general drift of these selections is toward a policy of residential dispersion that would, at the same time, bring minorities into spatial contact with added job opportunities. Therefore, we have here a policy dichotomy relative to other prescriptions which follow that advocate a rehabilitated ghetto.

the home and the factory

NATIONAL COMMITTEE AGAINST
DISCRIMINATION IN HOUSING

Severe labor shortages in suburbs and unemployment in ghettos, dwindling open space, a polluted environment, and increased large-lot zoning are among the irrational contrasts of the Tri-State New York region's unworkable development policies rooted in institutionalized racial and economic discrimination.

That profile and the magnitude in distance and numbers of the separation of Negroes and Puerto Ricans from suburban economic growth emerge clearly in the interim report of a study being conducted by the National Committee Against Discrimination in Housing (NCDH). . . .

The study is the most comprehensive undertaken to date of the interrelationship of job and housing patterns and access for minority workers in the suburbs of any metropolitan region. . . .

From The National Committee Against Discrimination in Housing, "NCDH Report Describes Unworkable Development Policies Rooted in Institutionalized Discrimination," *News from NCDH* (New York: Thursday, April 9, 1970), pp. 1–5 *passim*.

Among the facets of regional development profiled in the NCDH report are:

1. *The tradition of housing filtering down from upwardly mobile families to lower-income families and used as stepping stones as earnings improved "is meaningless to the black household if such housing is in a central city and the job sought by the household's breadwinner is in the suburbs."* The availability of "filtered-down" housing for minorities in suburbs convenient to employment locations will likely be the unusual coincidence rather than the usual case. The added cost of providing new housing in appropriate locations for lower-income groups is a social cost which society should assume as the price of undoing past years of neglect of, and discrimination against, blacks and Puerto Ricans.

2. *The growing trend in the region toward concentration of housing—which the report calls Europeanization—may well be essential to conservation of land, because it would act as a brake on continuing environmental deterioration due to unplanned urbanization without regard for land, water or air.*

   However, the Europeanization process under which high land and money costs are giving the regional housing market a strong multi-family and attached housing cast is on a collision course with most suburban zoning. Present zoning patterns of one- and two-acre lots most often result in a waste of land and exacerbation of sewage and solid waste disposal problems; higher densities permit economical treatment of sewage, solid waste incineration, and smoke control.

3. *The universal complaint of suburban employers about labor shortages reflects the abnormality of labor force distribution due to separation by income and race.* Most jobs are population-based. As many as 70 percent relate directly to the consumer, ranging from dentists to retail clerks. Jobs in goods production are a shrinking proportion of the labor force. Without being able to live in the suburbs, minority representation in population-based suburban employment must be minimal.

4. *The elementary fact that for every job producing goods and services for the national market, two jobs are necessary to serve the local population has evidently been ignored or defied by decision-makers, with a prominent role played by the real estate industry and suburban officials.*

5. *While the resident minority populations of both New York and Newark have increased dramatically over the past decade, the options left open to those who cannot avail themselves of nearby job opportunities because of education and skill factors have been either a longer journey to work or unemployment.*

6. *The suburban counties studied which experienced the largest increase in total employment over the period have also been those which enlarged their resident minority labor force least significantly: Nassau:* 122,000 more jobs in 1959–67; resident minority labor force up 7500 and total minority population up from 3.6 to 4.9 percent during 1960–68; *Bergen:* 75,000 more jobs, 1959–67; resident minority labor force up only 3000 and total minority population increase less than .5 percent. . . .

7. *Opening the suburbs to publicly-assisted housing for low and middle-income households must be an essential objective in any plan to provide a sufficient labor force for the various suburban sub-markets as required by suburban businesses and ghetto-bound lower-income minorities.* Presently, Federal and state laws permit local veto of subsidized housing. In most cases rezoning is also required to build publicly-assisted housing. Judicial intervention to protect minority rights and the possible conflict of interest between local homeowners [and] business interests seeking new industry may be forces that result in revision of present policies.

8. *Concentration of publicly-subsidized housing in central cities, mainly in ghettos, is rationalized by many whites as a solicitous regard for keeping intact the city neighborhoods of Negroes, Puerto Ricans and other low-income groups.* Such devotion by minorities to the blight and lack of opportunity that marks their neighborhoods in preference to outlying employment and housing, if accepted as true, would be a trait of minority groups alone.

9. *Speculation over what would be the preferences of mi-*

norities *for housing as between city and suburb if they had a choice is futile and, essentially, dishonest.* It can easily be resolved by building housing in both city and suburb that is within the means of minorities and, thereby, providing the same freedom of choice whites take for granted. The concentration of publicly-assisted housing in central cities is not in deference to the desires of minorities, but rather is in deference to the desires of suburbanites who exclude such housing from their communities.

10. *Costs and inconveniences generally rule out reverse commuting.* With 70 percent of all new jobs being created outside New York City, and all growth in manufacturing jobs outside, residence within New York City severely reduces the opportunities to take advantage of such jobs.

Unless massive numbers of Negroes and Puerto Ricans have opportunities opened to them to live in the suburban communities that are within convenient travel time to new employment concentration, they will have to forego jobs already there as well as vast numbers of new jobs projected for such locations. . . .

"The dimensions of the problem for the region and the nation," the report comments, "will require stronger open housing laws and more efficient enforcement; but this will not suffice by itself. It will require a supply of housing at costs scaled to the earnings of minority workers in nearby industries throughout the region; but even this will not suffice. It will require fair employment practices and training programs geared to tap the full potential of the minority labor force as if the security of America depended upon it; but this by itself will not suffice.

"It will take a national commitment to do it comparable to World War II's commitment to victory; in the words of William James, 'the moral equivalent of war.' "

housing: private failures,
public needs

CHESTER HARTMAN

The first issue I would like to discuss with you is the question of the costs of a program run by the public sector versus a program run by the private sector.

In the various proposals I have heard and discussions I have engaged in over the last few months about what has been called unleashing the private sector, I find there is, explicit or implicit, an assumption that somehow if the private sector can be convinced to do the job, we are going to wind up with a much less costly program than might otherwise be the case.

In my opinion that is an untrue assumption and a rather dangerous one, because it tends to postpone the realization we all must come to that at this time we have to be spending billions where we are now spending only millions.

It seems that in an age where we can, with incredible facility, spend $5 billion for anti-ballistic-missile systems, several billion dollars on supersonic transports, we still have not been willing to come to the realization that these kinds of billions, billions of Government tax moneys, must be spent in solving our urban problems.

I made some estimates, for the compendium, that just for solving the housing problem alone we would need somewhere in the neighborhood of $7 to $8 billion a year. The financial realities of our urban problems can't be skirted or wished away by some magic wand called the private sector. The realities are such that the gaps in the housing field between the incomes of people who need decent housing and the cost of producing decent housing are very great and they can only be met through a program of Government subsidies.

In the area of economic development and creation of jobs in the ghettos it is quite obvious that the commitment to guarantee profits, the tax credits offered, the reimbursable risks for business

From Chester Hartman, Testimony before The U.S. Joint Economic Committee, U.S. 90th Congress, 1st Session, Subcommittee on Urban Affairs, October 4, 1967 (Washington: Government Printing Office, 1967), pp. 192–94 *passim*.

housing and jobs

corporations that can be convinced to locate in the ghetto are all going to be extremely costly, and we shouldn't pretend there is any magic about a private sector solution.

Second, I have some very deep doubts, based upon my own readings and observations about corporations in the private sector, as to how widespread and how deep and long lasting is going to be the private sector's involvement in the solution of these urgent social problems.

It seems to me it is one thing to persuade a few corporations known to be progressive, a few key executives who are known to be socially responsible, to pioneer in carefully planned experiments, but there are going to be counterpressures from the stockholders and within the organization itself. . . . I don't think you are going to find a mass movement within the corporations themselves toward an altruistic sense of helping out with social problems.

There is also the question of a possible competitive disadvantage that corporations which are willing to put their resources, manpower, and managerial skills into this field of urban problems may find themselves in, vis-a-vis other corporations in the same field who are not willing to risk similar resources in these experiments.

There is the question of corporate image, too. How long will a corporation be willing to get involved in what is essentially a minor part of its operations which can very severely damage its own corporate image through difficulties which may arise in the process of social experiments? We have had instances, in New York, of insurance companies which have been very reluctant to get involved sponsoring housing developments, following their experience in the 1940's and 1950's when these companies found themselves in the position of landlords having to impose rent increases on their tenants; they feared their main business—insurance—would suffer because of this.

In short, my reading of the nature of the corporate beast leads me to believe that its own goals, motivations, and inner dynamics are not consonant with its playing a major role in the solution of social problems.

The third, and last, issue I would like to raise with you is the question of control. I think if we are at all sensitive to the demands coming out of the ghetto right now, possibly the principal issue, if there can be called one single issue that stands out, is the demand of the ghetto residents to control their own institutions, the economic and political forces that shape the community.

On the other hand, the primary feature of the American corporation is its concern with power and control, extremely centralized control to shape a corporate environment conducive to maximizing the profits and competitive position of the corporation. There is bound to be a clash here. That large corporations will include in their decisionmaking processes members of the ghetto community seems to me highly unlikely. And, it seems highly unlikely that they will be sympathetic with many of the key demands of the ghetto. They won't be able to communicate effectively with the people in the ghetto community. Similarly, the imposition into the ghetto of a powerful outside force with its own demands and agenda is going to lead to a great deal of resentment; may lead to very destructive behavior, and is not likely to produce an atmosphere of success. Therefore, I think one of the major issues we have to discuss is the question of who controls what in the ghetto; from this vantage point, at least, suggestions to bring private corporate enterprise into the ghetto seem to run counter to the major thoughts and trends within the ghetto itself.

11 prospects for black business

INTRODUCTION

The miniscule volume of black business today is perhaps the best measure of its prospects under even the most favorable policy stimulants. Even those who, like *The Wall Street Journal,* evince a cautious optimism are prone to anticipate that an expanding "black capitalism" will involve at best a relative increase in *small* business. The dominant corporate sector is and will remain almost completely white. There is even a serious question as to whether black minority participation in the large corporate nexus, as recommended by Richard America,[1] would signify anything beyond a slight tendency to further the cause of equal employment and promotional opportunities for black workers employed in that sector.

Furthermore, as pointed out by AFL-CIO president George Meany in the following selection, public aid to black small business under the present spatial pattern of economic activities would seem to imply a hardening of the segregated ghetto economy. Perhaps with help blacks could reduce the black–white discrepancy in the proportion of business proprietors in the population, but whether this would increase black "indepen-

---

[1] See Richard F. America, Jr., "What Do You People Want?", *Harvard Business Review* (March–April 1969), 103–112.

241

dence" depends largely upon one's views of the status of small enterprise in the business world and in the economy as a whole. The question of the degree of "independence" is particularly pertinent in what Eugene Foley considers the more promising case of the franchisee. In rural areas, perhaps the neglected black farmer or sharecropper could achieve both a greater degree of independence and a firmer entrepreneurial status through the formation of rural cooperatives. This possibility is explored below in the selection by The Rural Advancement Fund. Still, one has the impression that an inordinate amount of attention has already been devoted to a policy facet that promises only minute results.

black capitalism:
pro and con

"to replace dependence
with independence"

THE WALL STREET JOURNAL

While "black capitalism" surely is no poverty panacea, it's hard to see that it deserves the condemnation it has received from organized labor.

In the Presidential campaign Richard Nixon advanced the idea cautiously. Drawing funds from private and public sources, a program would be set up to help black employees become employers. "The first need," he said, "is to replace dependence with independence." . . .

Already, however, the AFL-CIO Executive Council has ren-

From "Labor and Black Capitalism," editorial in *The Wall Street Journal* (New York: March 12, 1969) p. 16. Reprinted with the permission of *The Wall Street Journal.*

prospects for black business

dered its verdict: Black capitalism is "anti-democratic nonsense" and an "illusion."

Nine out of every 10 persons who work are employees, the council noted; "only a small number of people can move into the economy's mainstream through self-employment and small business." True enough. Yet it's also worth noting that, among working nonwhites, an even larger proportion are employees—more than 97 of each 100. Is it really so antidemocratic to try to help minority groups get a larger piece of the action?

Black capitalists, like white capitalists, will sometimes fail. They will need assistance from, among others, the already considerable Negro business community.

They will need help, too, from white businessmen, and they are already beginning to get it. Some companies are providing technical and management advice. More tangibly, corporations like Xerox have contracted to buy products produced by black-owned shops and factories. Even scattered successes could do a lot to lift the morale of minority Americans.

Before such activity can be fairly dismissed as an illusion, the critics should be prepared to suggest something more constructive. Unfortunately, about all that the AFL-CIO has to propose is more of its old familiar prescription: Raise the Federal minimum wage and beef up Federal welfare and other programs.

Certainly it is an illusion that a higher minimum wage will mean increased incomes for all of the poor. All too often, it has instead priced lower-skilled workers out of the job market. This effect has been compounded by a steady increase in union-negotiated starting wages. The dismal record of recent decades should also have demonstrated that more is needed than mere continuation and expansion of the same old Government approaches.

If the unions would try a little fresh thought, they could be of a great deal of help. They have, for instance, made some progress toward opening up the apprenticeship programs, in the building trades and elsewhere, but they still have a considerable distance to go.

Fresh thinking is of course needed in many areas. It's regrettable that Government, after assembling unemployment statistics for so many years, is only now beginning to collect information on job opportunities. Besides aiding job seekers, this information could provide guidance for private and public job training programs. The job-opening study long was opposed by the unions, which feared that the findings would induce cuts in Federal welfare outlays.

President Nixon has yet to spell out all the details of the Government's role in black capitalism or, as the Administration now prefers to call it, "minority enterprise." In some ways the proposal may be objectionable, either on grounds of principle or practicality.

Unlike the AFL-CIO's more-of-the-same idea, however, it at least represents an attempt to turn away from proven failures, to start anew with the people themselves.

"a dangerous,
divisive delusion"

GEORGE MEANY

. . . America's goal must be the rapid elimination of ghetto conditions and the ultimate elimination of the ghetto itself.

Some people . . . have urged that this route be abandoned for an emphasis on so-called "black capitalism."

At its best, this policy is an illusion. In a society where 90 percent of those who are at work are wage and salary earners—on private and public payrolls—only a small number of people can move into the economy's mainstream through self-employment and small business. Thus sole or major emphasis on this policy would undermine or kill the jobs-skills-education-housing measures that are essential for the overwhelming majority of Negroes and other minorities.

At its worst, "black capitalism" is a dangerous, divisive delusion—offered as a panacea by extremists, both black and white, some businessmen who see a chance for profit and a few well-intentioned, but misguided, liberals.

Attempts to build separate economic enclaves with substantial

From George Meany, "Economic Progress of Minorities," statement by the AFL-CIO Executive Council, Bal Harbour, Florida, February 21, 1969 (mimeographed).

federal tax subsidies within specific geographically limited ghetto areas is apartheid, anti-democratic nonsense.

It is also unworkable, for the ghettos are, in fact, a part of the nation, their inhabitants are Americans, and small pockets of urban or rural poverty cannot be made into viable, separate economic entities. The gross national product, produced by the inter-dependent national economy, should be shared fairly by all Americans.

Moreover, the "black capitalism" proposals to create huge, new tax loopholes for business to locate in ghetto areas is also bad tax policy. If enacted, these loopholes would attract small sweat-shops or some marginal plants of big companies—with little additional employment at decent wages, but with considerable tax benefits to the companies.

Some legislative proposals for separate economic enclaves would create development corporations, in each ghetto area, with authority to control the economic life of the area. Such control could be used by extremists to harass businessmen, black and white alike, within these geographically defined enclaves.

Separatist economic schemes offer no hope for the solid advance of the overwhelming majority of disadvantaged minorities into America's mainstream. But they do present a real threat of further division, additional conflict and bitter frustration.

a small business program,
for the ghetto

EUGENE P. FOLEY

In order to strengthen the role of Negro owned small businesses in the ghetto and thereby create not only additional employment opportunities but also symbols of success in contrast to the rest of the ghetto, an aggressive small business program for the ghetto should be developed. It is essential to keep in mind that an important aspect of the ghetto's economic development, as

From Eugene P. Foley, *The Achieving Ghetto*. (Washington, D.C.: The Washington National Press, 1968), pp. 142–47.

well as the ultimate liberation of the Negro businessman, is the full involvement of normal commercial financial institutions and services in the ghetto. The trade contracts, business opportunities, and financial assistance they can offer are far greater than anything the federal government can devise.

An aggressive small business program for the ghetto should include:

1. Re-institution, re-emphasis, and liberalization of the Title IV and 6 × 6 programs of the SBA. [Loans up to $25,000 by the Small Business Administration with government counseling until the enterprise can operate independently.]

2. Development of high risk casualty and theft insurance policies by the major insurance companies similar to high risk automobile collision insurance policies. Most casualty and theft insurance companies do not insure in Negro areas; this applies to white businessmen as well as Negroes. A progressive, risk-taking businessman cannot operate boldly without such insurance; this is true any place, but especially in the ghetto.

3. The banks must be brought into the commercial financing of the very small business. The SBA has proved that the risk is not as great as feared. Banks have now been offered a further incentive because under Title IV of the Economic Opportunity Act they can obtain 100 percent guarantees by the SBA.

4. Franchising arrangements must be encouraged for Negro businessmen. One of the most promising opportunities for young Negroes aspiring for a business career, but lacking money and experience, is in this field. Franchising is an arrangement by which a firm (the franchiser) which has developed a successful pattern or formula for the conduct of a particular kind of business extends to others (the franchisees) the right to engage in the business provided they follow an established program. Typical examples of franchise arrangements are the Howard Johnson Restaurants, A & W Root Beer Stands, and Holiday Inn Motels.

Among the services franchisers provide to the franchise operators are the following: (1) location analysis and counsel, (2) store development aid, including lease negotiation, (3) store design and equipment purchasing, (4) initial employee and management training and continuing management counseling, (5) advertising and merchandising counseling and assistance, (6) standardized procedures and operations, (7) centralized purchasing with consequent savings, and (8) financial assistance in the establishment of the business.

Needless to say, the franchisee must provide a financial return of some kind to the franchisor. This may take the form of an initial fee ranging from $1,000 or less to over $100,000. In addition to the fee, or in place of it, the franchisee may pay royalties based upon a percentage of his sales. There are variations from one industry to another. In the case of soft ice cream, for example, the franchiser's principal source of profit is derived from sales of the franchiser's sales of merchandise to his franchisees—such as the mix used in preparing the cream, together with cones, napkins and other accessory items.

In a way, the franchisee is not his own boss because, in order to maintain the individuality of his system and to protect its good will, the franchiser usually exercises some degree of continuing control over the operations of his franchisees and requires them to meet stipulated standards of quality. The extent of such control varies. In some cases, franchisees are required to conduct every step of their operation in strict conformity with a manual furnished by the franchiser. In others, there is a very loose arrangement.

Depending on the form of arrangement, control, services offered, etc., the franchise can be an excellent way for a Negro to enter business. The U.S. Commerce Department has developed a Franchise Business Opportunities Program. This program identifies franchise firms which do not discriminate on the basis of race, color, religion or national origin in the sales, terms or conditions of their franchises. As of March 6, 1967, 249 franchisors had agreed to the terms of the Commerce Department's program. What is needed now is local encouragement and application of this potentially valuable program by civil rights leaders, poverty warriors, and municipal officials. It is another good example of how existing tools are lying unused because of a lack of focus and purpose in the area of Negro business and the ghetto economy.

  5. Negro businessmen must organize their own business associations until such time as they are freely admitted into the local chambers of commerce and other trade associations. Such associations will help give the Negro businessman a sense of identity and a channel of communication for success stories. In addition, they provide a vehicle for representing the individual Negro merchant's views and complaints on rent-gouging, licensing, traffic-routing, and zoning, as well as his interests in the anti-poverty program, city hall, and civil rights.

the black rural cooperative

RURAL ADVANCEMENT FUND

For the marginal tobacco farmers of Baxter County,[1] forming their own cooperative has become a source of hope and even a labor of love.

With tobacco as their one cash crop, they have been growing poorer every year. Tobacco acreage allotments set by the government have been steadily cut, reducing the amount they are entitled to plant and market. Smaller volume makes it harder for small farmers to compete with large, affluent planters who have the advantage in the machinery they can afford, the credit they can get, and, because they are white, their easy access to the technical advice of county agricultural experts.

Baxter's black tobacco farmers, who even find themselves discriminated against at the tobacco auction, know their one-crop operations cannot last. Mechanization has already begun on many of the large farms, and when the full transformation comes, the small farmers dependent on hand labor will be hit hard. Some have tried supplementary crops but have been unable to find local markets. Their produce rots on the truck.

Since 1967, when the local anti-poverty agency introduced

From *A Co-op is Born* (New York: Rural Advancement Fund of The National Sharecroppers Fund, Inc., 1968).
[1] Baxter is a fictitious name, adopted to protect the people of the actual county (eds.).

prospects for black business

them to the concept of the farm cooperative and the National Sharecroppers Fund agreed to provide technical assistance through its field staff, the idea of forming a co-op has more and more stirred their imagination. They see a way to relinquish their dependency on tobacco and gradually move into crops like vegetables that bring more money. They are encouraged that letters to food processors far afield have brought responses of interest in buying what they grow.

And so they are organizing to learn to grow new crops, to save on supplies and machinery by buying together, and to produce the substantial volume that will guarantee them bargaining power and markets in advance.

But they are also uniting to have some control for the first time over their lives. And to become, in the larger sense, a community. For most of them it is a new experience to take part in technical training, to stand up and express themselves at meetings, and to try to solve their problems as a self-governing group. Most of them have never before belonged to any such organization. This cooperative is *theirs*. They are running it. . . .

After a two-day NSF workshop in February 1968, committees and temporary officers for the nascent cooperative emerged. . . .

A legal committee began working on by-laws and an applications committee sat down with staff from the local anti-poverty agency, NSF, and the Agricultural Extension Service to draft a proposal for an OEO grant. What they produced together brought a $53,000 training grant to put the principal building blocks of the cooperative in place.

Because other of the South's new cooperative ventures have suffered from lack of technical preparation, Baxter is laying a firm foundation for its co-op in a feasibility study of the area and in extensive technical training for members. Poorly educated, self-taught in farming, and held back all their lives, they must overcome important gaps in knowledge.

Outside consultants who are experts in planning for cooperatives are studying land, soil, climate, resources, and markets to apprise the farmers of which crops offer the greatest chances for success.

Meanwhile, under . . . grant, ten farmers have been trained by NSF to serve as paid "outreach specialists," carrying the message of the co-op's potentials to people who have not yet been drawn in. It is in a sense a membership campaign, because

the black rural cooperative   249 the co-op will need the strength of numbers. But the outreach workers have been trained to be the couriers of other news as well. Few poor farmers take part in social security; many are uncertain about welfare regulations; most have been systematically excluded from government programs such as soil testing. In isolated farmhouses, the co-op's representatives are educating others of the poor in their rights.

When they have made their decisions about crops, those who have joined the co-op will begin five months of training under the tutelage of a young agricultural college graduate who has now been hired. The co-op's program has many facets. It will upgrade the skills of low-income farmers in both conventional and new, specialized areas of agriculture. It will teach them marketing and bookkeeping principles. It will explore other co-op ventures such as credit unions, buying clubs, forestry, and profit-making opportunities with small industry.

And it will investigate with government the possibility of manpower-training programs to free those who are tied to the poverty of sharecropping or seasonal farm labor. Hopefully, it will provide transitional skills for those who choose to leave Baxter for the cities.

The co-op's members will choose several of their number to grow demonstration plots of selected crops and to run a small experimental program in raising feeder pigs. They have been assured of Extension Service and Farmers Home Administration backing. Any profits from the demonstrations will be returned to the co-op's treasury. The farmers know that as their treasury grows, it will place in their hands the freedom to make their community prosper and develop.

Baxter's co-op is still in [the] process of being born. But by mid-1969 the farmers will have hired a business manager, obtained contracts from processors, and begun to grow their crops with their newly-acquired knowledge. . . .

. . . the idea of black people organizing for any purpose raised suspicion among much of Baxter's white population. The uneasiness increased when white Vista volunteers came to help the co-op and chose to live with Negro families. The increased activity and the disregard for tradition brought the sheriff poking about regularly to find out what "all those meetings were about" and who the "outsiders" were. . . .

Far from being intimidated, the small farmers are beginning to understand their co-op as a potent instrument for coping with their whole range of problems—economic, social, educational, and even political. An articulate though impoverished farmer whom NSF hired in the early months as a community aide has now organized a dozen families living in primitive homes into a self-help housing group. With NSF's new housing director as a guide and with low-interest FHA loans, they plan to begin building their houses soon, contributing their labor to one another.

Other farmers talk of the co-op's organizing a community center, of building the swimming pool black children now do not have, and of establishing their own tobacco warehouse. Some believe the cooperative must eventually buy land with its profits. They feel it is the only way to release the area's sharecroppers from bondage.

the ghetto

President Nixon's Council of Eco-
INTRODUCTION   nomic Advisers, in the following
                   excerpt, seems to have a more opti-
mistic view of black business prospects than was evident in the
preceding chapter. It should be noted that the Council is specifically referring to black *ghetto* business, and appraisal of its
discussion should therefore be made in the light of the criticisms
of ghetto business articulated in the introduction to, and selections contained in, Chapter 11. The Council also stresses the fact
that most jobs are still in "central cities," an emphasis different
from that in Chapter 10, Housing and Jobs, which focused upon
the *future growth* of jobs. It should be noted as well that any
definition of "central city" will ordinarily encompass an area
much larger than the ghetto and therefore sustains the relevance
of what was said in Chapter 10 about informational and commu-
tational barriers to employment stemming from the distance between ghetto residence and nonghetto job locations.

The ghetto may be seen as an "economy," a "quasi-economy,"
or a "colony." In any case, what these terms all endeavor to
highlight is the dependent and disadvantaged status of ghetto
dwellers in that setting. The status differential, as emphasized in
Part 1 of this book, is economic, social, educational, psychological, and political. Richard Cloward and Frances Piven, in
their innovative forecast, argue that big business no longer needs
white racism and the old ghetto, and that it is prepared to transform the ghetto into a subsidized, still spatially separated, market

for itself. But they assert that corporate giants themselves will intrude into ghetto society with material improvements in such a way as to supplant the role of municipal government at precisely that moment in history when blacks are on the threshold of wresting the control of city government from whites. Presumably this corporate strategy would also make unrealizable the goal of greater black neighborhood power through local governmental subunits, proposed to alleviate ghetto political disadvantages by The Advisory Commission on Intergovernmental Relations.

But Clarence Funnyé, reporting on a black workshop on economics, endorses those participants who would break away from all proposals premised upon the continuation of ghetto existence, whether improved, alleviated, or politically strengthened. The central task, Funnyé implies, is to achieve deghettoization—to break out of the prison: "Dig it, we ain't no more native to the ghetto than the white man is native to America."

private enterprise in
ghetto development

U.S. COUNCIL OF ECONOMIC ADVISERS

Reconstruction of the cities will require deeper involvement of private enterprise.

The major asset of private business is its efficiency in accomplishing specific tasks at minimum cost. The Federal Government has recognized the contribution business can make. For example, local housing authorities are now permitted to turn over much of the planning, site acquisition, and supervision of construction of public housing to private developers. This "Turnkey" policy has reduced costs and greatly cut the time required to produce public housing.

From The U.S. Council of Economic Advisers, *Economic Report of the President Together with The Annual Report of the Council of Economic Advisers* (Washington: Government Printing Office, January 1969), pp. 174–76 *passim*.

Without government inducements, profits are low in ghetto areas—a deterrent to private investment. Despite higher prices, retail business has difficulty thriving in the ghetto. Investing in new housing for low-income families—particularly in big cities—is usually a losing proposition. Indeed, the most profitable investment is often one that demolishes the homes of low-income families to make room for businesses and higher income families. Much of the blemished reputation of early urban renewal programs came from pursuing the most profitable development of renewal areas.

Many business leaders are willing to sacrifice some profits in order to invest in the ghetto, but they cannot be expected to shoulder the major part of a financial burden that is properly the responsibility of all society.

Participation by the private sector is also limited by the large scale normally needed to make a ghetto project economically viable. Costs are far lower and prospects for permanent improvement far greater if redevelopment of an entire neighborhood is undertaken in a relatively short period. Only the largest corporations are likely to be able to afford efficient renewal efforts.

Government aid to provide profit opportunities will be needed to induce significant participation by the private sector. The Federal Government can provide such aid by direct subsidies to firms willing to build under its program specifications. Alternatively, a tax credit or a deduction from taxable income could be given for a broad class of ghetto development expenditures.

Three considerations bear on the choice of the proper techniques for attracting private enterprise into ghetto reconstruction.

First, the efficiency of Federal assistance is reduced if subsidies are paid for activities that would have been undertaken anyway. Tax incentives automatically apply to all investment in the subsidized category. Even in the most depressed urban areas, some investments are still being made without subsidies.

Second, a dollar of direct expenditure and a dollar of tax incentive have identical effects upon the budget, requiring either a reduction in other Federal programs or an increase in taxes. One technique adds to Federal expenditures; the other lowers Federal tax receipts.

Finally, tax incentives are not effective for encouraging indigenous businesses. Large corporations, earning profits in other

the ghetto

operations, benefit from tax incentives, but firms operating only in the ghetto—where profits are low—receive less benefit. New firms often receive no benefits from tax incentives since fledgling enterprises typically earn low profits. Since support of new, ghetto-owned businesses is a particularly promising vehicle for promoting ghetto development, a more direct form of assistance for these firms is necessary. Such firms need loans and management assistance as well as the subsidies that would be provided to established businesses through tax incentives.

The Federal Government has moved to assist indigenous businesses. Projects in Model Cities areas must, where possible, be constructed by labor and businesses from the "model neighborhood." The Small Business Administration, through federally guaranteed loans and technical assistance, aided 2,300 minority-owned businesses in fiscal 1968. It plans to raise this number to 6,500 new firms in fiscal 1969 and 14,000 in fiscal 1970.

The Federal Government can also assist in establishing other social institutions. Community Action Agencies, supported by the Office of Economic Opportunity, provide a fulcrum for involving the residents of low-income areas in the revitalization of their neighborhoods. These agencies also provide a single, knowledgeable source of information on the programs available to assist the poor, as well as supplying many of these services themselves. . . .

Most jobs are in the central cities. Even in sectors such as manufacturing, wholesale and retail trade, nonprofessional business services, entertainment, and government, with relatively more jobs in lower skill occupations, the ratio of employment to population is over 40 percent higher in the cities than their suburbs. Employment in the city is also less physically dispersed than in the suburbs, and public transportation is more readily available.

For the foreseeable future, most ghetto residents will continue to have a greater chance of finding a job in the central city. Job vacancies created by normal attrition are far more numerous than those created by entirely new positions, and consequently the number of job openings is greater in the city with its much larger total employment. . . .

corporate imperialism
for the poor

RICHARD A. CLOWARD / FRANCES F. PIVEN

The "urban crisis" has clearly become a full-blown political crisis. Just as clearly, national elites are responding by fashioning the outlines of a plan to forestall further violence. The plan features public subsidies to induce private enterprise to redevelop the ghetto—at both high profit and low risk. . . .

The new urban program is being pressed by an alliance of political and corporate leaders, with representatives of labor and traditional civil rights organizations bringing up the rear. . . . The Urban Coalition which met recently in Washington brought together 800 national political leaders, mayors, officials from labor and civil rights and such stalwarts of corporate enterprise as Andrew Heiskell, chairman of Time Incorporated; Henry Ford II, chairman of the Ford Motor Company; David Rockefeller, president of the Chase Manhattan Bank, and Irwin Miller, chairman of Cummins Engine Company.

The urban alliance could have substantial economic impact. Public subsidies for the ghetto are now pitifully small. By using public funds to guarantee profit, however, huge private investments can be turned toward the ghetto. . . .

. . . How do we account for the "statesmanlike" responses of elites at a time when the wider public seems goaded to new expressions of racism?

The answer is not difficult to find. First, corporate enterprise no longer has major stakes in domestic racism. Historically, racism helped to perpetuate a caste system that produced a surplus of cheap black labor. That surplus was used against white workers, chiefly to undermine wage levels; more directly, blacks were hired as scabs and goons to impede efforts by whites to unionize. The resulting antagonism between blacks and whites was one aspect of a history of pervasive conflict among ethnic groups in America, leading them to turn upon one another rather than against oppressive classes, thus accounting in good measure for the absence of a cohesive working class. However, antago-

From Richard A. Cloward and Frances F. Piven, "Corporate Imperialism for the Poor," *The Nation*, Vol. **205**, No. 12 (October 16, 1967), 365–67 *passim*.

the ghetto

nism has been most acute between poor blacks and whites. Nor has that conflict subsided: it now extends beyond the labor market, erupting in bitter struggles to control neighborhoods, schools and city government.

With automation and the corporate management of markets, low-skilled and low-paid labor has become a relatively unimportant factor in the profits of much large-scale urban enterprise. Consequently, racism is no longer needed to depress wages and inhibit unionization. The racist attitudes of the working and lower-middle classes persist, but these attitudes, and the ghettos they help to produce have become anomalies—vestiges of an earlier era of industrial organization.

Indeed, racism is beginning to exact some costs from corporate enterprise. Violence in the cities disrupts the civic stability on which huge, bureaucratized enterprises depend. Note, for example, that department store owners are prominent in the spate of local communities and commissions formed in the wake of the riots. Nor is it any accident that insurance companies, faced with huge losses in property damage, are at the forefront in proffering investment funds for redevelopment of charred ghettos.

Now, too, there is the promise of profit to be made in removing poverty. Redevelopment promises to be a huge business, running into billions of dollars—provided that public funds and public powers are employed to eliminate risk and guarantee profit. Far-seeing corporations like Litton Industries and U.S. Gypsum have been alert to these possibilities for some time, undertaking research and demonstration projects (often put forward as "civic" activities) to explore cost-saving materials and new building techniques so as to create a product within reach of the ghetto market. Industry's technical explorations have not accomplished much to reduce costs, but that doesn't matter: public subsidies will bridge the gap.

For their part, politicians are in trouble, and the alliance is a way out. Urban disorder has made them vulnerable; they must act to end it or face defeat at the polls. However, they are not free to indulge the outraged sentiments of their working- and middle-class constituents, for repression would alienate blacks all the more and might lead to worse violence. Blacks are also becoming a major electoral force in the cities, a fact which cannot be ignored much longer. Nevertheless, white racism prevents political leaders from securing legislative approval for programs to pacify the ghetto. The corporate alliance solves this dilemma: relatively small amounts of public money can be used to stimulate relatively large private investments. . . .

The new program, in brief, is impelled by the threat of disruption and the promise of profit. It will work to curb violence, and to secure gains for political and corporate leaders alike. The ghetto is also likely to be somewhat better off economically for being absorbed into corporate spheres.

. . . The economy of the ghetto is now run by relatively small entrepreneurs who are somewhat vulnerable to local pressure, such as consumer boycotts and rent strikes. The new managers of the ghetto will be huge quasi-public development corporations (like the New York Port Authority) insulated from effective political control and endowed with powers to issue bonds, condemn property and form webs of relations with private investment companies, large-scale contractors and management companies. Industrial firms will spin off new subsidiaries to exploit opportunities for subsidized profit in employing ghetto people. And predominantly white unions will absorb these workers, thus neutralizing whatever potential that separate Negro unions might have had as an instrument of ghetto power. The ghetto has nothing much to offer which corporate enterprise needs—skilled labor, entrepeneurial skills or raw materials. It is even too poor on its own to attract corporate products on any large scale. Governments will thus convert the ghetto to a subsidized market, and life conditions will be improved; but no Negro-controlled economic institutions are likely to emerge, nor will the ghetto have the resources to influence the operations of outside corporate enterprise.

The greatest danger to blacks is that the new corporate role will help to erode the power of municipal government, and this at a time when the black is about to obtain control of the city. . . .

Impending changes in the relations of federal and local government will mesh well with corporate intervention, further weakening the traditional powers of city government. The federal government is beginning to use the vast resources of its grants-in-aid programs to create metropolitan-wide administrative agencies to cope with pollution, blight and other urban problems. As agents of federal power, the metro bureaucracies will supersede local government as channels for federal money. Since these

the ghetto

new administrative complexes will be largely removed from popular control, the blacks of the ghettos—even as they reach electoral majorities in the cities—cannot hope to influence them greatly. But the metro bureaucracies—manned by an emerging class of planners and technicians—will find congenial counterparts in the corporate world. In other words, just as black majorities come to power in the city, much of that power will be usurped by an alliance of national corporations and political leaders, as well as by federal-metropolitan bureaucracies.

There is not likely to be much opposition to these developments, however. Churchmen and union leaders have already given their blessing. Traditional civil rights leaders have special reason to be pleased, for their symbolic hegemony over the ghetto has been undermined. . . . It was not without reason that traditional civil rights leaders joined with the President and leaders of the insurance business to announce the billion-dollar pledge of corporate funds to the ghetto.

It is possible to imagine that militant leaders in the ghetto will resist the intrusion of corporate giants, but it is much easier to see how their resistance will be overcome. The new corporate imperialism will be mediated through a host of intervening subsidiaries and management structures, many located in the ghetto itself. Advocates of "participatory democracy," "decentralization" and "black control of black affairs" will find these themes turned against them as they are invited to endorse and participate in the new corporate subsidiaries. Even now business leaders in some cities are cultivating black activists, often over the protestations of local politicians befuddled by the curious twist in alignments.

If grants-in-aid were to be funneled through city governments, as in the past, and not through quasi-public and private corporate structures, black municipal leaders could convert these funds into the jobs, services and facilities required not only to improve economic conditions but to consolidate a black electorate as well. Under such circumstances, local government would serve blacks as it has served other groups by providing a base for power in state and national affairs. Once absorbed in local corporate subsidiaries, however, blacks will become instruments of national corporate power. Their economic lot will be improved somewhat, to be sure, but their long-term economic prospects depend on their potential political power, and that will be diminished.

neighborhood power

ADVISORY COMMISSION ON
INTERGOVERNMENTAL RELATIONS

As the nation has debated the "crisis in the cities," a growing body of opinion has pointed to the need for a greater "involvement" of the neighborhood within the large city. The complaint is frequently voiced that the distance between the neighborhood and the city hall or the county building has lengthened continually until the distance is figuratively one of light-years rather than blocks or miles.

The "maximum feasible participation of the poor" or the establishment of "neighborhood centers" may not be a panacea for all the social ills of our large, impersonal cities, but they can be constructively useful under certain circumstances. The Commission consistently has favored maximum flexibility in State legislation governing the organization, structure and financing of local government. . . .

Much can be said for the need to stimulate individual neighborhood improvement and self-improvement. City governments should be authorized—*not required*—to create neighborhood subunits of government with election of the local leadership and limited powers of taxation such as a fractional millage on the property tax to be collected by the city or county as a part of the property tax bill and returned to the neighborhood for use as its governing body determines. Per capita taxation or periodic neighborhood association "dues" might be authorized.

The enabling State legislation should make it clear that such subunits as may be created by the city or county *may be dissolved by them at will.* The purpose here is to permit the creation of *subunits of existing local governments—not the creation of new local units.* It is not our intention to suggest a further fragmentation in local government structure in metropolitan areas but rather to make it possible for existing large units of local government to harness, through the neighborhood subgovernment process, some of the resources and aspirations of its inner communities. The Commission is aware that this proposal

From The Advisory Commission on Intergovernmental Relations, *Fiscal Balance in the American Federal System: Metropolitan Fiscal Disparities,* Vol. 2 (Washington: Government Printing Office, October 1967), p. 17.

the ghetto

will not draw high marks from purists in the fields of political science or public finance. However, in this time of crisis, change and challenge in our congested urban areas, political leadership at the State and local levels should not shrink from experimentation but be ever ready to seek more effective institutional arrangements to encourage the active participation of citizens in the affairs of their neighborhood and their local units of government.

"we don't all have to be
in the ghetto
just to be brothers"

CLARENCE FUNNYÉ

The Workshop on Economics—Black Self Help, which was to deal with the "formation of black economic concepts and developing an independent black economic system in which the Black Nation can survive collectively," was led by Sonny Carson of Brooklyn CORE who admitted "I don't know nothing about economics" and a sociology student from the University of Chicago who blew hard about East African history while rejecting any suggestion of irrelevance of Tanzania land and mineral wealth to the plight of urban black Americans, who have neither land nor wealth.

Elsie Y. Cross presented a competent paper on cooperatives which, like other papers, was received tolerantly but quickly pushed aside to discuss "slave debt" owed by the Federal Government. Reginald Jones of Brooklyn, whom Carson described as one of the brightest men on the scene, noted that 10 acres and a mule, promised each free slave family and never delivered by the Federal Government, was at 4 per cent interest now worth over a quarter of a million dollars and the blacks could use this

From Clarence Funnyé, *Black Power and Deghettoization: A Retreat to Reality* (New York: The National Committee Against Discrimination in Housing, Inc., 1969).

money to develop their own community. Jones also suggested that "can-shaking" (appealing to ghetto dwellers to put some coins in a can) could yield millions of dollars which could be used to bring industry into black communities which could then become self-sufficient. Traditional cheer-rally rhetoric—hardly ever taken seriously.

Not all of the audience applauded. Several actually challenged Carson's qualifications to lead the discussion. Carson was honest —he didn't expect to have to lead the number one workshop. Cyril Tyson of New York was supposed to be chairman. But he never showed up.

Sonny was only doing what he could to pinch hit, but the challenges pressed on. . . .

One delegate shouted that the assembly was continuing to bullshit, that people didn't come hundreds of miles to hear jive-time clichés about ghetto gilding and economic development of ghettos while ghetto income continues down in both absolute and relative terms—blacks are locked into central cities while industries and jobs move out—and new industrial development accelerates in all-white suburbs.

A brother from Detroit angrily asked: "How in hell we're gonna talk about economic development when the bulk of black people are being separated by training or distance from jobs which have formed the base economy of black people? We going to just feed on each other?"

A cute sister chimed, "Yeah how? Driving into here we saw dozens of factories outside the city . . . no brothers out there making any that bread . . . we can't all live on the industry that can be built in ghettos."

The panel leaders were reeling now. They did not expect to talk about regional or even citywide considerations. Previous black power rhetoric had only programmed them for "bringing industry into our own community." Alfred Rhodes shot back that those were "white men's factories out there in the suburbs"—and all hell broke loose.

"What the hell you mean white men's factories?" a brother from Chicago shouted. "When your government takes from tax money 40 million bucks and gives it to some 'private' airplane company to build some goddam SST plane, baby that factory is yours no matter where he builds it—west hell or an all-white suburb—and you better start getting your stuff together and figure out some way to get out there and get some that action."

Carson called for order, but the assembly chorused "let's hear the brother." The brother paused and pressed on. "We been sold a lot a junk about bringing industry into our own communities. . . . Check it out. See how much land a modern factory takes up, how much vacant land is there in 'our communities'? Man, just to build a tot lot we have to tear down three houses and move 30 families . . . and the already overcrowded ghetto—what you call 'our community'—gets even more crowded. It's land-locked by white suburbs, not getting bigger, just getting higher, and babies keep being born and needing more space and where they gonna live? Where will their apartment buildings be? Where we gonna put those damn factories you gonna bring in?

"While some of you untogether niggers fighting each other about control of a lousy $400,000 poverty program, another white factory gets $4 billion in government funds to build a space ship or some such stuff—and they set up in the wide open country, build houses for whites, and you don't even notice. I say we got to get our eye back on the ball. Sure, control your own communities—but don't just stop there. You're not just citizens of the ghetto. Watch what the man is doing in economic, national and regional affairs. Watch where the subsidies are going for construction of bridges, highways, regional sewer plants, waterworks, missile test centers, anything and everything.

"Don't buy this bull that just because you might want some clean air and green grass for your kids that makes you some kind of imitation white man. Dig it, we ain't no more native to the ghetto than the white man is native to America. Fact is, if it weren't for him, we'd be back in Africa where we'd have more fresh air, open space and green grass than anyone in the world."

(Cheers and applause.)

Now the brother was slowing down—pacing himself for effect —he had the audience—now thoughts were being planted. "All I say is we should check out the action wherever it is. We don't all have to be in the ghetto just to be brothers. Calling a prison a community don't make it so."

This was it, out in the open on the floor: the long smoldering ideological conflict between people interested in "how now?" Between cheer-rally types whose forte is the anti-white or pro-black "blow hard," who see the future of black communities limited to "control" of Model Cities or anti-poverty boards and the government funds coming into the community—between these people and those who see both anti-poverty and Model Cities as diversionary non-solutions intended to absorb community energy and obscure the fact that the traditional urban ghetto ("our community") is fast becoming the western white man's instant concentration camp, and who also see community survival directly related to the number of brothers who can escape the ghetto and that a community of culture and spirit does not depend on geographical confines—especially if those confines facilitate physical destruction.

The brother had brought it out into the open—that sub-surface struggle which had been straining to get a full hearing. For three years now—since the decline of the traditional civil rights phase —the latter forces had been in partial retreat, while ghetto builders sneeringly asked "what's so good about being next to a white man?" (integration) Now the answer is, "nothing—except being able to watch that mother. . . ."

A planner from Brooklyn noted that "Harlem is already efficiently encircled and could be completely isolated and closed off in 20 or 30 minutes by a single regiment," but that if half of the present residents—say 200,000—lived strategically all over the city, such an obvious capture would be less tempting to white planners and blacks could still "control Harlem."

Already white planners are developing black new town schemes to *re-confine* the brothers who have escaped to the suburbs. An article appearing in the August 1968 issue of *Progressive Architecture* urges that a black new town be built on 6,000 acres of Fort Dix land in New Jersey. The fort would serve a double purpose, providing training and employment for black workers and instant urban stability.

Julius Brown, a Los Angeles economist, said the separatist brothers were buying a virgin pig in a blanket—that the few dozen non-thinking cliché peddlers were leading some unsuspecting people down a garden path. It's no accident that the articles most loudly espousing total black ghettoization have been in white publications including the liberal *New Republic*. The intellectual basis for Floyd McKissick's and Roy Innis's separatist positions were said to have been formed by Fran Piven and Dick

Cloward, white sociologists from Columbia University's School of Social Work [see pages 256–59].

The separatist brothers were taken aback by vigorous attack of brothers who urged blacks to "become city dwellers as opposed to ghetto dwellers." The new breed brothers had made a good point about turning one's back on the billions of dollars given suburban plants for development of [the] SST while squabbling over Model Cities peanuts. Previously such thoughts would have been put down by anti-white clichés ("the brother just wants to rub shoulders with whitey") but the separatists had done no homework and slogans were being battered down in the face of reality.

13 income maintenance

INTRODUCTION

Accumulating evidence flatly contradicts the strongly held fear of majority whites that, given a choice, people—especially black people—prefer public welfare payments to earning their own livings. The Office of Economic Opportunity has reported that, in its experiments over three years with poor people receiving income supports, there has been no significant decline in *earned* income. Indeed, despite any work requirement and despite the failure to provide day-care programs for working mothers with children, the recipients of such supports often use the opportunity not to stop work, but to seek out even more productive, higher-paying jobs. This broader research supports Michael T. Boskin's findings in the Oakland ghetto which follow. Furthermore, it lends statistical support to proposed programs of income floors as advocated by The President's Commission on Income Maintenance in the first selection and reported by Dr. Sherwood O. Berg.

The need for careful planning in coverage and administration of any such programs is, however, quite evident in the last selection from *Ramparts*. A failure to consider local institutions and attitudes, as in the American South or elsewhere, would quickly render any such program ineffective, if not perverse, in its impact.

In no sense can income floors substitute, in the case of the able, for a meaningful opportunity to participate fully in the economy. Meanwhile, for a large proportion of welfare recipients who are innocent victims of circumstance, income floors may well be preferable to the current welfare morass.

cash grants for the poor

SHERWOOD O. BERG

The President's Commission on Income Maintenance Programs . . . made recommendations for modification in our present welfare system and for certain types of income supplement designed to aid the poor in America. The report was compiled after some 22 months of hearings, study, and research. . . .

. . . Taking the U.S. Government's figure of $3,553 for a nonrural family of four as the poverty line, 25.4 million Americans were still caught in poverty in 1968.

Of those who are below the poverty line, we find that:

—one-half of all poor families live in the South.
—two-thirds of all poor families are white.
—one-fifth of the poor are over 65 years of age.
—two-fifths are children under 18.
—over one-third of the poor live in families in which the family head worked throughout the year.

In the latter case, among the so-called "working poor" the average gap between the family income and the poverty line exceeded $1,000. . . .

An examination of the poor people in this country clearly demonstrates that the overwhelming majority are clearly the innocent victims of circumstances. In 1966, it was estimated that after subtracting the children, the aged, the disabled, the women heads of households, and those who worked all or part of the

From Sherwood O. Berg, "Conclusions of the President's Commission on Income Maintenance," talk at The 1970 National Agricultural Outlook Conference, Washington, D.C., February 19, 1970, pp. 1–7 *passim* (multilithed).

year, only about 176,000 presumably able-bodied male heads of households did not work. In any case, the vast majority of poor people are very largely the helpless victims of circumstances. The combination of age, racial discrimination, disability, prior responsibility for the care of small children, underemployment and full employment at low wages, and involuntary unemployment represent the reasons why all but the smallest percentage of poor people have not been able to do anything about their own situation. . . .

The Commission concluded that there must be a larger role for cash grants in fighting poverty than we as a nation have acknowledged in the past.

The main recommendation of the Commission was for the creation of a "universal income supplement," financed and administered by the Federal Government. Direct payments would be based on income needs to all members of the population. By making payments to all in need, regardless of where they live or in what type of family they live, the pressure presently placed, for example, on the working father with a low income to desert in order to make his family eligible for AFDC would be gone. The payments would vary by family size and would provide a base income for any needy family or individual.

The Commission suggested a basic grant of $750 per adult and $450 per child to families with no other income, which would amount to a total of $2,400 for a family of four with two adults and two children.

The basic grant is combined with a provision for families to retain a portion of their earned income as an incentive to become or remain a part of the labor force. The Commission proposed specifically that the family's grant be reduced by only 50 cents for each dollar earned up to the break-even point (the point at which the family no longer receives the universal income supplement because the amount deducted from the grant equals the grant itself). Being able to keep half of one's earnings above the basic grant would be a considerable incentive to seek a job or to remain in one's present employment. Every dollar earned on the job would always mean more income. Everybody who quit work would automatically receive less income. . . .

The Commission's proposal does not include a work requirement, nor would it, by any stretch of the imagination, be a guarantee of income equality for all. But it would be a step in the direction that everyone would have some income to become a part of the community.

Since an income of $2,400 for a family of four is still far below the poverty line, the Commission has not chosen this level of income supplement because of its adequacy. It was chosen, in part, because it is a practical program that can be implemented in the near future. Furthermore, there is little doubt that even this relatively low level of income supplement will make a vast difference in the living conditions of the poor. The impact of such a program on the financial position of a family of four, including the amount of supplement and the total income by level of other income, can be readily demonstrated (Table 13-1).

Table 13-1

Total Income Situation: $2,400 Basic Income Supplement
with 50 Percent Retention Rate on Other Income,
Family of Four

Other Income	Income Supplement	Total Income
$ 0	$2,400	$2,400
500	2,150	2,650
1,000	1,900	2,900
1,500	1,650	3,150
2,000	1,400	3,400
3,000	900	3,900
4,000	400	4,400
5,000	0	5,000

The Commission also recommended that Federal participation in existing public assistance programs be terminated. One objective is to replace the existing *categorical* public assistance system with a *universal* Federal program. . . .

what's the price tag?

The recommended plan would increase net Federal budget costs by an estimated $7 billion in 1971. If states which now make assistance payments above the recommended initial level of the Federal programs were to make supplementary payments to present recipients up to their current standards, state and local

cash grants for the poor   269 spending would be reduced by one billion dollars. Thus, the estimated net added cost of the recommended program to all levels of government would be $6 billion in 1971.

The income transfers would mean an increase in the disposable income of the 10.5 million households of 36.8 million persons under the plan. $5 billion of the increased income would be received by the estimated 8 million households poor prior to receiving payments, and the remainder by households a little above the poverty line. Over one million households would be removed from poverty, while all of the poor would have significantly higher incomes. Over half of the increased income would be received by households at present not receiving public income transfers.

These costs are not insubstantial. However, the costs of not acting should also be considered. The child who grows into a mentally retarded adult because of protein deficiency is a cost, whether he is institutionalized, or whether he is giving the society much less than he would otherwise be able, or whether we count the human cost of just being an inferior human being.

We . . . have a trillion dollar economy. Can it be that we cannot afford less than one percent of this for the truly deserving in our society? . . .

. . . the level of this universal program, which equitably and simply transfers cash income to the poor, can be raised in the future. With such a basis we shall have gone far towards solving the critical problem of poverty in this nation.

incentives and
guaranteed income

MICHAEL J. BOSKIN

The negative income tax is a device designed to use the individual income tax system as a vehicle for closing a portion of the

From Michael J. Boskin, "The Negative Income Tax and the Supply of Work Effort," *The National Tax Journal*, Vol. **XX**, No. 4 (December 1967), 353–66 *passim*.

poverty gap, i.e. the differential between the actual income of the poor and poverty-line income. . . .

It is apparent that the tax rate used is the crucial determinant of the proportion of the poverty gap that the negative income tax will close. Why not use a 100 per cent rate and close the entire gap? It seems reasonable to assume that at extremely high rates, the poor might be induced to reduce the supply of work effort they are willing to offer at given wage rates. . . . Give them a negative income tax allowance, the argument goes, and they will stop working and "live off public funds." . . .

The purpose of this paper is to begin to evaluate the hypothesis that the adoption of a negative income tax as an anti-poverty measure would lead to a substantial reduction in the amount of work effort supplied by the poor at given wage rates. . . .

To determine if a negative income tax might cause some poor to retire earlier than planned, we asked,

Have you had any opportunities for paid employment since you retired?

Looking towards the future, do you plan to keep on working as long as your health permits, or retire at a certain age, or haven't you thought about it much? (asked only of those who appeared to be over 45)

The retired (who numbered only six) to a man did not have any opportunities for paid employment since they had ceased working. As for the retirement plans of the relatively elderly working poor, most thought that they would work as long as their health permitted, or had not given the matter much thought; very few thought that they would retire at a certain age. When asked if they were covered by social security, most did not know!

. . . To more directly determine the extent of the potential work disincentive, a series of direct and indirect questions was asked to determine the extent of indebtedness among the poor, how satisfied they are with their present stock of consumer durables and savings, what they would be likely to do with an added income, and whether they thought they might decrease their work effort if given an added income. Among the questions asked were:

Do you own a television or a car?

Did you pay cash or make payments?

Suppose a friend or relative left you a gift or inheritance of $500, what would you most likely do with it?

Suppose you received an additional $500 per year, what would you most likely do with this added income?

Do you think you might work less because of this added income?

If a friend or neighbor came to you for advice and asked you what you thought would be a safe savings cushion set aside for emergencies, what would you tell him?

What about your own savings goals, are you satisfied with the amount you have saved?

About 29 per cent of the interviewees owned a television and 24 per cent owned a car. Of those who would say, two-thirds purchased the car on payments; making payments will commit the worker to a continued stream of income, and would temper the disincentive tendencies of the negative tax. As for the most likely thing to do with $500, anything and everything was mentioned. Only 14 per cent mentioned the possibility of saving all or part of the gift; the most frequently mentioned items fell into two broad categories: consumer durables such as radios, televisions, hi-fis, and occasionally even cars, on the one hand, and nondurables such as food, clothing, medicine, etc., on the other. Also frequently mentioned was the payment of debt (19 per cent); for those in debt, we can again expect minimal disincentive effects. As expected, answers to the safe savings cushion covered a remarkable range, from $100 or $200 to the ambiguous "as much as you can." The data was difficult to meaningfully aggregate; perhaps $400 to $500 was the median. The majority were not satisfied with the amount they had saved, but judging from the low response to the $500 questions, were not prepared to sacrifice consumer goods in favor of saving. On the $500 per year question, three persons brought up the possibility of working less (although none had on the $500 gift question). This forms what I call the strong disincentive group. When directly asked if they thought that they *might* work less, only four more responded in the affirmative, forming the middle disincentive group; 66 per cent flatly declared that they would not; 18 per cent were undecided. To make sure that we included all those who might be subject to a disincentive, the undecided group was winnowed on the basis of their answers to other questions,

Table 13-2
Disincentive Group—Hypothetical

Type Disincentive	Per Cent
Strong (3/87)	3 + %
Middle (4/87)	5
Weak (3/87)	3 +
Strong + Middle (7/87)	8
Strong + Middle + Weak (10/87)	12

and the weak disincentive group of three more persons was added. The results are summarized in Table 13-2. It should be noted that the results are a practicable upper limit; first, we have *not* winnowed the strong and middle groups (for example, to exclude those above poverty incomes) and second, the question was carefully worded to obtain a yes response from those who thought only that they *might* be subject to a work disincentive, not just from those who thought that they *would* be subject to one. . . . Median income among the poor is approximately $1,900. A negative income tax at a 50 per cent rate would give the median poor person $550; $500 was selected because of the rounded nature of the figure. We thus have a rough measure of a practicable upper limit to the percentage of the poor subject to a work disincentive (at least with a marginal rate of 50 per cent) based on their own evaluation of how they would react in a hypothetical situation. We know that about 12 per cent of our sample might be subject to a work disincentive; what we really want to know is the amount by which total work effort will decrease. We will again adopt the technique of figuring a practicable upper limit. We reasoned above that the practicable upper limit to the decrease in work effort for an individual would be a decrease just sufficient to equate pre-tax and post-tax income. A worker behaving in this manner will have a decrease in work effort function that is a function of the tax rate t and his pre-tax income. Depending on the tax rate, up to a certain limit the worker can decrease his work effort by 100 per cent; with a 50 per cent tax and a $3,000 poverty line, any worker earning $1,500 or less can stop work entirely and receive the same, or more, income. Above $1,500 (or in general, tX), the possible decrease declines rapidly, reaching two-thirds at $1,800, one-half at $2,000, and one-fourth at $2,400. Remember these are unlikely practicable upper limits. Assuming an average decrease in work effort of two-thirds, which we believe overstates the decrease by well over 100 per cent, we present the results in their most highly reformed manner in Table 13-3. Again, the estimates are arrived at by taking the upper limit of those who believe that they *might* be subject to a disincentive and assuming that every single one of them reduces his work by the maximum practicable amount. Even with these upper limits, our estimate of the decrease in work effort is only 8 per cent!

Table 13-3
Total Decrease in Work Effort

Type Disincentive	Per Cent	At	Decrease
Strong	3	2/3	2%
Middle	5	2/3	3.3
Weak	3	2/3	2
Strong + Middle	8	2/3	5.3
Strong + Middle + Weak	12	2/3	8

. . . We have much qualitative evidence to support the order of magnitude of our quantitative estimate. The poor are not satisfied with their levels of consumption or saving, many are in debt, some have institutional rigidities surrounding their job, few have opportunities to obtain additional work and perhaps most importantly their wives do not want them at home. At least a dozen times during interviews with wives, they claimed that they did not want their husband to receive welfare, that it was socially degrading to have the neighbors see him around the house during the day, and that they only wanted him to work fulltime all the time. . . .

In conclusion, we state only that the negative income tax is an attractive device for closing the poverty gap substantially and quickly, and that, although additional research is needed among other poor groups, it appears feasible from the disincentive standpoint. Perhaps more important, when the poor were asked,

Would you rather see the government provide free services such as housing, education, etc., or spend the same

income maintenance

amount of money by giving it directly to poor people to
spend as they wish?

the respondents voted two-to-one in favor of the negative income
tax.

the nixon program and
the southern rural poor

LINDA HUNT / GARY HUNT / NANCY SCHEPER

To those who know the South, . . . Nixon's [income main-
tenance] plan is far from a panacea. Like the programs which pre-
ceded it, the family assistance plan side-steps all of the most
troublesome obstacles to the elimination of poverty in the South.
First, the wholesale migration of young blacks from the rural
South has left behind hundreds of thousands of elderly men and
women who live together or alone without children. These
people constitute one of the most depressing collective tragedies
of the region, but because they are not eligible to receive "family
assistance" under Nixon's welfare system, they will be forced to
rely on the unfair and inadequate food programs already in existence.

But even for those who are eligible to receive the family assistance benefits, Nixon's new program is a dismal disappoint-
ment. It cannot even guarantee, for example, that Southern
blacks will ever see their family assistance checks. Black farmers
in the South live within a credit economy which fosters a chain
of dependency upon white landowners and local shopkeepers.
Despite their long hours of hard work, the black farmer and his
family invariably end each farm year even more in debt than before. A 1967 survey by the Southern Rural Research Project
(SRRP) of 242 heads of black farm households revealed that

while half of the families worked an average of nine to ten hours a day on their farms (nearly 20 per cent of them worked as much as 11 to 15 hours), two-thirds of these same families ended the 1967 farm year deeply in debt.

In order to make it through the winter the black tenant is dependent upon the high-interest loans and credit which he can get from his landlord or local merchant (often the same man). And again each spring at planting time he finds himself in the position of borrowing against the value of his future crops as well as against the credit of any government checks coming his way (cotton subsidy and diversion checks or welfare payments). Often he signs these checks over to his creditors without seeing them or otherwise verifying their exact amount. Nearly 40 per cent of those black farmers interviewed had signed a paper handing their government checks over to some other person—most frequently their landlord or another local creditor.

Bookkeeping between tenant and landlord and between farmer and the general store is purposely kept loose and informal. The tenant can get as much credit as he needs, but he is neither given access to the "books" nor handed receipts or statements of his real financial standing with his creditor. Always in debt, he can never find out exactly how much he owes. This age-old feudal relationship works to the decided advantage of the landowner, who can consequently cash in on any federal checks coming from new programs designed to alleviate the poverty of tenant farmers. Although there is an SRRP lawsuit before the Supreme Court challenging the right of landlords to take federal checks from tenant farmers in payment for past debts, there is as yet absolutely no legal apparatus to prevent this same practice from swallowing up the checks received under Nixon's new welfare scheme.

Under the surplus commodity and food stamp programs there was at least a minimum built-in safeguard for hungry blacks. No white landlord or shopkeeper would or could demand that the farmer "sign over" his free food "doles" or his food stamps. . . .

But the most disastrous part of Nixon's plan is what he presents as the core of the program. In his words: ". . . it is time for a new federalism in which power, funds and responsibility will flow from Washington to the states and to the people." More precisely, this "new federalism" would in effect be a gift of unfettered control to local white racists. What it would mean for

income maintenance

Southern black farmers is less federal surveillance of increased funds and power in the hands of the same Southern-born and Southern-bred white authorities who have always subverted federal funds away from the blacks and into the pockets of the white and wealthy power structure.

Through an extensive study of the relationship between black farmers and the farm programs of the U.S. Department of Agriculture (USDA), SRRP field workers learned exactly what does happen to federal programs that are locally controlled in the South. The most powerful discriminatory weapon of federally-employed county administrators is their ability to withhold information about the various farm programs—a weapon which they employ to the hilt. The SRRP found for example that 97 per cent of all black farmers interviewed had *never* received any help or advice from any of the powerful Agricultural Stabilization and Conservation Service (ASCS) community committees, and that 95 per cent had never received any help from the ASCS county committees. The local offices of these two committees—which virtually control the economy of Southern cotton farming—are invariably run by whites, even in such counties as Wilcox, Alabama, where 80 per cent of the population is black. A 1965 report by the U.S. Commission on Civil Rights states that at the time the study was taken there were no Negroes employed in professional, clerical, or technical positions in the ASCS in the entire South. As of 1968 there was *one* black person thus employed.

The same SRRP survey revealed that 95 per cent of the black farmers interviewed had never received any help or advice from any member of the Farmers Home Administration (FHA) County Committee, the agency which approves all federal farm loans in each county. The Civil Rights Commission report showed that in all the 1500 county offices of the FHA, as well as in all the national and state offices, only about 40 Negroes were employed as professionals. Clearly, it is the intention of the local white administrators of this essential program to reserve loans insofar as possible for whites.

Most black farmers do not know how to defend themselves against the conspiracies of these white-controlled committees, for they are rarely aware of the benefits available to small farmers under the various farm programs—if they happen to know of their existence at all. Most rural blacks in the deep South, for example, had never heard of federal subsidies or price support checks until they were informed of them by civil rights workers in the early 1960s—although these checks had been rightfully theirs since the 1930's. Private "arrangements" between county agents and white landlords directed the federal checks belonging to black tenants into the pockets of their landlords. . . .

Like the farm programs in the South, federal welfare assistance, too, had been undermined by county agents acting as representatives of the local white "establishment." These officials have worked to exclude as many Southern blacks as possible from the benefits of the various welfare programs—a policy which has resulted in the massive exodus of jobless, impoverished blacks from the rural South. These same federally-employed county agents have fought to keep the USDA commodity distribution and food stamp programs out of many of the poorest counties in the South. Such officials automatically oppose any program that might give black people "something for nothing."

It is difficult to imagine that local administrators will assume the burden of informing the illiterate black farmers of the South about the new family assistance program. . . .

Nixon has called for a "gesture of faith in America's states and localities." Behind that gesture is a vote of confidence for the same local Southern agents who have refused to accept food stamps or surplus commodities in hundreds of starvation counties, and a tacit approval of the same authorities who have systematically disqualified black farmers from federal assistance under the cotton subsidy program, diversion program, and small farm loan program. . . .

Given past experience with the handling of federally-financed programs on the local level, it becomes all too evident that Nixon's emphasis on "work-fare" could be insidiously used as a mechanism for disqualifying needy people from receiving *any* aid.

In his address to the nation Nixon remarked: "A guaranteed income establishes a right without any responsibilities; family assistance recognizes a need and establishes a responsibility. It provides help to those in need, and in turn requires that those who receive help work to the extent of their capabilities. There is no reason why one person should be taxed so that another can choose to live idly."

Such a statement could only be made on the assumption that

income maintenance

there is plenty of decent, well-paying work available for those who are willing and able to acquire the proper skills—a doubtful postulate when applied to the country at large and a blatant fiction in the case of the South, which remains an area of chronic unemployment. Despite "forward-looking" Southern officials' ongoing flirtation with big business, the annual increase in available industrial jobs is only about half the number of farm jobs eliminated yearly by agricultural automation. (It might be added that Nixon's anti-inflation policies can only discourage industrial expansion in the South.)

If the general unemployment situation in the South is grim, meaningful jobs for blacks are virtually nonexistent in states like Alabama, Mississippi, Georgia and South Carolina. If black men and women are forced to accept whatever employment is offered to them, those who will truly profit will be the rich white farmer, the owner of the sawmill, the contractor—that is, those who will be provided with a work force which is even more desperate than it was before. At present, a black man can at least refuse to accept work-gang conditions and work-gang pay and still be eligible for food stamps. But under the new family assistance plan he could easily find himself with nothing at all to fall back on. . . .

With his added emphasis on job training Nixon expects to curtail the massive migration of Southern blacks to the Northern cities. But that cannot happen as long as there are so few skilled jobs to be had in the rural South. Newly-trained personnel would in fact *have* to migrate to either a Southern or, more likely, a Northern city in order to get work.

Nor will the migration be stemmed by the supposed "leveling" effect of the welfare reform, for Nixon announced in his speech that the states would be expected to individually supplement the federal benefits—a plan which naturally reinforces the same disparities that have existed between the states up until now, with Northern states making substantially greater contributions to the welfare system than Southern states.

Displaced black farmers from rural Alabama will continue to become hardcore, cynical, and resentful ghetto dwellers of Northern cities. The fuel for the fiery explosions in American cities has been kindled in the peaceful cotton fields that have starved the Negro into migration. . . .

To feed the hungry black Southerner requires not further federal expenditure, but rather a commitment to a fair and just transferal of land ownership—away from the white absentee land-owners and into the hands of those who have actually worked the land for generations: the black tenant farmers. The black American wants nothing less than his birthright—a meaningful place within a viable economic system that allows him control over his own destiny.

14 employment and the price level

INTRODUCTION

In this final chapter on policy choices, we return to the aggregate level. From Thurow to Tobin (pages 282–85) there is one overriding theme: all particularistic, microeconomic programs can have efficacy only in the context of full employment, regardless of whether or not the federal government assumes the role of employer of last resort. Even former Representative Thomas B. Curtis (pages 286–87) would presumably subscribe to this dictum.

But in our times we seem always to be trying to walk the tightrope between high employment and inflation. In recent years we have witnessed an administration so frightened by the inflationary threat that it has been prepared to generate substantial unemployment to try to arrest that threat. For blacks, it must be remembered, the unemployment rate ordinarily runs twice the national average rate and they are last-hired, first-fired. Hence, anti-inflationary policies are of grave concern to those interested in eliminating the disadvantaged status of blacks. In view of an apparently overwhelming consensus that "moderate" average unemployment (6 percent?) is to be preferred to moderate inflation, we are pleased to present in the last selection in this chapter the results of a research project of the University of Wisconsin Institute for Research in Poverty, directed by R. G. Hollister and J. L. Palmer. They point out that since we consider

281

inflation as a "tax," then we should also be aware that an anti-inflation policy based upon the creation of greater unemployment is also a "tax" imposed by virtue of such unemployment. Such a "tax" clearly falls with differential severity upon blacks. If Hollister and Palmer are nearly correct, this represents a dramatic breakthrough on the policy front affecting black Americans.

a full employment policy
is crucial

JAMES TOBIN

The most important dimension of the overall economic climate is the tightness of the labor market. In a tight labor market unemployment is low and short in duration, and job vacancies are plentiful. People who stand at the end of the hiring line and the top of the layoff list have the most to gain from a tight labor market. It is not surprising that the position of Negroes relative to that of whites improves in a tight labor market and declines in a slack market. Unemployment itself is only one way in which a slack labor market hurts Negroes and other disadvantaged groups, and the gains from reduction in unemployment are by no means confined to the employment of persons counted as unemployed. A tight labor market means not just jobs, but better jobs, longer hours, higher wages. Because of the heavy demands for labor during the second world war and its economic aftermath, Negroes made dramatic relative gains between 1940 and 1950. Unfortunately this momentum has not been maintained, and the blame falls largely on the weakness of labor markets since 1957.

The shortage of jobs has hit Negro men particularly hard and thus has contributed mightily to the ordeal of the Negro family, which is in turn the cumulative source of so many other social

From James Tobin, "Improving the Economic Status of the Negro," *Daedalus* (Fall 1965), 880–84 *passim*. Reprinted by permission from *Daedalus*, Journal of the American Academy of Arts and Sciences, Boston, Massachusetts, Volume **94**, Number 4.

employment and the price level

disorders. The unemployment rate of Negro men is more sensitive than that of Negro women to the national rate. Since 1949 Negro women have gained in median income relative to white women, but Negro men have lost ground to white males. In a society which stresses breadwinning as the expected role of the mature male and occupational achievement as his proper goal, failure to find and to keep work is devastating to the man's self-respect and family status. Matriarchy is in any case a strong tradition in Negro society, and the man's role is further downgraded when the family must and can depend on the woman for its livelihood. It is very important to increase the proportion of Negro children who grow up in stable families with two parents. Without a strong labor market it will be extremely difficult to do so.

It is well known that Negro unemployment rates are multiples of the general unemployment rate. This fact reflects both the lesser skills, seniority, and experience of Negroes and employers' discrimination against Negroes. These conditions are a deplorable reflection on American society, but as long as they exist Negroes suffer much more than others from a general increase in unemployment and gain much more from a general reduction. A rule of thumb is that changes in the nonwhite unemployment rate are twice those in the white rate. . . .

Persons who are involuntarily forced to work part time instead of full time are not counted as unemployed, but their number goes up and down with the unemployment rate. Just as Negroes bear a disproportionate share of unemployment, they bear more than their share of involuntary part-time unemployment. A tight labor market will not only employ more Negroes; it will also give more of those who are employed full-time jobs. In both respects, it will reduce disparities between whites and Negroes.

In a tight market, of which a low unemployment rate is a barometer, the labor force itself is larger. Job opportunities draw into the labor force individuals who, simply because the prospects were dim, did not previously regard themselves as seeking work and were therefore not enumerated as unemployed. For the economy as a whole, it appears that an expansion of job opportunities enough to reduce unemployment by one worker will bring another worker into the labor force.

This phenomenon is important for many Negro families. Statistically, their poverty now appears to be due more often to the lack of a breadwinner in the labor force than to unemployment.

But in a tight labor market many members of these families, including families now on public assistance, would be drawn into employment. Labor-force participation rates are roughly 2 per cent lower for nonwhite men than for white men, and the disparity increases in years of slack labor markets. . . .

In a tight labor market, such unemployment as does exist is likely to be of short duration. Short-term unemployment is less damaging to the economic welfare of the unemployed. More will have earned and fewer will have exhausted private and public unemployment benefits. . . .

. . . one more dimension of society's inequity to the Negro is that an unemployed Negro is more likely to stay unemployed than an unemployed white. But his figures also show that Negroes share in the reduction of long-term unemployment accompanying economic expansion.

A tight labor market draws the surplus rural population to higher paying non-agricultural jobs. Southern Negroes are a large part of this surplus rural population. Migration is the only hope for improving their lot, or their children's. In spite of the vast migration of past decades, there are still about 775,000 Negroes, 11 per cent of the Negro labor force of the country, who depend on the land for their living and that of their families. Almost a half million live in the South, and almost all of them are poor.

Migration from agriculture and from the South is the Negroes' historic path toward economic improvement and equality. It is a smooth path for Negroes and for the urban communities to which they move only if there is a strong demand for labor in towns and cities North and South. In the 1940's the number of Negro farmers and farm laborers in the nation fell by 450,000 and one and a half million Negroes (net) left the South. This was the great decade of Negro economic advance. In the 1950's the same occupational and geographical migration continued undiminished. The movement to higher-income occupations and locations should have raised the relative economic status of Negroes. But in the 1950's Negroes were moving into increasingly weak job markets. Too often disguised unemployment in the countryside was simply transformed into enumerated unemployment, and rural poverty into urban poverty.

In a slack labor market, employers can pick and choose, both in recruiting and in promoting. They exaggerate the skill, education, and experience requirements of their jobs. They use diplomas, or color, or personal histories as convenient screening devices. In a tight market, they are forced to be realistic, to tailor job specifications to the available supply, and to give on-the-job training. They recruit and train applicants whom they would otherwise screen out, and they upgrade employees whom they would in slack times consign to low-wage, low-skill, and part-time jobs.

Wartime and other experience shows that job requirements are adjustable and that men and women are trainable. It is only in slack times that people worry about a mismatch between supposedly rigid occupational requirements and supposedly unchangeable qualifications of the labor force. As already noted, the relative status of Negroes improves in a tight labor market not only in respect to unemployment, but also in respect to wages and occupations.

Sustaining a high demand for labor is important. The in-and-out status of the Negro in the business cycle damages his long-term position because periodic unemployment robs him of experience and seniority.

A slack labor market probably accentuates the discriminatory and protectionist proclivities of certain crafts and unions. When jobs are scarce, opening the door to Negroes is a real threat. Of course prosperity will not automatically dissolve the barriers, but it will make it more difficult to oppose efforts to do so.

I conclude that the single most important step the nation could take to improve the economic position of the Negro is to operate the economy steadily at a low rate of unemployment. . . .

employer of last resort:
a make-work technique

THOMAS B. CURTIS

. . . Insistence on maintaining aggregate demand in the society by having the Federal Government supplement whatever the private sector does not spend can remove discipline from governmental programs to such an extent that poor and redundant programs proliferate and smother healthy growth. I think an examination of the present proliferation of welfare programs reveals that this is exactly what has occurred in recent years. . . .

I regret that another attempt is made . . . to make the terms "maximum" and "full" employment appear to be synonymous. This robs the student of the fruitful dialog which occurred at the time the Employment Act of 1946 was enacted, over the differences implicit in these two terms. The term "maximum" was used to convey the idea that society through its governmental sector could do no more than create the economic climate which hopefully would attain full employment in the economic sector. The term "full," on the contrary, was used to convey the idea that Government could and therefore must guarantee employment for all. The concept of Government being the employer of last resort is a similar corruption of the meaning of terms. The term "employment" has implicit in it economic employment. Employer of the last resort has, of course, the connotation of "make-work," not of economically useful work. I think most people react unfavorably both to welfare as a way of life and "make-work" as a technique to make welfare as a way of life more palatable.

Welfare to help people get on their economic feet is not resented, on the other hand.

The basic question thus remains. Are there sufficient jobs to be filled, of the kind the people as we have them can fill? The evidence, I believe, shows that there are. Accordingly, there is no need for the pessimism and inhumanity which calls for guaranteed incomes or Government to be the employer of last resort.

From Representative Thomas B. Curtis, supplementary view, in The U.S. Congress, Senate Joint Economic Committee, *Report: Employment and Manpower Problems in the Cities—Implications of the Report of the National Advisory Commission on Civil Disorders*, 90th Congress, 2nd Session, Report No. 1568 (Washington: Government Printing Office, September 16, 1968), pp. 16–18 *passim*.

There is reason for optimism which calls for guaranteed opportunities for our people to be gainfully employed throughout their lifetime.

impact of inflation
on the poor

ROBINSON G. HOLLISTER / JOHN L. PALMER

. . . the public discussion of inflation and the policy issues related to it have been pervaded by the general presumption that the poor are hurt by inflation. At the very least, our evidence makes clear that this has been a presumption and not a proven fact; we feel the evidence indicates that the presumption should be that the poor are *not* hurt by inflation.

One might conjecture that the idea that the poor are hurt by inflation has gained currency because of a tendency to generalize from piecemeal considerations and isolated cases. If the money incomes of the poor are fixed then price rises will cause a deterioration in their economic well-being, but one must go the next step and consider whether the same process which generates the rise in prices is not likely to generate rises in the income of the poor as great or greater than the rises in prices. Similarly, though there are some poor families living on incomes from fixed value assets or pensions vulnerable to inflation, it should not be concluded that the majority of the poor are in this circumstance.

Both of these considerations are particularly important when the use of policy instruments with a broad impact is being considered, e.g., fiscal and monetary policy. With respect to the first consideration, it might be concluded that the policy instrument (reduced aggregate demand or tighter money) might be adequate to stop rising prices but is it not likely to generate also processes

From Robinson G. Hollister and John L. Palmer, *The Impact of Inflation on the Poor,* discussion paper, Institute for Research on Poverty, University of Wisconsin, 1969, pp. 45–51 *passim* (mimeographed).

which will reduce the incomes of the poor, perhaps by more than the reduction in price rises? Regarding the second consideration, if there are special situations of inequity within a subgroup of the population, then one should try not to use broad policies to deal with those relatively isolated cases. More particularistic policies can usually be found to deal with particular circumstances. For example, . . . if it should happen to be a subgroup of the poor receiving a particular type of transfer payment whose incomes are deteriorated by inflation, then it makes little sense to use fiscal and monetary policy in order to stop inflation for their benefit alone (this example may seem ludicrous, but we suggest that a careful examination of much of the arguments about anti-inflationary policies reduce to this sort of reasoning). It seems eminently sensible instead to make a policy decision to raise automatically their transfer payments to keep pace with the price rises. . . .

We want to be clear that the tenor of our arguments should not be taken to be one of advocating a purposeful policy of generating strong inflation. We merely wish to attempt to correct what has struck us as an extraordinary imbalance in the public and academic discussion of these issues. The presumption that inflation necessarily hurts the poor simply is not supported by evidence on the recent United States experience. . . .

If we are going to talk about the "tax of inflation," it might be useful also to talk about the "tax" imposed by unemployment. If, through government policy, we can adjust aggregate demand so as to foster more or less inflation and more or less unemployment, then it seems reasonable to think of unemployment as a cost of government policy, a "tax" imposed through unemployment. We might ask therefore on whom does the "tax of unemployment" fall? It falls very heavily on the poor. Surely if middle or upper income people were asked if *they* themselves were willing to bear the "tax of unemployment" in order to remove the "tax of inflation," they would answer, resoundingly, "no!" It is very clear that the "tax of unemployment" is a very inequitable tax; it is not clear that the "tax of inflation" falls extraordinarily heavily on *any* population group—its impact may be spread rather broadly across the population.

Many people have talked about the necessity to have a "slight rise in unemployment" or even a "slight recession" in order to halt the current inflation. They sometimes point to "slight recessions" in the past which have "shaken out" the inflationary factors in the economic structure. We would like to point out that there is a tendency to define a recession solely in terms of what happens to the rate of growth of output. In these terms the recession of 1957–58 looks "slight" and short-lived—the rate of growth of output returned to a normal level in the next year. But a recession could also be defined in terms of the unemployment rate and on those grounds the 1957–58 recession was substantial and lasted nearly eight years—unemployment rates did not return to their 1957 levels until late in 1965.

In the past few years we have seen increasing emphasis put upon public and private training and hiring programs for the poor. These are important programs but their effectiveness is highly dependent on the existence of tight labor markets which provide the incentives to employers to undertake extraordinary efforts in behalf of the poor. . . . It seems evident that if every time some inflationary pressure appears, a rise in unemployment is going to be generated to halt it, employers are not going to feel that the pains of training and learning to deal with marginal workers are worthwhile. Thus, even a "slight rise in unemployment" is likely to seriously threaten these manpower training programs which have been so painfully launched. Just to get an idea of how important a "slight rise" in unemployment is, if we take the estimates from our regressions . . . a "slight rise" of one percent[age point] in the unemployment rate is likely to put one and a half million people into poverty who would not otherwise have been there. The National Alliance of Businessmen's JOBS program for hiring the hard-core poor has as a three year goal 500,000 jobs. Thus, if for every job, three persons are lifted out of poverty, it would seem that a one percent[age point] rise in unemployment would wipe out the entire gains of the three year JOBS program.

We would like to suggest that a *long term* commitment to tight labor markets, even in the face of some inflation, may be a key to the development on the part of private sector employers of effective programs to cope with training and employment problems of the hard-core poor. . . . With continued tight labor markets we should expect improved performance on both sides; the employer will have improved his training skills and the workers will have overcome that initial difficult experience of adjustment to regular employment.

impact of inflation on the poor   289

Furthermore, the European experience in the early 1960's of absorbing immigrant workers into the employed labor force without greatly lowered productivity is promising. The evidence on this experience is very sketchy, but it does suggest that large numbers of difficult-to-train workers can be rapidly converted into effective workers. In the early 1960's, Germany was recruiting over 100,000 foreign workers annually. These workers were largely unskilled and had major language problems and yet seemed to have been absorbed rather rapidly with relatively short periods of training. Labor productivity in Germany continued to grow. Switzerland has absorbed foreign workers to such an extent that they make up nearly one third of her labor force. It is hard to believe that the problems of absorbing unskilled foreign workers speaking a different language are less difficult than those of dealing with the hard-core poor. The United States equivalent of the German absorption of 10 thousand marginal workers a year would be roughly 300 thousand per year, about twice the annual rate set as a goal of the JOBS program. We repeat, however, that if every time markets begin to really tighten and prices rise, the government uses fiscal and monetary policy to cause labor markets to slacken, then employers will take slack markets as the norm and will not feel it worthwhile to invest their time and money in learning to make effective workers out of those on the margins of the labor force.

epilogue

a policy for the seventies

A. PHILIP RANDOLPH

It is perhaps indicative of the way most Americans think that in our debate about the racial crisis we often ignore fundamental economic considerations. Blacks, as well as whites, are guilty of this error of omission. We all seem to think that the two races are separated only by "the color line," to borrow the phrase of W. E. B. Du Bois, when in fact they are equally separated by a class line.

The difficulty with this way of thinking is that it implies that the injustices from which Negroes suffer would disappear were we somehow able to eliminate racial prejudice and discrimination. But this is far from the truth. The problem of racial discrimination is not the reason why our society tolerates a high degree of unemployment and is willing to increase unemployment to combat inflation. Nor is it the reason why we do not build enough decent housing for everybody. If our schools are starved for funds, or if our health care system is primitive by West European standards, or if automation and cybernation are making millions of jobs obsolete, these problems will not be solved simply by changing the racial attitudes of whites. They are fundamentally economic problems which are caused by the nature of the system in which we live.

This system is a market economy in which investment and production are determined more by the anticipation of profits

Prepared especially for this volume by A. Philip Randolph.

291

than by the desire to achieve social justice. In such a system, the needs of all poor people—black *and* white—cannot be met since it is not profitable to build low-income housing or to have health benefits that all can afford. Moreover, because the nondefense public sector of the economy is starved for funds, our government does not have the resources to do those things the private economy ignores. Most important, it cannot act as the employer of last resort, giving jobs to people who cannot find work during periods when plants are operating well below their full capacity.

While these problems affect poor people of all races, they hurt blacks most severely because they comprise such a disproportionate number of the poor. But in thinking of a solution to the problem, we must avoid at all costs the idea of a black solution, i.e., that a separate black economy is a realistic or desirable alternative. Separatism will only aggravate the problems from which blacks suffer because it will isolate them from the mainstream of the economy where the best jobs are to be found. Historically blacks have been isolated in this way, so it would hardly be a "solution" to perpetuate the conditions which have already caused so much misery.

The solution to the economic problems of black America must consist of two major components. The first is that we must strive towards a full employment economy. A booming economy will bring with it expanding employment opportunities, and this will tend to help blacks even more than whites since blacks suffer from higher rates of unemployment. This is exactly what happened between 1960 and 1968, a period of economic expansion, when nonwhite employment increased by 19 percent while the total rise in employment was only 15 percent. Among nonwhite adult men, the unemployment rate dropped from 9.6 to 3.9 percent. This, in turn, increased the economic power of blacks both in absolute terms and in relation to whites. Between 1960 and 1967, the median income of nonwhite families rose from 55 to 62 percent of the median income for white families.

The Nixon Administration's disastrous economic policies are reversing this positive trend. Since Nixon assumed office, the unemployment rate has gone up almost two full percentage points. This means that nearly two million more people are out of work today [1970] than in January, 1969. Blacks, as usual, have been hurt worst of all. Even promising training programs set up by private industry have been closed down. Blacks, the last to be hired during the boom, are now the first to be fired during the bust. This situation can be remedied only if we move once again toward an economy of abundance.

The second part of the solution to the economic problems of blacks has to do with the role of the Federal Government. In "A Freedom Budget for All Americans,"[1] I outlined what I consider to be a real war on poverty. It doesn't consist of a scattering of little programs designed to solve little problems, but a massive, comprehensive, and rationally planned program which can attack poverty at its roots.

The Freedom Budget rests upon the fundamental assumption that only the government in Washington possesses the resources to deal with the complex and intractable problems of poverty. Since private industry neither can nor will employ all of the poor, the government must become the employer of last resort. Since private industry cannot build the 2.6 million housing units which the 1968 Housing Act earmarked as the necessary annual production quota over a ten-year period, the government must construct far more housing, particularly low-income housing, than it has ever done before. And the government must also be willing to pay for the modernization of our systems of education, health, and welfare.

Where will we find the money to pay for all this? More money is already escaping taxation through tax loopholes than would be required to pay for the whole Freedom Budget. In addition, the Freedom Budget could be financed out of the growth in tax revenues that derive from the annual increase in the Gross National Product. The money is there; we just don't have the political will to spend it. And until we do—until there is a majority political movement in America that is committed to using our nation's abundant resources to solve our grievous social problems—the economic injustices which afflict black America will persist. Rather than talk about the psychological aspects of racial prejudice, we would do far better to apply our time and energy to building such a political movement in the hope of creating a truly just society.

---

[1] See A. Philip Randolph, "A Freedom Budget for all Americans" (New York: A. Philip Randolph Institute, October 1966).

list of authors

MARCUS ALEXIS is professor in the College of Business Administration at the University of Rochester. He has done major research in black consumption patterns.

ALAN BATCHELDER is professor of economics at Kenyon College and economist with the Harvard Development Advisory Service. Much of his professional research has been in the area of black economics.

SHERWOOD O. BERG is Dean of the Institute of Agriculture at the University of Minnesota.

MICHAEL J. BOSKIN is a member of the economics faculty at the University of California, Berkeley.

KENNETH E. BOULDING is professor of economics at the University of Colorado and former president of the American Economic Association.

THOMAS J. BRAY is a staff writer for *The Wall Street Journal*.

VERNON M. BRIGGS, JR., is professor of economics at the University of Texas. His major interest is in manpower problems.

KENNETH B. CLARK is professor of psychology at the City College of the City University of New York. His excerpts in this volume are from *Dark Ghetto*, which won first prize in the social science essays at the First World Festival of Negro Arts.

RICHARD A. CLOWARD and FRANCES F. PIVEN are professors in the School of Social Work at Columbia University in New York City.

THOMAS B. CURTIS was a Representative to the United States Congress from Missouri.

W. E. B. DU BOIS was a critic, author, scholar, historian. A major civil rights leader, he was a founder of the NAACP. He received his doctorate from Harvard and was professor of Latin, Greek, and economics. *Black Reconstruction in America* is the most famous of his many works.

JOHN EGERTON is an educational analyst and staff writer for the Southern Education Reporting Service, Nashville, Tennessee.

JAMES FARMER was one of the founders of CORE (the Congress of Racial Equality) and former program director of the NAACP. He is now a professor at New York University.

EUGENE P. FOLEY has been active in initiating problems to stimulate black business as former Administrator of the Small Business Administration and as Assistant Secretary of Commerce for Economic Development.

CLARENCE FUNNYÉ was former NCDH (National Committee Against Discrimination in Housing) Director of Field Services.

DANIEL R. FUSFELD is professor of economics at the University of Michigan and President of the Association for Evolutionary Economics.

D. PARKE GIBSON is President of D. Parke Gibson Associates, Inc., of New York, a management consultant firm.

GEORGE and EUNICE GRIER have conducted research on the racial attributes of housing for the Washington Center for Metropolitan Studies and the Anti-Defamation League of B'nai B'rith.

PHYLLIS GROOM researches for the Office of Publications of the United States Bureau of Labor Statistics.

CHESTER HARTMAN is professor of urban planning at the Harvard-MIT Joint Center for Urban Studies.

KYLE HASELDEN was on the staff of *The Christian Century*.

WILLIAM L. HENDERSON and LARRY C. LEDEBUR are professors of economics at Denison University.

DALE L. HIESTAND is on the economics faculty at Columbia University and Senior Research Associate in the Conservation of Human Resources Project.

ROBINSON G. HOLLISTER and JOHN L. PALMER are, respectively, professor in the department of economics at the University of Wisconsin and economist associated with the Stanford economics department. Both have been with the University of Wisconsin Institute for Research on Poverty.

LINDA HUNT, GARY HUNT, and NANCY SCHEPER all write for *Ramparts* magazine.

W. H. HUTT was Dean of the Faculty of Commerce and Director of the Graduate School of Business at the University of Cape Town and is now Professor Emeritus. He has since taught at numerous universities in the United States.

F. RAY MARSHALL is professor of economics at the University of Texas and an expert on black participation in the labor movement.

GEORGE MEANY is the President of the American Federation of Labor and Congress of Industrial Organizations.

TRIENAH MEYERS is a Staff Assistant to the Administrator in the Economic Research Service of the United States Department of Agriculture.

GUNNAR MYRDAL is professor of international economy at the University of Stockholm. The monumental study of United States race relations, *An American Dilemma,* is the best known among his numerous books.

RICHARD P. NATHAN was Associate Director of Research of the National Advisory Commission on Civil Disorders (the Kerner Commission) and is now Assistant Director of the United States Bureau of the Budget.

LLAD PHILLIPS, HAROLD L. VOTEY, JR., and DAROLD MAXWELL are economists associated with the University of California, Santa Barbara.

MAHLON T. PURYEAR is President of Manpower Consultants, Inc., of Pelham, New York. He has been involved in technical education and has been consultant to numerous governmental agencies. He was formerly on the staff of the Urban League.

A. PHILIP RANDOLPH is President of the A. Philip Randolph Institute. He organized the Brotherhood of Sleeping Car Porters, which became the strongest black labor union, was President of the Negro American Labor Council, and was a leading organizer of the 1963 civil rights march on Washington. He is widely regarded as the elder statesman of the black civil rights movement.

LEE SOLTOW is professor of statistics at Ohio University. He has major research interests in the field of income and wealth distribution.

NEIL V. SULLIVAN is the Superintendent of the Berkeley Unified School System.

LESTER THUROW is professor in the department of economics and management at the Massachusetts Institute of Technology. He was formerly with the President's Council of Economic Advisers.

JAMES TOBIN is professor of economics and chairman of that department at Yale University. He was formerly with the President's Council of Economic Advisers and the Cowles Foundation for Research in Economics.

RUDOLPH A. WHITE is professor of industrial relations and Director of Academic Affairs in the College of Business and Industry, Mississippi State University.

MALCOLM X was the outstanding spokesman for the Black Muslim movement and founder of the Organization of Afro-American Unity. The excerpt in this work is from *The Autobiography of Malcolm X.*

WHITNEY M. YOUNG, JR., was Executive Director of the National Urban League and former Dean of the Atlanta University School of Social Work. *To Be Equal* was his first full-length book.

list of authors